Urban
Development
in Australia

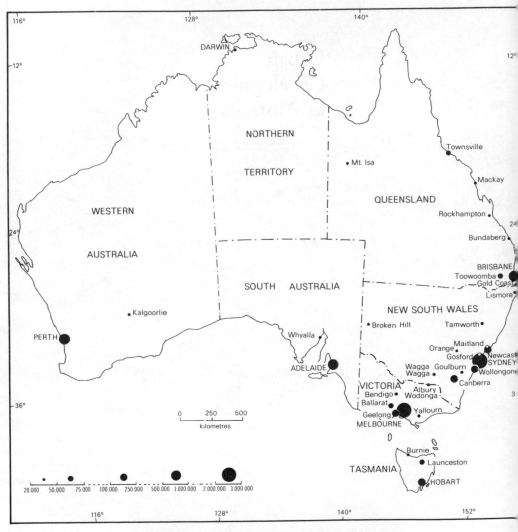

Urban centres with populations over 20 000: 1971.

Urban Development in Australia

A Descriptive Analysis

MAX NEUTZE

Head, Urban Research Unit
Australian National University

GEORGE ALLEN & UNWIN
SYDNEY   LONDON

First published in 1977 by
George Allen & Unwin Australia Pty Ltd
Cnr Bridge Road and Jersey Street
Hornsby
NSW 2077

National Library of Australia
Cataloguing-in-Publication entry

.Neutze, Graeme Max, 1934–
    Urban development in Australia.

    Index.
    Bibliography.
    ISBN 0 86861 000 3
    ISBN 0 86861 008 9 Paperback.

    1. Cities and towns—Planning—Australia.
    2. Cities and towns—Australia—Growth.
    1. Title.

309.2620994

Set in 11 on 12 point Bembo by Academy Press, Brisbane
Printed by Hogbin, Poole, Sydney

To Peggy

PREFACE

This book derives from one facet of research of the Urban Research unit, and other members of staff and students have contributed much to the development of the ideas it contains. Two research projects in the Unit on the process of urban development aimed to sort out the major influences, concentrating much of their efforts on small study areas in Sydney and Melbourne. The detailed results were published by the Unit in a series of monographs and by the Australian Institute of Urban Studies (Urban Research Unit, 1973). This book includes any interpretation of the more general results of those two projects, but I have also tackled some questions which require data for whole urban areas and have not confined my attention to Sydney and Melbourne.

The book is intended to contain the 'information about urban development that every student and policy-maker should know' and also contains interpretations of the information. I intend to follow it with a volume on urban development policies.

Ken Johnson, Lyndsay Neilson and Elzo Vandermark were involved in the Sydney and Melbourne projects. Patrick Troy, Peter Harrison and I have worked together for much of the past ten years as a team. I cannot distinguish which ideas were originally theirs and which were mine. In addition Peter Harrison read the whole transcript and made many valuable suggestions for improvement. I am also indebted to June Harries for typing, to Leo Pancino for drawing the maps and diagrams and to Jenny Craik and Jenny Norman for research assistance. The faults, errors and shortcomings that remain are mine.

MAX NEUTZE

CONTENTS

1 Introduction

In recent years there has been a rapid increase in the level of interest in urban studies, both in Australia and overseas. Australians have long been aware of the fact that most of their fellow countrymen live in cities and that they are more concentrated in a few large cities than people living in almost any other country. We have recently realised that cities are not simply a collection of houses that happen to be close to each other and to factories, shops, offices and parks. Unless the various activities that occur in cities are arranged in a reasonably efficient way relative to one another the costs to individuals and governments can be very high. Not only are journeys to work long and costly for the worker but the provision of transport and other parts of the infrastructure is likely to absorb a high proportion of the funds available for investment in Australia. Which cities grow and how they grow influences the costs of accommodating and servicing growth and affects the welfare of people living in them.

In Australia one of the central questions that has been asked over many years is whether the few large cities are becoming too large. There has recently been a revival of interest in this question with the increasing awareness of the pressures which large cities put on the natural environment. This interest of environmentalists reinforced a long-standing interest in the economics of city size and the possible advantages of diverting some of the growth of population and employment from the large cities. Even if further growth in the large cities causes increased costs, diversion of growth elsewhere is not the only solution. Some of the problems can be overcome by decentralisation of population and employment *within* the existing large urban regions, or by a more appropriate allocation of land between different uses. Many of the disadvantages of very large cities are felt particularly by those who cannot afford to live in the more desirable suburbs but have to accept a polluted physical environment, poor housing and a low level of services. Diversion of population growth can help to relieve the pressure on housing and services within the large cities, but whether growth is diverted or not, more resources still need to be allocated to improving living conditions, especially for the many poorer families who will continue to live in the large cities.

Conversion of rural land to urban use is particularly important in determining the future shape of Australian cities. The subdivision pattern, the street layout and the location of different land uses and facilities which are determined at that time persist for many decades. Good planning at that stage is crucial. While more mature cities in other countries may be developing more by changing and redeveloping established areas, Australian cities are still growing mainly by spreading at the fringe. The efficiency of the rural-to-urban conversion process also affects the supply and price of land for expansion. In turn that affects the price of housing and other property elsewhere in the urban area.

The establishment of the National Urban and Regional Development Authority by the McMahon Government in 1972 and the ambitious urban programmes of the Whitlam Government from 1973 to 1975 signalled a revival of interest in these issues at a national level. They had previously been of concern to the national government in the 1940s, when the Commonwealth Housing Commission (1944) and the Department of Post-War Reconstruction (1949) developed far-sighted plans for the urban and regional dimensions of post-war Australia. The Commission was largely responsible for the Commonwealth State Housing Agreement of 1945, which was designed to be a major instrument in improving the urban areas of Australia, but eventually came to play a restricted though valuable welfare role in assisting poor families to get adequate housing. During the fifties and sixties the state and metropolitan planning authorities in the major cities, and local councils in smaller centres, were mainly responsible for guiding urban development. Their efforts have borne only limited fruits, partly because the planning authority has usually been regarded as simply another authority with its own programmes, rather than being responsible for an important aspect of development—its location—that needs to be taken into account in formulating almost all investment plans and in all aspects of government policy.

Another related problem confronts those who attempt to influence the way urban centres develop. We know very little about urban development and we understand even less about why it occurs in a particular way. Our limited knowledge affects urban policy at all levels. Even the professionals in planning authorities have sometimes seen only the physical aspects of development without understanding its social, economic or political aspects. Those in other government departments understand different aspects but few have anything like a general understanding of the whole process. Politicians often think of urban issues in simple or segmented terms—they do not link transport isses with questions about housing or sewerage. It is little wonder that the general population finds it difficult to comprehend urban policy when it is no more than a convenient umbrella for a whole series of often disparate programmes. We understand little about either the structure of our cities or how they have been changing under the influence of increasing prosperity, improving transport and changing production technologies.

This is not a book about policy, but it is a book about the way Australian cities have been changing and about the structure and functioning of those cities. Although it is not about policy it is for policy-makers, both present and future. It is written in the belief that a better understanding of our cities is necessary if policy decisions are to be well made and to achieve their objectives.

The dearth of information about cities which has inhibited earlier planners and analysts of Australian cities makes this book less complete and less informative than it might have been. Apart from census material, very little information about Australian cities is available on a comparable basis. Only in the very recent past has data about the price and supply of land and housing begun to be collected in a systematic manner, and even now the data are collected from different sources and relating to different sorts of sales in different cities. Except for the journey to work, our information about transport within cities comes mainly from periodic transportation studies conducted at different times, by different firms in different cities, which collected and published data on different bases. Reliable land use information is very scarce and it is not possible to make direct comparisons between any two cities, or within one city, to find out how the use of land has changed over time.

The emphasis in the book is on descriptive analysis. Theories about why cities grow in particular ways are not very powerful, and until we are reasonably confident that our information is reliable it seems premature to use it to test the theories that have been developed and tested overseas, sometimes using data which is not much better than our own. Some of the data about changes in population density over time is presented as a test of alternative explanations (theories) of why population densities are higher closer to the city centre.

Urban development can be examined at two quite distinct scales. Firstly, distribution of development between different towns and cities can be described, and the relative rates of growth of large and small centres, and of centres in different parts of the country, compared and analysed. The functions that different centres perform can also be compared. This area of study is sometimes called 'regional' rather than 'urban'. Although this book includes some description of this inter-urban dimension of development, most of the emphasis will be at the second or intra-urban scale. At this scale most of the emphasis is on the pattern of development within cities, the extent to which they spread over large areas at low density or are concentrated in small areas at high density, how the land within the urban boundary is used and how goods and people are transported from one part of the urban area to another.

Because of the limited availability of information, different topics are treated at very different levels of detail. In few places is it possible to describe all urban areas in a comparable way. Attention is concentrated on the five mainland state capitals, partly because there are better data about them, but also because they house 60 per cent of the national population. Even among them the information available is very variable. It is generally best for Sydney and Melbourne because they have been more intensively studied. Some parts of the book concentrate on those two and others take Sydney alone, largely because the Sydney Area Transportation Study carried out in that city in 1971 provided more data about transport and land use than are available for any other city, and it can be conveniently linked to the 1971 Census data. The Urban Research Unit was fortunate in being able to get copies of much of the basic data collected for the Study.

Concentration on Sydney and Melbourne can be justified for other reasons. Not only are they the largest—housing over 40 per cent of the national population in 1971—they also show many of the characteristics of Australian urban development, including its problems, most clearly. They show something of what the smaller centres will be like if they continue to grow. Sydney stands at one extreme in the urban pattern because it is the largest and also because its site is more confined than that of any other mainland capital. Its city centre is far from the geographical centre of the urban area and transport is impeded by sunken river valleys which at the same time provide some of the most attractive locations for residential and office buildings in Australia. It can only spread to the west. As a consequence transport within Sydney is costly, there is more high density development in the inner parts of the urban area and land prices within a reasonable distance of the city centre are higher than in any other city. Finally some kinds of data are presented for one city (usually Sydney) when a similar situation exists in other major cities, and where comparisons between different cities are either not possible or not very revealing.

Urban development can be described in different ways, for example as a physical, social, economic or political process. The emphasis in this book is on the physical and economic aspects of development, but the important role of government in urban development is also highlighted in many parts. People in cities are more interdependent than they are in rural areas because they live close to one another and come together to work and for education, recreation, cultural and social activities. Many services have to be supplied to all members of the community rather than to individuals. For this reason governments are important and the economics of cities derives more insights from the study of collective action and public finance than from the economics of the free market.

There is very little discussion of policy issues in this book. Rather it contains the kind of information necessary for policy discussion. The selection of the material was, however, determined to a large extent by the policy issues which are important in today's cities. A volume dealing with policy issues, which will depend heavily on the understanding of urban development described in this book, is being planned. To give some flavour of the relevance of the book to policy, the introductions to a number of the chapters mention policy issues.

The book commences with an historical description of the development of Australian cities. Even in a relatively young country like Australia, there is a large legacy from the past of housing, other buildings, streets and services. Because the established parts of cities change only slowly, many of the characteristics of Australian cities in the 1970s can only be understood by going back into the past and finding out, for example, when and why the suburban railways were built along their present routes, and how the pattern of terrace houses in the inner suburbs emerged. Chapter 2 is necessarily selective, concentrating on the distribution of population, transport and the provision of housing and utility services. These are some of the areas where the influence of the past has been strongest, and where it also constrains the policy choices available today.

The most common measure of the rate and distribution of urban growth is population growth. Chapter 3 examines the rate at which the population of different urban centres has been growing and analyses their growth into the parts due to internal migration, overseas migration and natural increase. Internal migration as a factor in urban growth has often been exaggerated and it receives careful attention in this chapter, using the information collected at the 1971 Census about movements between 1966 and 1971.

Within cities one of the most obvious trends in the location of population is suburban sprawl. Chapter 3 shows that the period since the Second World War has been one of suburban expansion, and urban growth can best be understood as the 'filling up' of successive areas at increasing distance from the city centre. Areas do not, however, fill up completely before growth spills over, and since about 1960 there has been an increase in the population of some inner suburbs with flat redevelopment, though only in Sydney has this effect been significant.

The fact that people who live in cities usually work some distance from where they live is one of the main reasons we need large and costly urban transport systems, but very little comprehensive information is available about where people work. Chapter 4 devotes most of its attention to workplaces within Sydney, and how they have changed over time. Suburbanisation of jobs has tended to follow suburbanisation of homes and has occurred at very different rates for different kinds of jobs. Consequently the central business districts are becoming increasingly specialised as office employment centres. Although specialisation of job locations within cities is the main focus of attention, Chapter 4 also shows that the major cities themselves differ in the proportions of different kinds of jobs they offer and the kinds of industries they contain, which in turn affects their urban structure.

The relative importance of different activities within cities and their arrangement relative to one another is reflected in the way land is used. Land is the main scarce resource of cities and controls over land use are the way in which changes in the urban area are planned and controlled, so it is surprising that there is so little data about the way land is used within cities. Chapter 5 summarises some of the data which are available and also looks at the closely related aspect of cities—transport—which has been intensively studied and measured. The two topics are related since transport is needed to provide a link between where people live and where they work, shop, go to school or meet other people. It is also needed to move goods around urban areas. A good deal of attention is given to the effects of changes in land use patterns on the transport system, and in particular to the reasons why the use of public transport is declining while use of private cars increases.

For a considerable period after the Second World War it appeared as though Australians could increase their housing standards almost indefinitely. One reason was that a high proportion of Australian families were able to become owner-occupants, which proved to be a very good way to buy housing in periods of modest inflation and relatively low interest rates. However, during the late sixties and early seventies increasing housing standards were threatened by rapidly increasing land prices and interest rates, which reinforced one another in making it increasingly difficult to buy housing. Chapter 6 examines the evidence for changes in housing standards and the evidence for the recent increase in housing costs, and concludes that there are signs that even existing housing standards might be difficult to maintain.

It is seldom recognised that urban development absorbs about half of the total funds available for investment in Australia. Chapter 7 attempts an estimate of the investment in urban development and its main component parts. Although the precise percentage is sensitive to the way urban development is defined, even the restricted definition used in this chapter accounts for over half of gross fixed capital formation. The chapter makes it clear that by no means all of the investment in urban development is required to cater for population growth and, within Sydney, only some kinds of building activities are concentrated in the rapidly growing fringe suburbs. Most urban development takes the form of marginal spread, but redevelopment and adaptation are beginning to become more significant in the larger urban areas. The final part of the chapter examines the ways in which the savings of individuals and the surpluses of firms and public authorities are channelled into providing finance for urban development.

Chapter 8 draws together information about the significant and changing role of different government authorities in urban development. As in the previous chapter the significance of this role is assessed in the three main parts of urban development—land development, provision of public services, and building. Governments also play an important, though different, kind of role in planning and controlling urban development. All three levels of government are involved, though the state governments play the most prominent part. The fact that responsibility for different functions is divided between the three levels of government and between departments at each level, and that some of the important functions are performed by authorities which are not directly responsible to any elected government, has important implications for how urban policies can be formulated and implemented.

The final chapter identifies five main classes of individuals and organisations involved in urban development and describes how they interact to determine the way Australian cities grow and change. Any decisions can only influence the future development of cities, most of whose features are determined by the legacy of past development and the physical features of the site. It is rare for developments over any short period to have more than a marginal effect on a city, and the best way to understand a number of the characteristics of Australian cities is to find out how the topography has influenced the location of transport routes, industrial areas and high income residential areas. Interactions between decision-makers described in the chapter occur in many different ways: some through the market, others through government bureaucracies, and still others through political processes.

Any book on a subject as large as urban development in Australia must be highly selective. This introductory chapter has outlined some of the reasons for the selection of material in the following chapters. But beyond these reasons the selection is to some degree idiosyncratic. It reflects my own view about what are the important features of urban development in Australia. They are important partly because they help to show the results of the processes which are described in the final chapter, but mainly because it is necessary to know that these changes are occurring, and to have some understanding of why they are occurring, before we can make any significant progress in solving the important policy problems which are currently facing Australian cities.

2 An Historical Perspective

Australia's cities, more than most aspects of our contemporary economic and social life, are a product of the past. Much of their physical fabric is at least several decades old. Our understanding of the reasons for the present structure of Australian cities is greatly enriched by learning something of how they have expanded over time, how transport facilities developed and how an increasing range of services was provided. A simple example of the influence of past development can be seen in the case of housing. Although we have no accurate data on the age of dwellings we know that each year new building only adds 2 to 3 per cent to the stock of houses. The number of occupied dwellings in Australia shown in the 1961 Census was only 24 per cent less than in 1971, and in 1947 only 49 per cent less. Relatively few of the dwellings counted at either of these censuses have since been demolished, so most of our housing is a product of the period before 1960—roughly half was built before the war. Their size and other features were designed to satisfy the tastes and demands of those periods. Although offices, shops, factories and warehouses may have somewhat shorter average lives than houses and flats, there is still a lot of building of all kinds which dates from before the Second World War, and even before the First.

Even when the buildings themselves are replaced many other features of cities, such as the pattern of subdivision, remain unchanged. The streets with their water, gas and sewerage mains, and sometimes with their tram lines, have usually remained almost unchanged from initial surveys and construction. For this reason the ten-chain grid of streets, which was used by the colonial administration of New South Wales (Jeans, 1972) in planning towns at the beginning of the nineteenth century, before Victoria and Queensland were separated, can still be seen in a large number of towns in eastern Australia, towns ranging in size from Melbourne to some very small villages. Suburban railway routes, parks and recreation areas, schools and other civic buildings remain over very long periods. Groups of buildings such as shopping, commercial and industrial centres often remain in the same location even though the individual buildings are replaced. Towns and even villages are very rarely moved, though the less well located occasionally decline dramatically, especially when a new kind of transport is introduced. Nevertheless, given the extent to which the initial features of urban development determine city features over long periods, this study must be set in an historical context.

Many of the physical features of the sites on which cities are built—their topography, geology, soils, liability to flooding, climate and natural vegetation—have a profound influence on the way they develop. This influence is felt so strongly through history that in this book it is described along with the historical development. For example, the early stock routes and tracks avoided swampy ground. The settlements established along these routes were subsequently linked by suburban rail services and arterial roads. The pattern of development of Sydney, especially before the Bridge was built, cannot be understood without taking into account the barrier imposed by the harbour. There was a good deal of daily travel across the harbour, but residential development, and especially growth of employment, was slower to the north than to the south and west.

This chapter describes the main features of the development of Australian cities since the mid-nineteenth century. Much of the data extends from some time in the second half of that century to about 1971, but the discussion concentrates on the period up to the Second World War. The post-war developments will be examined in later chapters dealing with individual aspects of development.

One of the main themes running through this chapter is the importance of transport and communication in shaping the pattern of urban development in Australia. In the first section it will be argued that the development of mechanised transport relatively soon after initial settlement of most of the country allowed a great deal of trade within Australia, and between Australia and overseas, and inhibited the growth of major regional centres outside the colonial capitals. In the second section the provision of suburban train and rail services is shown to have contributed to the spread of relatively low density suburbs around the city centres. Later sections describe the development of the utility systems transporting water, wastes, energy and information, which are needed when people locate in cities at urban densities.

The Size Distribution of Urban Settlements

The high proportion of the population of each of the Australian colonies and states found in its capital city has caused a great deal of comment, among both earlier commentators (Coghlan, 1896, 47) and recent historians (Butlin, 1964, 181–99). As early as 1901 more than 37 per cent of the populations of four states were found in their capitals and over one-fifth in the other two. Figure 2.1 shows that except during a few periods, such as the depressions of the 1890s and the 1930s, that proportion has tended to increase steadily since the gold rushes of the 1850s. During the nineteenth century Hobart was also an exception for special reasons. Although metropolitan boundaries were not defined in a consistent way prior to the 1966 Census, this is likely to have little effect in changes over long periods, but could affect changes in shorter periods (Linge, 1965; McCarty, 1970).

Both McCarty (1970) and Turner (1967) have argued that this high concentration was due to the fact that Australian urban growth came mainly from overseas migration, while in most other countries it came mainly from rural-to-urban migration. In those countries urbanisation has drawn people previously engaged in largely self-sufficient farming into industrial and commercial jobs in the towns and cities. Workers were released from farming as it became more commercial, more specialised and more capital-intensive. This process occurred in Britain and a number of other

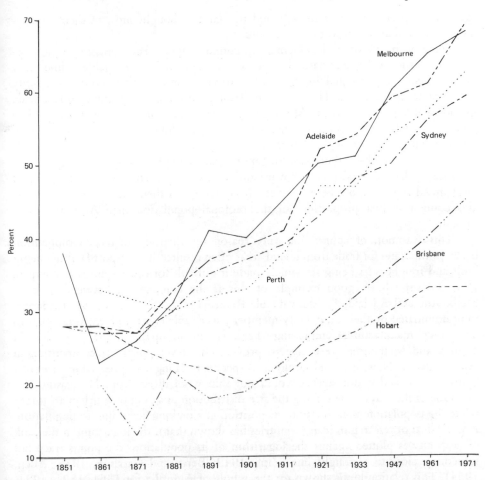

Figure 2.1 Capital city population as a percentage of colonial/state population: 1851–1971.
Sources: 1851–1891—Linge (in press); 1901–1911—McCarty (1970); 1921–1971 —Censuses and Year Books.

European countries in the eighteenth and nineteenth centuries. It is still occurring in areas such as western France and southern Italy. Even in the United States and Canada the eastern regions were settled in the first instance mainly by farmers who led a relatively self-sufficient existence, and urbanisation involved a degree of rural depopulation (Lampard, 1968; Hirsch, 1973, Ch.9).

By contrast Australia, like the western United States, New Zealand and the southern parts of South America, never had a peasant agriculture. From the beginning Australian farmers concentrated on commercial agriculture, producing almost solely for the market rather than for their own consumption. The wheat and wool producers sold nearly everything they produced, and most of the wool was exported to other countries. The only exception may have been in the first few years in the Hawkesbury and Derwent valleys. But once settlement spread beyond the Blue Mountains, agricultural production was for sale and the farmers bought most of their requirements rather than produce for themselves.

Some of the industrial development in countries with large peasant farming populations was located where natural resources such as coal were available, while other developments were located in the market towns where workers could be readily recruited from the farms. The result, in Western Europe for example, was a wide spread of urban development. Although some cities have become much larger than others, especially in the twentieth century, they rarely house as large a proportion of the regional population as the Australian state capitals. Some of the colonial entrepôt cities, such as Bangkok, Rangoon, Singapore and Colombo, came to dominate their countries' urban settlements because urbanisation occurred after the development of mechanised transport, but because of the high density of their rural populations they also contain smaller proportions of the regional population than Australian state capitals.

This was not, of course, the only reason for their dominance. Competition between the states for trade from inland areas often resulted in transport facilities being built and freight rates being set which made it difficult for other centres to compete with the capitals. A good example of this is the competition between Sydney, Melbourne and Adelaide for the valuable Riverina trade (Cloher, 1975). Trade unions, dominated by their capital city members, were able to set uniform wage rates to discourage manufacturers employing cheap labour in smaller centres. Traders in Sydney and Melbourne were able to prevent the development of competition in centres such as Newcastle and Geelong, respectively (Linge, in press). For example, Sydney stock and station agents would not ship wool direct from Newcastle.

One of the ways of describing the size distribution of a country's urban areas is to relate the population of each city to its position in a ranking according to population. A good deal of research in many countries has shown that if the logarithm of the rank of each city is plotted against the logarithm of its population, the points trace out something close to a straight line (Zipf, 1949; Berry and Garrison, 1958; Allen, 1954). This relationship is shown for the whole of Australia for 1861, 1891, 1921, 1947 and 1971 in Figure 2.2. It is reasonably close to a straight line. The main deviations occur among the largest cities, and reflect the dominance of Sydney and Melbourne in particular, and to a lesser extent, Adelaide, Brisbane and Perth. Up to a population of some 70 000 in 1971 the urban size distribution is similar to that observed in other countries, with a slope close to -1.0 in the logarithmic relationship (Zipf, 1949; Allen, 1954). Above that size the effect of the small number of medium-sized cities (only five centres between 75 000 and 600 000) can be seen. The picture has remained much the same over most of Australia's recent history, though there is a clear tendency for the curve to become steeper, especially since 1947, reflecting more rapid growth in the larger than the smaller centres.

If this relationship is plotted for each state, on the grounds that the colonies and the states have been relatively, though decreasingly, independent, an even more marked steep section joins the largest centre to the second largest (Figure 2.3). Another way to measure the dominance of the largest city is to calculate the ratio of the total population of the next, say four, cities to the population of the largest. If the linear logarithmic relationship holds, and if the slope is equal to -1.0, as suggested by Zipf (1949), and as appears to hold, for example, in the United States (Mills, 1972b), that ratio should be about 1.28. The actual ratios are shown for each state, for a selection of years, in Table 2.1.

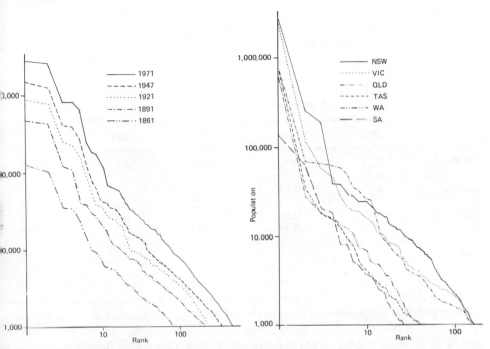

Figure 2.2 Rank-size relationship for Australian towns over 1000 population: 1861–1971.
Source: Censuses.

Figure 2.3 Rank-size relationship for towns in each state over 1000 population.
Source: Censuses.

On this evidence the degree of metropolitan dominance has been greater in Australia than in most other countries, including the western United States and New Zealand (Robinson, 1962), which were settled by external migration at about the same time. There are many reasons and we can only explore them briefly. Firstly, a number of Australian cities started as convict settlements—not only Sydney, Hobart and Brisbane, but also smaller centres like Newcastle and Port Macquarie. Although Perth was first settled by free settlers it took on the role of convict settlement later, during a very important stage of its development (1850 to 1868). The convict settlements were not dependent for their economic well-being on exports from their rural hinterlands. Rather, the services they exported were custodial and were paid for in supplies from Britain and in the salaries of troops and officials. The demand for supplies for convicts and troops provided a market for what the farmers produced. The large convict settlements were well established and could easily serve the growing demand for urban services as the hinterland was settled and developed.

Secondly, the colonial capitals were able to attract much of the industrial development which began in Australia in the later part of the nineteenth century (Linge, in press). They contained the greatest concentration of buying power in the community; through them passed the exports of wheat and wool from the interior and the imports of both consumer goods and the raw materials required for manufacturing. They were also the best places to recruit workers and they had few competitors. As a result, despite the rapid development of rural Australia between 1861 and 1901, and the greatly improved transport network, the capitals, apart from Hobart, were able to maintain or increase their proportion of the colonial populations.

TABLE 2.1   *Ratio of the Total Population of Next Four Centres to the Population of Largest Centre: 1861–1971*

	1861	1891	1921	1947	1971
NSW.	0.21	0.15	0.08	0.13	0.19
Vic.	0.32	0.19	0.12	0.10	0.10
Qld.	1.10	0.49	0.41	0.32	0.30
SA.	0.24	0.11	0.08	0.08	0.10
WA.	0.65	0.36	0.19	0.15	0.10
Tas.	1.22	0.76	0.81	0.75	0.84

Source: Censuses

Although contemporaries complained about migration from rural areas to the state capitals in the second half of the nineteenth century, this cannot account for much of their growth. Despite the increase in the *proportion* of the population in the capital cities, the number of people in the non-metropolitan areas of the colonies/states continued to increase. Indeed, when the pattern of Australian urban development was being formed in the late 1800s the non-metropolitan, and even the non-urban, populations were still growing. They did not always retain all of their natural increase but, except during the 1880s, migration from rural areas made a relatively small contribution to the growth of the urban centres (Butlin, 1964, 181–3). When people did move out of rural areas they were less likely to move to local country towns than in the older peasant economies, where many families had lived in the same area, or even the same village, for many generations. The Australian rural population was more mobile and more likely to move directly to a large city.

The natural environment in Australia discouraged the establishment of self-sufficient farming in most places. The soils were not sufficiently fertile and the rainfall was too low. The only economically viable kind of farming was extensive grazing, and later, where soils and rainfall permitted, extensive cropping. It would have been very costly to produce the wide variety of crops and animal products required to meet the farmers' own needs.

Australia's geography produced a settlement pattern which made the establishment of large inland towns unlikely. The agriculturally productive parts are found in a crescent around the east and south coasts, which is broken into a series of narrower crescents. A broken coastal strip of varying width and productivity is separated by rugged fault mountains from a broad band of tablelands where rainfall is still adequate but soil fertility generally low. This is mainly a grazing area producing fine wool at a low stocking density. Goulburn, Armidale and Bathurst lie in this band. Most lines of communication run along the coast and along the tablelands rather than crossing the ranges. A further band where the soils are more fertile and the rainfall still adequate supports the wheat-sheep belt. As the rainfall declines further inland cropping gives way again to extensive grazing (*Atlas of Australian Resources*, 1973). Only the wheat-sheep belt is productive enough to support much urban development and it is too narrow to support large regional centres.

The country towns which did develop provided services which were needed closer than in the capital city, and served as links between the farms and the capital cities. They were collecting points for farm products on their way to the cities and ports, and distribution points for the requirements of the farming community that were imported or produced in the capital cities. A limited amount of processing, for example flour milling, wool scouring and tanning, took place in towns and rural areas, and some manufacturing for the local market in the largest of them. Manufacturing developed in the Victorian gold towns in the 1850s and 1860s. Engineering firms were established for mining equipment and continued in general engineering, serving a wider market and absorbing much of the labour from the declining employment in mining. During these two decades the non-metropolitan centres housed a large part of the colony's rapidly growing manufacturing workforce. Although later, manufacturing grew much more rapidly in Melbourne (Linge, in press), some industries, such as woollen mills, are still mainly located outside Melbourne. Other towns could not compete with the capitals for most of the manufacturing and commercial activity which served a colonial or state-wide market, for only the state capitals had transport links with all other parts of the states.

In some countries mineral deposits formed the basis of large concentrations of population, which subsequently took on the general functions of cities. In Australia few large cities depend on mining—the first was Broken Hill in the 1880s, but the two most important today are the coal towns of Newcastle and Wollongong. Some of the other mineral deposits which have been important in Australia's development are in locations so remote and unproductive that most of the processing is done elsewhere. Examples are Broken Hill's base metals, though Broken Hill was the third largest centre in New South Wales until overtaken by Wollongong, Mt. Isa's copper, Kalgoorlie's gold and Yampi Sound's iron ore. The iron ore deposits west of Spencer Gulf in South Australia are used in the steel and ship building industries at Whyalla, but only as a result of pressure from the State Government. Coal from central Queensland and iron ore from the north of Western Australia are largely exported at present. Gold mining led to the establishment of a number of towns in Victoria and New South Wales but it was not sufficiently important nor sustained for long enough, for them to become large inland cities. The Victorian gold towns were larger and became permanent because they relied on deep mining, whereas the alluvial mining in New South Wales gave rise to less permanent settlements.

Compared with most of the 'colonial' countries, Australia was settled relatively late, so that a large proportion of its development has taken place since the introduction of mechanised transport. The railways were the first, and in many ways the most important, influence. The maximum length of railways open in Australia was some 44 000 km, in 1941. Of this 4 per cent was opened by 1871, 15 per cent by 1881, 35 per cent by 1I91 and 46 per cent by 1901. This large volume of railway building occurred while the Australian population was expanding from 1.2 million in 1861 to 2 million in 1901. It was during this period, following the gold rushes of the 1850s, that the Australian economy began to take on a more permanent shape and many country towns were established. The original settlement of much of inland Australia was by squatters who produced wool which was transported to the coast by bullock waggons. It was only when railways were built that wheat production became possible. Later, with the development of refrigeration, beef and mutton could be produced for export.

The railways not only facilitated moving the produce out, but also reduced the costs of bringing the farmers' requirements from the ports and factories. Butlin (1964, 184–93) has shown that towns served by railways tended to expand more rapidly, but because adjacent states built railways of different gauges it was difficult, as long as rail was an important means of transport, for a rival centre to grow between two capitals and draw custom from more than one state. In addition the railway rates were tapered with distance so that goods could be transported more cheaply within a state than across state boundaries.

The particular pattern of railway investment reinforced the dominance of the capital cities. The lines radiated out from the capitals so that often the cheapest way to get goods from one country town to another was through the capital. Queensland was exceptional in that the main routes from the inland areas went to the coastal ports such as Townsville and Rockhampton instead of directly to Brisbane. For some time the connection between these ports and Brisbane was by coastal shipping so that the ports played an important role as trans-shipment points. Only later was the coastal rail connection completed (Lewis, 1973). Along with the fact that it is in one corner of the state, this helps to account for the much smaller proportion of the state's population found in Brisbane than in the other mainland capitals. Feeder lines to the ports were also built in South Australia, but only after Adelaide had established its dominance, and mostly after the ports were linked with Adelaide. Hobart is also small relative to the state population. Launceston, the state's second city, gained equal legal status with Hobart as a port, and gained more from the mineral developments of the 1880s. Despite its virtues as a site for a penal settlement, and the quality of its harbour, Hobart turned out to be badly located to serve as the economic capital of an island with most of its productive land in the north, and its main economic ties north to the mainland.

It is important not to exaggerate the influence of mechanised transport as a reason for the capitals *becoming* much larger than other towns. Metropolitan dominance was established in Australia before mechanised transport became significant (Cloher, 1975). The seventies and eighties were the major period of railway expansion, but by that time the entrepôt port functions had become very important in relation to pastoral production and gold mining. The railways enabled them to maintain that position as their hinterland areas expanded in production and population.

Despite the advantages the capitals enjoyed there have been periods when individual non-metropolitan towns have grown more rapidly. For the most part this has been due to mining. Gold in the nineteenth century, coal and various non-ferrous metals in the early part of this century, and more recently iron ore and bauxite have produced boom towns. Other towns have grown rapidly because of expansion of agriculture in their hinterlands. Examples are Toowoomba on the rich Darling Downs and Griffith in the Murrumbidgee Irrigation Area. Rapid growth also occurred with the creation of the national capital at Canberra and the growth of tourism and recreation on the Gold Coast, south of Brisbane.

Most of the accessible parts of the coast lack good natural harbours suitable for overseas shipping. As a result overseas trade was concentrated in the capitals and, to a lesser extent, in a few other ports such as Newcastle and Geelong. Had there been more good harbours coastal shipping may have assumed a more important role in stimulating the growth of regional centres.

The dominance of the capital cities was reinforced by the fact that each was the centre of a separate colonial administration until the turn of the century. Since Federation in 1901 the states have remained responsible for most of the aspects of government and administration which involve direct contact with the population. The infant Commonwealth Government remained in Melbourne for many years, and its employees boosted the workforce of that city. It was not until 1927 that the Commonwealth Parliament was transferred to Canberra, and only in the 1950s and 1960s were many departments transferred.

Government in Australia evolved in a way which reflected economic development. Whereas in Europe and the United States the first demands for many functions of government appeared at the local level, Australians relied much more on the central colonial governments. While the parish, the shire and the municipality in other countries took the initiative in education, police protection, fire protection and welfare services, these and many other functions were provided by the governors and the colonial administrations in Australia. This could be easily understood in the convict settlement colonies but it was not confined to them.

Local government in Australia evolved in two phases. The first phase appears to have been part of the effort to get some independence from British rule, and was limited to the capitals and a few other cities. Adelaide had the first local council in Australia, founded in 1839; Perth, Sydney, Melbourne and Geelong all followed in 1842. Hobart had its first elected council in 1846 and Brisbane in 1859. Life did not run always smoothly for these early councils—the Adelaide council became legally defunct in 1843 and was not re-established for nine years, and the Sydney Corporation was dissolved in 1853 and a new council not elected until 1858.

The second phase involved the establishment of local government in the suburbs of the capitals and in country towns and rural areas. The colonial legislatures passed legislation permitting the incorporation of areas as shires or municipalities. The local residents, however, often seemed to prefer to avoid local taxes and continued to rely on the colonial government for services, even if it meant a lower level of services. Local government was voluntary, and a wide variety of local boards and councils were formed. This ended with consolidation of local government, and in some colonies/states compulsory incorporation. For example, in 1871 in Western Australia and in 1874 in Victoria, almost the whole of each colony was incorporated. In 1906 both Tasmania and New South Wales passed consolidating legislation. But although the whole of the desert and sparsely populated areas of Western Australia and Queensland are now governed by local authorities of some kind, 85 per cent of South Australia and 12 per cent of New South Wales are not part of a local government area and, except in Darwin and Alice Springs, there is no local government in either of the territories.

Although local government legislation in Australia derives to a considerable extent from British legislation, local authorities in this country have fewer functions than their British or North American counterparts. For example, they have almost no responsibility for education or police services and have been almost completely inactive in public housing. In part this is because they have only exercised some of the functions which are permitted under their various Acts. Especially in rural areas their activities have been mainly confined to roads and bridges—in fact in some states rural local authorities have been called 'road boards'. In the United States over half of all government employees are employed by local government compared with only one-tenth in Australia (Neutze, 1974; Joint Study into Local Government Finances, 1976).

Capital City Sites

The siting of the larger cities in Australia is of particular importance because the natural features of the chosen sites and their surrounding areas have had a large influence on the shape and form of subsequent development.

Sydney

After a brief stop in Botany Bay the first settlers moved to Port Jackson and chose the site at Sydney Cove because it combined a supply of fresh water in the Tank Stream with deep water close to the shore. This convenient location for establishing a penal colony proved a good place for an urban centre, with room to expand in most directions (Cumberland County Council, 1948; Winston, 1957; Stephenson, 1966). The harbour not only facilitated communications with the rest of the world but also gave access by boat to many bays and inlets, mostly on the southern shore, which were suitable for housing. One disadvantage was that the soil was relatively infertile on both sides of the harbour: to the east and south-east were sandhills and rocky areas near the coast, and to the south swamps, to the north the sandstone plateau was both infertile and deeply dissected. Further west the soils were more fertile, and a second settlement was soon established at Parramatta. Even further west, in the valley of the Hawkesbury river, more fertile land was found, though some of it is subject to flooding. And with the crossing of the Blue Mountains in 1813 Sydney became the capital of a huge developing region to its west.

West of Sydney, between Port Jackson and the Georges River, the Cumberland Plain spreads to Parramatta and Liverpool and then fans out to a width of over 50 km. It provided easy building sites for housing and industry. To the north of Port Jackson and again south of the Georges River are sandstone plateaux which are deeply eroded by streams. They are difficult and expensive to build on, though they provide very good views. Because of the rough topography north of the harbour, and because of the barrier of the harbour itself, until the Harbour Bridge was completed in 1932 Sydney spread much more rapidly to the south. Sydney's site, which restricts development in most directions, nevertheless provides many prime areas for development which contrast with the less attractive low-lying areas. The natural differences between parts of the site have contributed to the clear distinctions in development between different parts of Sydney.

Melbourne

By contrast, the site chosen for Melbourne in 1835 is topographically easier to develop, more uniform and less interesting (Grant and Searle, 1957; *Victorian Year Book*, 1973). The centre was located near falls on the Yarra River at a place where fresh water was available upstream and tidal water for ships was available downstream. Both east and west of the centre the land was flat or rolling. The Yarra was not an important barrier to travel and was bridged with a wooden structure in 1846. Once Sydney had filled the area between the very steep and rocky plateaux to the north and south (large parts of which were eventually reserved as national parks or military reserves) it could only spread west around a limited circumference. By contrast, Melbourne's location on the shore of a wide bay means that the further the city expands the greater is the circumference around which it can expand. Melbourne's site at the head of the bay also puts it deep into its hinterland and allows it to dominate trade at the expense of smaller centres.

The urban area has not spread evenly in all directions, partly for reasons of geology and climate. To the west and south-west of the city centre the Yarra flowed through swamp areas on either side, which remained unused until late in the century. Later they provided excellent sites for the construction of a port, very close to the city centre, a large railway goods yard between the port and the city centre and extensive industrial development further downstream in the Fishermans Bend area. While the soil to the east of the city centre is mostly a relatively fertile sandy loam, a few miles to the west and north are unproductive grey basaltic clays with a thick layer of hard acidic basalt at a relatively shallow depth in many places. The area is largely flat and treeless and trees are difficult to cultivate. The bare plain is exposed to wind and is an unattractive place to live. Furthermore the average annual rainfall varies from below 500 mm in the west to over 800 mm in the east. Partly as a consequence, urban development extends only about 15 km from the city centre to the north and west compared with 25 to 40 km to the east and south-east, and even further around the bay shores.

Although Melbourne was sited so that the port could be adjacent to the city centre, the inadequacy of the Yarra River wharves soon became obvious. The larger overseas vessels began to berth at Port Melbourne in the bay, and the first railway line in Australia was built between Melbourne and Port Melbourne in 1854. Port Melbourne was not a satisfactory port, however. The Melbourne Harbour Trust was formed in 1876 and between 1884 and 1892 the Yarra was shortened by the cutting of the Coode Canal and a large dock was cut from the West Melbourne swamps, close to the city centre. Although bridging of the Yarra above the port is relatively cheap there has been no bridge below the port. As a result all traffic between south-east and south-west Melbourne has to pass through the congested areas of the city centre. A 'Lower Yarra Crossing' is under construction.

Brisbane

Brisbane was established from Sydney in 1825 as a penal settlement for the more intractable convicts. The site was chosen where a ridge runs towards the Brisbane River and where a stream running into the river provided fresh water. Barracks were built on the ridge at a location which was easy to defend against attack—one of the few cases in Australia of a defensive choice of site. Since the settlement's communications with the outside world would be by ship it needed to be on the navigable reaches of the Brisbane River. That river was a much more formidable barrier than the Yarra, and settlement on the south bank was restricted until the first bridge was erected in 1865, and then the cost nearly bankrupted the City Council (Greenwood and Laverty, 1959). Brisbane's riverside wharves downstream from the city centre have served it over a long period but it was decided in 1974 that most will be replaced by a new port at the mouth of the river.

Brisbane has experienced serious flooding on a number of occasions. Disastrous floods occurred in 1893, 1897 and again in 1974. In 1864 and 1869, local flooding was serious enough to flood the ground floors and basements of premises in the main shopping street. In the latter part of the nineteenth century the city council and the State Government cooperated in extensive work on storm water drainage to relieve problems of local flooding. But the large-scale general flooding affects a considerable area of low-lying land which cannot be economically protected. However, the floods have been infrequent in this century and much of this land has been developed for housing and other purposes.

Queensland became a separate colony in 1859. Although Brisbane was the most important centre, it was located in one corner of a very large territory and less well placed than most of the other colonial capitals to dominate its hinterland. Ipswich, further upstream, was the graziers' choice for a capital. The Darling Downs, inland from Brisbane, was first explored and settled overland from New South Wales. For many years in the nineteenth century, north and central Queensland looked to Sydney as their economic capital, rather than to Brisbane.

Adelaide

The site for Adelaide was chosen more deliberately than that for most other Australian cities (*Report on the Metropolitan Area of Adelaide*, 1962). Colonel Light, in 1836, chose the area about six miles inland from the Gulf of St Vincent, astride the Torrens River. Almost midway between the coast and the edge of the Mount Lofty Ranges, the centre of Adelaide remains, like Brisbane but unlike Sydney and Melbourne, close to the geographic centre of the urban area. Like the other colonial settlements Adelaide needed a port, but in this case the city centre was not built nearby, partly because only a limited amount of sandy and swampy land was available for development near the only suitable harbour. The first railway in the colony was built to connect Port Adelaide with the city in 1856.

The Adelaide Plain between the ranges and the sea is easily developed. Perhaps its main limitation is that the soils have only a limited absorptive capacity, which led to Adelaide becoming the first city in Australia to install water-borne sewerage. The foothills of the ranges themselves provide some land suitable for development, especially where they open out towards the coast to the south. The steeper slopes are expensive to develop though, and are being kept free from urban development as far as possible because of the scenic backdrop they provide for the city. North of the present urban area there is a wide plain suitable for development.

Perth

The site for Perth was also deliberately chosen, some distance from the port of Fremantle (Stephenson and Hepburn, 1955). The first settlers arrived in 1829 and established a settlement on the north bank of the Swan River some 15 km from Fremantle. The river itself was easily bridged just upstream from the site of the first settlement. In some respects the site of Perth is like Adelaide's, in this case between the Darling Ranges and the sea, although the Darling escarpment is further from the coast, lower, less scenic, and more broken. Very little of the land in the ranges is too steep for building.

Most of the site is sandy and relatively unproductive agriculturally. Most of the land along to the foreshore is higher than further inland, creating a number of poorly drained areas unsuitable for building. Nevertheless the sandy soil over much of the area has a high level of absorbency, and the introduction of water-borne sewerage was less urgent than in most Australian cities.

Hobart

Hobart was the second choice for a settlement in south-eastern Tasmania. The first, in 1803, was at Risdon on the opposite bank of the Derwent estuary. The more permanent settlement, established in the following year, was sited where Sullivan's Creek gave a good supply of water and where there was deep water close to the shore.

Although it has a fine port, Hobart is hemmed in by Mount Wellington, and the difficulty of crossing the Derwent estuary restricted the development of the easier terrain on the east side of the river. In 1964 a high level bridge was completed, only to be cut in an accident in 1975. When the main reason for a settlement in Tasmania was to protect the sea lanes of Bass Strait, it is surprising that this south-eastern site was chosen. A settlement was in fact established on the Tamar, near present-day Launceston, in the same year as at Hobart, but the capital remained the administrative centre and the main convict settlement.

Canberra

The Australian constitution required that the federal territory 'shall be in the State of New South Wales and be distant not less than one hundred miles from Sydney'. The instructions for the selection of the city site included the requirements that it should be

carefully considered 'from an hygienic standpoint, with a view to securing pictures-
queness and also with the object of beautification and expansion'. The actual site,
selected to 1909, straddles the flood plain of the Molonglo River, which was dammed
to form Lake Burley Griffin in 1964. Most of the surrounding area is a rolling plateau
broken by a series of hills. This topography has lent itself to the development of the
city in a series of separated 'towns', but has not been a serious barrier to transport. To
the south, steeper country will limit development. With a rainfall of only about 500
mm, heavy summer irrigation is required to maintain the lawns and other non-native
vegetation so much a feature of the city.

Establishment of Canberra as the national capital began with the opening of
Parliament House in 1927. The subsequent depression, war and post-war shortages
curtailed its development, and only in the mid-1950s was its growth accelerated so
that it is now very much a city of the automobile age.

Suburban Transport and City Expansion

The effects of the transport system on the spread of the city at different periods can explain many of the features of modern cities. Until the mid-1950s transport within
Australian cities and towns was on foot, or by horse or bullock wagon, except in those
few locations served by boat. At this time, for example, the best way to transport
goods between Sydney and Windsor was via the Hawkesbury River and the open sea.
Because most people walked, cities developed as compact settlements. This is shown in
maps of Australian cities in 1861 which indicate that the areas occupied were small
—Sydney's population was only 96 000 and Melbourne's 125 000. Although overall
population densities were not high, by comparison with cities in other parts of the
world, the houses and shops—mostly single-storey—were clustered close together
with open areas separating the clusters.

Gross municipal population densities were not high even by present-day suburban
standards. In Melbourne, for example, in 1861, nearly half of the population lived in
municipalities with less than 20 persons per hectare. By 1891 this had shrunk to about
one-third, and over 40 per cent of the population was in municipalities with more
than 40 persons per hectare. In 1971 the comparable percentage had fallen to 10.
Even these figures understate residential densities as photographs and maps surviving
from this period show large open areas between houses. Hence the gross municipal
population densities are much lower than the population densities in residential areas.

The first means of mechanised transport which made an impact on Australian cities
was the steam railway. The first railways in Australia were built in Sydney and
Melbourne, and those two cities have developed extensive suburban systems.
Suburban railways in the other state capitals developed later and remained less impor-
tant (see Chapter 5). Following the 1854 opening of a line linking Melbourne with
Port Melbourne, a line was opened in 1855 between Redfern, an inner suburb of
Sydney, and Parramatta, then a 'rural' centre at the head of the river. In the same year
Redfern was connected by a goods line to Darling Harbour, adjacent to the city
centre. Although the Parramatta line subsequently became a part of the suburban

system it was not originally designed to carry suburban traffic. The urgent need in Australia at this time was to provide a more efficient means of moving goods between the ports and the hinterland. It was claimed that the cost of transport doubled the price of goods sent from Melbourne to the goldfields (Butlin, 1962, 301).

The next line completed in the Sydney area was from Granville to Liverpool in 1856. From Liverpool and Parramatta, both of which were quite distinct settlements, lines were constructed to Goulburn, Bathurst and beyond before there was any further significant building in the suburban areas of Sydney. Even though there were few stations between Sydney and Parramatta on the original line they still seem to have attracted some urban development. Maps of Sydney in 1881 show the urban area spreading towards the west. It was not until 1884 that the line to the south through Hurstville and Sutherland was commenced, and in 1886 the line to the north, branching from the Parramatta line at Strathfield to Hornsby and later to Newcastle. All of these lines were primarily part of a state rather than a suburban system, linking Sydney with the west, the south-west, the Illawarra to the south, and with Newcastle and the lines radiating from it in the north.

The first purely suburban line was built from Hornsby to St Leonards in 1890 and continued to Milson's Point in 1893; it brought people living in the northern suburbs to the ferry for the harbour crossing to the city centre. Additional lines for purely suburban traffic were constructed during the 1890s and construction continued right through to the 1930s when the East Hills line (1931), the line from Sutherland to Cronulla (1939), and the link across the Harbour Bridge (1932), were completed. Finally the city underground loop was completed in 1956.

More of Melbourne's railway system was built specifically for suburban traffic. It was built earlier and assumed a more important role in the early development of suburbs. In 1857 the private company which built the first railway to the port had opened a branch to St Kilda. By 1878 suburban lines served Essendon, Brighton, Oakleigh, Williamstown and Hawthorn. During the rapid expansion of Melbourne from a population of less than 300 000 to 500 000 in the boom of the 1880s, railway building continued and virtually the whole of the present suburban railway system was completed by 1890 (Davison, 1970).

The earlier and more extensive system of suburban railways in Melbourne would be expected to encourage the population to spread further from the centre of employment and services and make it a less compact centre than Sydney. Compactness of development is difficult to measure using municipal populations—the only data available before the Second World War. One kind of density profile is shown in Figure 2.4. Municipalities are arranged in rings around the city centre, and the average population density in successive rings is shown. It shows that in 1891, Sydney's population density in the areas close to the centre was significantly higher than Melbourne's, even though its total population was smaller by almost 20 per cent. Melbourne's population was spread to more distant suburbs.

Although the fully developed suburban railway system in Melbourne continued to have an influence on its pattern of growth into the twentieth century, its influence in the nineteenth century should not be exaggerated. During the thirty years 1861 to 1891, the density of population in the cities and inner suburbs of both Sydney and

Melbourne increased markedly. By 1891 the inner suburbs of Melbourne had almost reached their maximum populations. It was during this period, between 1861 and 1891, that many of the terrace houses in the inner suburbs of both cities were built: more in Sydney than in Melbourne. Although there was also a geographical spread of population, it was mainly into the inner suburbs served by trams while the railways served the more remote suburbs (Davison, 1970, 177). In 1890, when most of Melbourne's suburban railways had been in operation for a number of years, it was estimated that they carried annually only some 36 million passengers (*Victorian Year Book*, 1892) or about 60 000 two-way journeys per working day, when the population was nearly 500 000. The whole New South Wales Railways, with much less suburban traffic, carried only 17 million passengers in 1890. It would appear that suburban railways in Sydney were not carrying many passengers up to 1890.

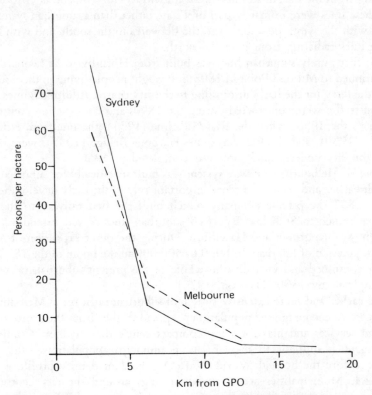

Figure 2.4 Municipal population density and distance from city centre: Sydney and Melbourne 1891.
Source: Censuses.

Table 2.2 shows the number of passenger journeys in Sydney and Melbourne by each mode of public transport at ten-yearly intervals. It shows the rise and subsequent decline in the number of rail and tram passengers. Bus services have developed more recently and, especially in Sydney, have become very important. The number of passengers carried is an imperfect measure of the volume of traffic, especially in the case of those modes where the average length of trip has changed. The numbers of passenger kilometres travelled are not recorded for most modes but the continuing spread of the metropolitan areas would be expected to increase average journey length, especially in the case of trains. For example, between 1940 and 1970 the length of the average suburban train journey in Melbourne increased 25 per cent, from about 12 to 15 kilometres.

TABLE 2.2   *Public Transport Journeys in Sydney and Melbourne: 1870–1970 (millions per year)*

		Railways[a]	Trams	Government buses	Private buses	Ferries
Sydney	1880	*	2	0	*	*
	1890	15	46[b]	0	*	*
	1900	23	62[b]	0	*	*
	1910	48	191	0	*	24
	1920	104	309	0	*	41
	1930	138	293	0	94	45
	1940	168	286	68	29	28
	1950	250	270	171	93	22
	1960	240	45	210	78	15
	1970	239	0	214	110	15
Melbourne	1870	5	0	0	*	
	1880	11	0	0	*	
	1890	36	45	0	*	
	1900	44	42	0	*	
	1910	80	75	0	*	
	1920	124	198	0	*	
	1930	150	198	4	*	
	1940	138	185	18	*	
	1950	184	204	60	*	
	1960	146	178	31	83	
	1970	138	111	22	78	

Sources: Sydney: *N.S.W. Yearbooks, N.S.W. Statistical Register*; T.A. Coghlan, *Wealth and Progress of N.S.W.*, various years; ABS, *Transport and Communications Bulletins; Sydney Area Transportation Study Report*, Vol.1, p.IV.29; Annual Reports of the Sydney Harbour Trust, and the Department of Government Transport.
Melbourne: *Victorian Year Book*, 1973. Annual Reports of the Commissioner for Railways, and of the Transport Regulation Board (private buses).

Notes: a In Sydney the railway journeys are those made within 22 miles of Sydney and Newcastle in 1890 and 1900, and thereafter within 34 miles of Sydney and Newcastle. In 1971 only 0.6 million journeys were in the Newcastle area.
b Estimated to exclude Newcastle and to take account of the effect of the 'penny fare' system.
* Not available.

Table 2.2 does not reflect the extent to which public transport was used by each city's residents because it does not take account of population growth. Figure 2.5 shows the number of journeys per head at census dates closest to the dates used in the table. The estimates are based on metropolitan populations which may vary from the catchment area of the public transport system. Journeys by private bus are omitted because they are not available before 1929 in Sydney or before 1961 in Melbourne. The table and the figure show that the most rapid increase in the use of public transport in the two cities occurred in the first two decades of the present century, and again during the Second World War.

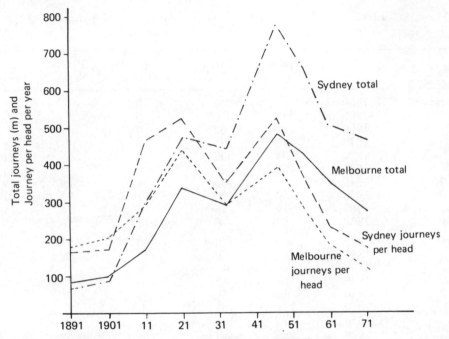

Figure 2.5 Public transport journeys in Sydney and Melbourne: 1891–1971. *Source*: Table 2.2.

Trams appeared somewhat later than suburban railways, and required less investment. They were more widely used than the trains and probably had a greater effect on city life and on the shape of development of Australian cities in the period before the Second World War. A horse tram route began operating from Redfern railway station to Circular Quay in Sydney, as early as 1861, but its heavy raised rails impeded other traffic and the service was discontinued four years later. In 1879 steam trams were introduced in Sydney (Birch and Macmillan, 1962, 168) and proved so popular that within six years there were nearly fifty kilometres of tramways. In 1893 the first electric tramway was opened. By 1910 nearly 90 per cent of the route in the 'Sydney and suburban' system was electrified, though steam trams still served Parramatta (10.9 km) and the Sutherland to Cronulla line (12.1 km). By 1905 there were 137 kilometres of route in the Sydney and suburban system, which had expanded to 222 kilometres in 1922. By 1890 trams carried some 46 million passengers, compared with only about 15 million on the suburban railway system.

Melbourne started rather later and adopted cable rather than steam trams. The first were introduced in 1885 and by 1891, 62 kilometres of track were open and in that year some 48 million passengers were carried. The new tram routes opened from the 1890s had electric trams but cable routes were not electrified until the late 1920s and the 1930s. Trams quickly proved popular. Within five years of the opening of the first route they were carrying 45 million passengers—more than the suburban rail system. Of course tram trips were shorter. They were particularly suitable for travel within what is now the inner suburban area.

Trams were used in all of the large Australian cities and provided the main means of transport for people living in inner and middle suburbs. In Sydney and Melbourne many routes extended to what was, up to the 1920s, almost the fringe of contiguous urban development. Tram routes served rich and poor suburbs alike, and did not have the working class image they had in Britain. Suburban railways served some of the same suburbs. Indeed according to Davison (1970) in Melbourne, 'the story of the part played by rail and tramways in suburban development is of the gradual and mutual interpenetration of each system on the other's catchment areas'. However, the railways were more suitable for the outer suburban and ex-urban commuter. The main development of low density suburbs in Australia began in the 1920s and accelerated after the Second World War. People living in these areas relied on automobiles and motor buses, which competed strongly with trams, and on the suburban railways.

Private bus services have played an important role in urban transport in Australia, filling gaps in the services provided by government trains and trams, providing feeder services to railway stations and cross-suburban services, and pioneering services which were subsequently taken over by government transport authorities. The earliest were the horse-drawn buses which operated in both Sydney and Melbourne before trains or trams. They provided transport mainly over relatively short distances and were not affected by the introduction of the suburban railways. Some routes were planned for future conversion to trams and the rapid expansion of tramways in the 1880s put many others out of business.

The next period when private buses became important came with the introduction of pneumatic-tyred motor buses in the 1920s, some of whose owner-operators received their mechanical training in the Services in the First World War. They were able to operate where there was too little traffic to justify tram lines. They fed both trams and trains, and were able to provide some services to the rapidly expanding low density suburbs. They also competed with trams in some areas, providing a more flexible service. There is very little information about their operations, but in 1929 in Sydney they carried nearly 100 million passengers—about two-thirds of the number carried by the suburban rail system.

In the 1920s the government public transport authorities became aware of a degree of 'wasteful' competition between private buses and government trams. It was also clear that buses could be operated economically on some routes not served by trams. As a result government bus services were introduced in the mid-1920s in Melbourne, and the early 1930s in Sydney. In Sydney they quickly became important, and even before trams began to be replaced by buses, in 1949, they carried something like a quarter as many passengers as trams, and far more than the remaining private buses. In Melbourne government buses, run by the Tramways Board, have never played a large role, perhaps because of the greater extent of the suburban rail and tram networks. In both Sydney and Melbourne private bus services operate mainly in the middle and outer suburbs, where load densities are relatively low. They provide services to railway stations and suburban employment and shopping centres.

The expansion of tram networks continued up to the early 1920s when it became more economical to serve some of the lower density routes with buses. After the Second World War, with the increase in road traffic volumes, trams were found to interfere with the flow of traffic much more than buses. Maintenance of both tracks and overhead wires is expensive. At the end of the Second World War the track and rolling stock had deteriorated badly, due to a lack of maintenance during the depression and the war, and as a result tram services have disappeared from all of the state capitals except Melbourne (and one route in Adelaide). Melbourne had a more modern system which is run by an independent Tramways Board rather than a government department. Melbourne is also fortunate in having a number of very wide radial roads, originally stock routes, which can cope with tram services and a large volume of motor traffic.

Figure 2.5 shows that since the turn of the century public transport has played a less important role in Melbourne than in Sydney. Melbourne's wider roads, especially the 'three-chain' radials, can accommodate more private vehicles, as reflected by Melbourne's slightly higher car ownership. In a survey in May 1970 it was found that 31 per cent of journeys to work in Melbourne were made by public transport compared with 37 per cent in Sydney (CBCS, 1972).

The expansion of train and tram services led to a rapid growth in the use of public transport per head up to the early 1920s. During the 1920s and 1930s there was little growth and the number of journeys per head fell during the depression, but the revival of economic activity in the late 1930s, and the war-time shortage of petrol, caused the use of public transport to reach new peaks. Its use fell off only gradually in the early post-war period so that the level was still very high at the 1947 Census. Thereafter, however, the use of public transport declined with the increasing ownership and use of private cars. Population and jobs also became dispersed away from the inner areas, where public transport is most effective, to the suburbs.

Car ownership allowed people to live away from public transport routes. This had a major effect on the growth and shape of Australian cities, especially allowing areas between railway routes to be developed. The most rapid expansion of car ownership occurred during the 1920s. There is no information about car ownership in urban areas before 1955, but the number registered per head in Australia, shown in Figure 2.6, grew rapidly in the 1920s, and then fluctuated between 65 and 80 per thousand until growth resumed after the Second World War.

The initial spread of car ownership was not at the expense of public transport. In fact the number of public transport journeys per head in Sydney in 1947 was about the same as in 1921. During, and for a few years after, the Second World War, a period of high employment and petrol rationing, greater use was made of public transport than ever before or since.

Since the Second World War car ownership in Australia has increased rapidly. Although less rapid than in the 1920s, the absolute growth, from 80 cars per thousand in 1950 to 330 in 1973 is much greater. The 1950s and 1960s were the periods when car ownership spread to the majority of Australian families. At the 1971 Census 74 per cent of private dwellings in Sydney and 77 per cent in Melbourne had one or more cars.

The effects of the development of intra-urban transport are evident in the spread of the cities. The advent of steam trams in Sydney and cable trams in Melbourne permitted suburban development on a large scale for the first time. Most of the development occurred relatively close to the centres and at a relatively high density. This was

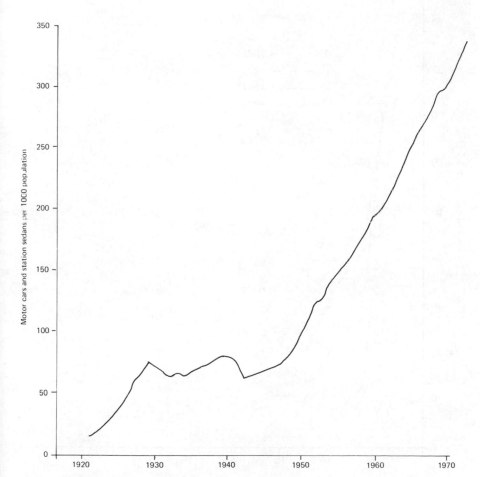

Figure 2.6 Motor car ownership per head: 1921–1973.

Note: Figures for 1921–24 are for New South Wales, South Australia and Tasmania only.

Source: ABS, *Transport and Communication*.

particularly true of Sydney where densities in the inner area were consistently higher than in Melbourne. Even in 1921 over 60 per cent of Sydney's population was found within what are now regarded as the inner municipalities, where the average overall density was over 30 persons per hectare.

Figures 2.7 and 2.8 show the changes in the population density at different distances from the centre of Sydney and Melbourne metropolitan areas from 1891 to

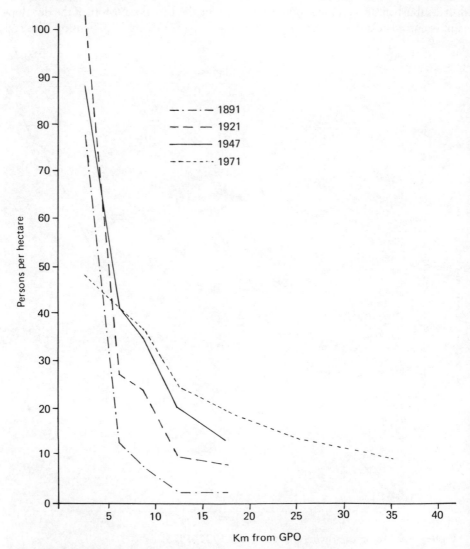

Figure 2.7 Municipal population density and distance from the centre: Sydney 1891–1971.

Source: Censuses.

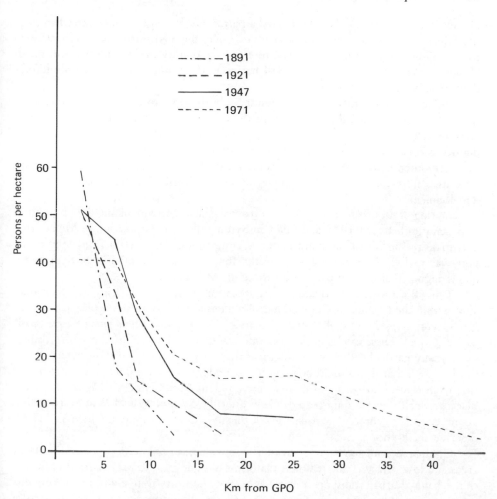

Figure 2.8 Municipal population density and distance from the centre: Melbourne 1891–1971.
Source: Censuses.

1971. The gradient of population density with distance from the centre has become less steep in both cities over the eighty years covered by the graphs. Densities in the inner municipalities have fallen as those in the middle and outer suburbs have increased as they became fully developed.

However there are interesting and important differences between the two cities, at least some of which resulted from the earlier development of suburban railways in Melbourne, and the more rapid growth of Sydney's tramway system between 1900 and 1920.[1] Sydney's topography, which makes access from the city centre to many of

[1] Sydney's tramway system trebled from 56 miles in 1900 to 177 in 1920 while Melbourne's less than doubled from 59 to 113 miles.

its suburbs more difficult, has also played a part. Sydney's higher inner-suburban density, already evident in 1891, was accentuated over the next thirty years as the density rose in Sydney and fell in Melbourne. In 1947 the density in this ring was still much higher in Sydney, but a very rapid fall between 1947 and 1971 left it little higher than Melbourne's.

Sydney has some relatively low density suburbs close to the centre on the north side of the harbour. Until the opening of the Harbour Bridge in 1932 these suburbs, although close, were not readily accessible to the centre. In addition their population density is reduced by very broken topography and the 'house-and-garden' development, favoured by councils in high-income areas. By contrast, in Melbourne there are few areas near the centre where topography or accessibility limits the density of development.

The ring of suburban areas 5–7.5 km from the city centre maintained their population densities between 1947 and 1971 in Sydney, but lost population in Melbourne. The main reason is that flat construction was much more important in Sydney in the post-war period. Population density in the inner and middle suburbs of Sydney remains higher than in comparable locations in Melbourne.

Table 2.3 shows the expansion of population in the various 'rings' of the urban area within the County of Cumberland. An alternative way to show physical expansion is with maps showing the developed area (*Sydney Area Transportation Study*, 1974, Vol.2, p.II.2). These can be misleading since, as the density profiles show, the distinction, at any particular time, between areas that are developed and those which are so thinly settled that they should be regarded as undeveloped, is rarely clear. The transition from rural to urban status of areas surrounding Australian cities has usually taken place gradually over a long period. Only after the Second World War were serious attempts made to consolidate urban development and restrict sprawl. Chapters 8 and 9 describe these efforts.

Compared with cities in most other countries Australian cities spread over large areas at a low density. One reason is that most of their growth has occurred in the era of mechanised urban transport. There has been no necessity to live within walking distance of jobs, shops and other services. Something like nine-tenths of the growth of most of the capital cities has occurred since 1881 when trams began to help the spread of the 1880s boom. Even in 1891, at the onset of a period of depression, when tram services were firmly established in Sydney and Melbourne, those two cities were only about one-fifth of their present size, and were not much larger in 1901, by which time many of the tramways were electrified. Suburban rail services, especially in Melbourne, also allowed people to live a considerable distance from the central areas that contained most of the jobs.

In the 1920s motor buses helped fill in and extend the areas served by the tramways. Perhaps even more important was the replacement of the horse-drawn wagon by the motor truck for transporting goods. It freed factories and warehouses from the need to be close to rail and port facilities and allowed employment to spread to the suburbs. At the beginning of that decade all of the state capitals, except Hobart, were less than one-third their present size: two-thirds of their growth has occurred in the age of the motor vehicle.

TABLE 2.3   *Distribution of Population Within Sydney: 1861–1971*

	City of Sydney[a]	Inner Ring[b]	Middle Ring[c]	Outer Ring[d]	Total
1861	79	14	11	24	1125
1891	214	130	60	43	447
1921	244	410	291	107	1052
1947	214	582	635	262	1694
1971	145	567	960	1110	2781
Percent of total					
1861	60.1	11.6	28.3		100
1891	47.9	29.2	22.9		100
1921	23.2	39.0	27.7	10.2	100
1947	12.6	34.4	37.5	15.5	100
1971	5.2	20.4	34.5	39.9	100
Density (persons per ha)					
1861	25.6	1.1	0.09		0.3
1891	73.3	9.8	0.27		1.1
1921	83.6	31.0	7.4	0.3	2.7
1947	73.3	44.0	16.2	0.8	4.3
1971	49.6	42.8	24.5	3.3	7.1

Source: Censuses.
  a The boundaries of the City of Sydney were considerably enlarged in 1949 and then reduced in 1968. The population shown is that within the 1949–1968 boundaries.
  b Mosman, North Sydney, Leichhardt, Drummoyne, Ashfield, Marrickville, Botany, Wool-lahra, Waverley, Randwick.
      Manly, Willoughby, Lane Cove, Hunters Hill, Ryde, Parramatta, Auburn, Concord, Strathfield, Burwood, Bankstown, Canterbury, Rockdale, Kogarah, Hurstville.
      Warringah, Ku-ring-gai, Hornsby, Baulkham Hills, Blacktown, Windsor, Penrith, Holroyd, Fairfield, Liverpool, Camden, Campbelltown, Sutherland.

As urban transport improved there was less need to crowd housing into areas within walking distance of factories and offices. It was possible for a large number of Australian families to live in detached houses on their own plot of land. The detached single family house, instead of being exceptional as in European cities, became the standard form of housing in Australia.

Housing

Housing has always been an important component of investment in Australia. Butlin (1959), presenting data for 1861 to 1938–39, comments that:

> Throughout the entire period, dwellings accounted for not much less than half total private capital formation—apart from short term fluctuations, the share of

housing remained about 45 per cent ... Half the private sector, one quarter of all Australian capital formation, year by year with limited variations—this was a formidable drain on resources just as it was a substantial stimulus to local industrial enterprise in the supply of building materials.

He also gives an account of the change in the nature of the demand for housing, from a demand for replacement of tents and other temporary dwellings by permanent housing, to a demand for accommodation for migrants in the 1870s and 1880s. The depression of the 1890s slowed down investment, but renewed activity in the early part of the century reached its peak in the boom of the 1920s. Another upswing in residential construction began after the Second World War with, for the first time, significant government encouragement and participation by public housing authorities. It was sustained by migration and the increasing standard of living.

Australian cities do not have a large heritage of old, small, high density housing. Even if all of the dwellings counted in Sydney at the 1901 Census had survived the next seventy years they would have accounted for only about one-eighth of those counted at the 1971 Census. If only those built of permanent materials (brick, stone or concrete) survived they would account for less than one-tenth. In Melbourne where there were more wooden houses, the brick, stone and concrete houses of 1901 would account for less than 8 per cent in 1971. In fact many wooden houses survive but expansion of commercial and industrial activities in the inner areas, road building and residential redevelopment have all resulted in the demolition or conversion of many houses of all kinds of construction. This is part of the reason for the declining populations of the inner suburbs, especially since about 1921. Because of the relative scarcity of old, small housing in the inner suburbs many poorer families have had to live in new, if modest houses on the urban fringes.

The wide spread of the suburbs, especially in Sydney and Melbourne, means long journeys for those who want to get to the city centre, and has resulted in two important changes in the pattern of urban development, especially since the Second World War. Firstly, shopping, service facilities and jobs have moved to the suburbs, partly to be closer to sources of labour and to customers. Retailing, manufacturing and even wholesaling have expanded in the suburbs while they have stagnated or contracted in central areas. However, as Chapter 4 shows, the central city remains by far the largest centre of employment. Secondly, more middle and upper income families are living near the city centres. Office jobs, entertainment and cultural activities are still highly concentrated in the centres and those who want to live close to them are increasingly demanding housing in the inner areas. This demand is being met by renovating some older housing and replacing some with high density flats. Apart from those accommodated in public housing, poorer families are displaced and being forced to live in less accessible parts of the city.

Some of the characteristics of housing in Australia since 1861 are shown in Table 2.4. Information about housing in the state capitals is not available before the turn of the century, therefore only state averages are shown for 1861 and 1891. The table shows a dramatic improvement in housing conditions in the last half of the nineteenth

TABLE 2.4 Characteristics of Australian Housing: 1861–1971

	NSW	Sydney	VIC	Melbourne	QLD	Brisbane	SA	Adelaide	WA	Perth	TAS	Hobart
1. Rooms per private dwelling												
1861	3.6	*	2.8	*	3.8	*	3.3	*	*	*	*	*
1891	5.1	*	5.2	*	5.3	*	4.2	*	4.1	*	*	*
1921	5.2	5.1	5.3	5.2	5.3	5.5	5.1	5.1	4.6	4.7	4.3	5.1
1947	4.8	4.8	5.0	4.9	5.0	5.2	4.9	4.9	4.6	4.7	5.0	5.0
1971	4.9	4.8	5.0	4.9	5.1	5.1	5.1	5.0	4.9	4.8	5.1	5.0
2. Inmates per room (private dwellings)												
1861	1.41	*	1.48	*	1.22	*	1.42	*	1.13	*	*	*
1891	0.93	*	0.94	*	0.94	*	1.25	*	*	*	*	*
1921	0.92	0.88	0.85	0.84	0.89	0.81	0.89	0.85	0.97	0.95	0.93	0.85
1947	0.78	0.77	0.74	0.74	0.76	0.72	0.74	0.74	0.82	0.80	0.79	0.78
1971	0.66	0.66	0.67	0.68	0.65	0.64	0.65	0.65	0.70	0.69	0.67	0.68
3. Percentage of private dwellings owner occupied												
1921	50	41	58	46	66	61	59	53	63	56	53	45
1947	48	40	53	40	61	60	57	54	57	55	53	49
1971	67	72	70	70	68	70	68	70	63	66	67	67
4. Percentage of private dwellings with brick, stone or concrete walls												
1861	29	*	15	*	8	*	63	*	*	*	40	*
1891	37	*	30	*	4	*	82	*	*	*	29	*
1921	43	78	29	47	2	3	80	84	35	61	23	52
1947	50	80	35	49	3	5	84	92	45	69	25	52
1971	51	67	54	63	17	21	86	92	63	78	36	45
5. Percentage of population living in private houses (including shared houses)												
1921	87	*	*	90	*	90	*	91	*	85	*	89
1947	79	*	*	86	*	84	*	89	*	87	*	85
1971	82	79	87	85	85	87	90	92	86	88	90	86

Source: N.G. Butlin (1964) for 1861 and 1891; Censuses for 1921, 1947, 1971.
* Not available.

century and a continued, though slower, improvement in the twentieth. By 1971 average housing standards were high and remarkably uniform across the states and capital cities. Chapter 6 takes up the question of housing standards in more detail. Between 1861 and 1891 the average size of dwellings increased markedly and there was a corresponding fall in the number of inmates per room. There was a continued, but slower, improvement in the next thirty years. By 1921 there were no great differences between the states, or between the state capitals and the remainder of the states, in the size of dwellings or room occupancy. Houses in Western Australia and Tasmania had somewhat fewer rooms, but even this difference has largely disappeared since 1921. The number of rooms per private dwelling is affected by the proportion of flats and other private dwellings to houses, as well as by the size of each type of dwelling. The effect of this can be seen most clearly in Sydney in 1971, where the relatively high proportion of flats was part of the reason for the smaller average number of rooms per dwelling.

Overcrowding of dwellings was a feature of the period immediately following the gold rushes, but since the late nineteenth century there has been a steady and fairly uniform decline in the average number of persons per room in private dwellings. Western Australia, with the smallest houses for the most part, has also had the most crowded. There have been only small and variable differences between the state capitals and the remainder of the area of each state.

There has been a good deal of disagreement about the extent of home ownership in the nineteenth century. Butlin (1964, 259–60) argues that it was high in the 1880s but fell considerably during the depression of the 1890s. There is no firm evidence before the Census of 1911, and in 1921, as Table 2.4 shows, the proportions in the states ranged from one-half in New South Wales to two-thirds in Queensland. The proportions were significantly lower in the capitals than in the other parts of each state.

Between 1921 and 1947 the proportion of owner-occupied dwellings fell in most states and in the capital cities. One reason was an increase in the proportion of flats, most of which were rented, as a result of the flat building boom of the second half of the 1930s. Very few dwellings were built during the depression, or the Second World War, or immediately afterwards. In the resulting shortage many families shared houses or rented rooms. The effects of this can be seen in the 1947 Census results. Between 1947 and 1971 there was a large increase in the proportion owner-occupied, especially in the capital cities, despite the flat building boom of the late 1950s and the 1960s which added large numbers of rented dwellings. Even though Sydney has a higher proportion of flats than any other state capital a slightly higher proportion of its private dwellings are owner-occupied. By 1971 the capital cities had caught up with the other parts of their respective states in the proportion owner-occupied. In the post-war period increasing numbers of families could afford to buy and get the advantages of home ownership in a period of inflation and take advantage of the government policies to assist home purchasers. The post-war influx of migrants into Australia might have been expected to reduce the level of owner-occupancy, for certainly relatively few migrants were owner-occupants before leaving for Australia. In Australia, however, they very quickly became owner-occupants, so that by 1971 overseas-born heads of households were more likely to own their dwellings than were those born in Australia.

The greatest variation in characteristics of housing between and within states in Australia is found in building materials. Queensland and Tasmania were well endowed with forests and most of their houses were built of wood, while at the other extreme, timber was scarce in South Australia, so brick and stone housing is the rule. Another cheaper wall covering, asbestos cement sheeting, popularly known as 'fibro', made its appearance between the wars and became very popular in the house-building boom of the 1950s. The large number of fibro houses built in this latter period resulted in a fall in the proportion of houses recorded as of 'solid' construction between the 1947 and 1971 Censuses in Sydney and Hobart. Many were also built in other states, though in recent years the proportion has fallen significantly.

The definition of dwelling types has been a continuous problem for census-takers. No consistent distinctions were used in the colonial censuses up to 1901. Even in 1921 self-contained flats were not distinguished from 'tenements'. 'Share of house' was used as a class from 1947 to 1966. In the early post-war period many houses were shared, but the proportion had fallen significantly by 1966. In 1971 shares of houses, which were probably much less common by then, would have been classified as non-self-contained flats. Table 2.4 shows that the percentage of the population living in private houses (including shared houses) has tended to decline. Most of that decline is due to the increase in the proportion of flats, first during the 1930s, and then during the 1960s. The proportion living in private houses reached a peak of nearly 83 per cent in Sydney in 1961. Since the Second World War the percentage living in non-private dwellings—boarding houses, hotels and hostels—has also declined quite substantially.

The relatively low density of most Australian cities, which was described in the previous section, is reflected in the composition of the housing stock. Both flats and high-density single family houses are relatively unimportant. Sydney has Australia's highest housing densities, but even there only 22 per cent of the private dwellings in 1971 were flats, and in Melbourne only 16 per cent. Sydney also had a larger stock of terrace or row houses (21 837, or 2.6 per cent of the total) than Melbourne (11 559, or 1.6 per cent of the total), reflecting its early, high density housing development and more restricted site.

House building in Australia has been mainly a private activity, with various forms of government assistance and participation. The first direct involvement occurred just before the First World War when each of the states legislated for the provision of public housing, and most actually built a small number (Jones, 1972). Immediately after the war the Commonwealth Government entered the housing field for the first time with its War Service Homes Scheme which gave financial assistance to ex-servicemen to buy or build houses. It financed one-third of all investment in dwellings in its peak year of operation, 1921–22 (Butlin, 1962). It continued at a significant level throughout the 1920s and at a much lower level in the thirties and forties before reviving after the Second World War. Between 1945 and 1970 the scheme provided finance for purchases equal to about 13 per cent of total completions. It was a scheme to finance house purchase rather than construction, and many of the houses purchased were not new. Most were built by private builders. In these respects it is quite different from the public housing operations of the states.

There was a revival of state interest in public housing in the late 1930s, following a number of inquiries into living conditions in the city 'slums'. The Commonwealth Government began to provide funds to state housing authorities immediately after the Second World War, following the recommendations of the Commonwealth Housing Commission (1944). While the War Service Homes scheme provided finance for house purchase, most of the homes built under the Commonwealth State Housing Agreement in the early post-war period were for renting, but from 1956 onward more State Housing Commission dwellings were sold. From 1945 to 1972 annual completions by the state housing authorities varied from 10 to 23 per cent of all new dwellings. The proportion tended to fall during the period. The Housing Commissions have played a more important role in smaller centres than in the major metropolitan areas. In 1971, 5.3 per cent of the houses and 7.5 per cent of the flats in Australia were rented from government housing authorities.

Utilities

Most government investment in urban development is in utility services and transport. Utilities provide some of the amenities that make urban life comfortable and convenient. Together with transport and housing they comprise most of the non-business physical plant of the cities. The most important are telephones, electricity and gas, water, sanitary sewerage and stormwater drainage. They require networks of pipes or wires which either connect a few supply or disposal sites with individual properties, or connect those properties with each other through centralised exchanges. The sites for both Sydney and Melbourne were chosen where there was suitable water, though in each case the chosen source became so polluted with wastes that it had to be replaced before the towns were many years old.

Australian cities were able to adopt technologies already in use in other countries for water supply, sewerage and drainage. There was a lot of argument and some long delays before their introduction while it was decided which level of government should be responsible. By the time major investment in these services was required the urban areas had already grown beyond the boundaries of the central cities. Unlike the case of the tramways and railways (especially in Melbourne), private companies did not take the initiative. The question to be settled was whether the cities should be given responsibility, even outside their boundaries, or special-purpose authorities created with metropolitan-wide responsibilities.

Water Supply, Sewerage and Drainage

The Legislative Council of the New South Wales Government passed an Act in 1850 allowing the infant Sydney City Corporation to construct a water supply system, pumping water from the Botany swamps, but the Corporation was not able to keep up with the growing demand for water with the expansion of the urban area, much of it outside the City boundary. The City of Sydney and a number of other municipalities established separate sewerage systems, draining into Port Jackson. In-quiries into water supply (1867) and sewerage (1875) recommended ambitious schemes for both services, covering the whole urban area. Work started in 1880 and in 1888 the Metropolitan Board of Water Supply and Sewerage was set up to take responsibility for both services (Aird, 1961).

Melbourne's experience was similar. Some twenty-two years after its foundation Melbourne received its first water from Yan Yean reservoir to replace the increasingly polluted supplies from the Yarra. Commissioners were responsible for the supply until 1860 when it became a direct colonial government responsibility. In the 1870s and 1880s Melbourne's water-borne wastes were either collected from cesspits or allowed to drain through open channels into the Yarra. A Royal Commission in 1889 recom-mended the establishment of a sewerage system, and an organisation to run the system and to take over the government water supply system. The Melbourne and Metropolitan Board of Works was established in 1891; work began in 1892 and the first connection was made in 1897.

The other mainland capitals had varying experiences. Adelaide established the first large-scale system of water-borne sewerage in Australia, becoming operational in 1881. Both Brisbane and Perth were slow to establish sewerage systems. It was 1923 before the sewerage system in Brisbane was extended far enough to justify a sewerage rate, despite the fact that an elected Water Supply and Sewerage Board had been es-tablished in 1909. Because individual waste disposal was easy in the predominantly sandy soil of Perth, work on the provision of mains sewerage there did not start until 1906. By 1911, 700 premises in Perth were connected and connections were begin-ning in Fremantle, but it was not until the 1930s that most of the houses were con-nected to sewers. Perth and Adelaide, like Melbourne, treated their sewage to a significant extent. Sydney is currently undertaking costly works for the treatment of its sewage at its ocean outfalls, although until the high volumes resulting from its re-cent growth of population and industry appeared, the ocean proved a more or less satisfactory receptor. Most of the sewage from Hobart and Brisbane is discharged into river estuaries.

It is somewhat surprising that Sydney, a smaller city than Melbourne in the 1880s, should have been nearly a decade ahead in installation of a satisfactory sewerage system. Ocean outfall sewers to Bondi and Malabar were completed in 1889. Sydney had the advantage of being able to use ocean outfalls for what was in-ititally untreated sewage, while Melbourne had to establish a farm at Werribee for treatment before discharge into Port Phillip Bay. The difference between the two cities was even more remarkable in that Sydney were sewered mainly during the boom years of the 1880s while Melbourne, where the boom in private development was more spectacular than in Sydney (Cannon, 1966; Barrett, 1971), only started to 'clean its house' in the depression years of the 1890s—an act of contrition for the ex-cesses of the boom years.

Table 2.5 shows the population served by water and sewerage services in four of the five mainland capitals. Comparable data is not available for Adelaide, though other information shows it to be close to fully sewered. A broad indication of the lags in sewerage services can be seen by comparing the population served by sewerage

TABLE 2.5   *Population Served with Water and Sewerage Services: 1891–1971*
'000

| | Sydney[a] | | Melbourne | | Brisbane | | Perth | |
	Water	Sewerage	Water	Sewerage	Water	Sewerage	Water	Sewerage
1891	365	129	487	—	*	—	*	—
1901	491	370	495	183	78	—	40	—
1911	696	540	588	516	121	—	73	*
1921	1110	745	789	717	207	—	171	*
1931	1307	1019	1024	949	327	70	221	99
1941	1539	1104	1181	1116	337	160	244	175
1951	1940	1380	1333	1209	472	196	303	212
1961	2340	1620	1836	1331	626	232	425	264
1971	2987	2477	2359	1898	807	565	637	313

Sources: Melbourne: Melbourne and Metropolitan Board of Works, 'Analyses of Accounts'.
Sydney: *N.S.W. Year Book, Australian Year Book.*
Brisbane: *Australian Year Book, Queensland Year Book.*
Perth: *Australian Year Book, Western Australian Year Book.*
a   Includes Wollongong.
*   Not available.

with that served by water services. The lags have been quite large in most of the cities. In 1971 less than half of Perth's population was connected to mains sewerage. The percentage of houses and flats in the major urban areas connected to mains sewerage, according to the 1971 Census, were:

Sydney	84	Hobart	89
Melbourne	87	Canberra	98
Brisbane	76	Newcastle	88
Adelaide	92	Wollongong	56
Perth	46	Geelong	92

Water supply has frequently been a cause of crisis in Australian cities. Decisions to invest in major new schemes have often been precipitated by severe shortages caused by prolonged drought. Australia has the most variable rainfall of any continent, and very large storages are required to ensure supply. Sydney is particularly subject to drought and needs very large capacity storages compared with its annual consumption.

Water supply in Australia is often expensive because of low rainfall near the major cities, competition for water from farm irrigation, and highly variable rainfall. The long drought in Sydney in the late 1930s and early 1940s hastened the construction of Warragamba Dam on a large tributary of the Nepean River. Its construction resulted in diversion of resources from other parts of the water and sewerage systems to such an extent that during the 1950s sewerage reticulation fell further behind population growth, and during a drought in the mid-1960s the Board had more water in its main storages than it could deliver to its customers through the mains. In 1976 the first water from the Shoalhaven scheme became available, though most of it has to be pumped.

Melbourne's water supply was developed relatively cheaply, exploiting the headwaters of the Yarra, until the 1960s. Tapping sources outside the Yarra catchment involves using water that would otherwise be available for irrigation. The cheapest alternative source would have been the Big River, which feeds irrigation schemes in the Goulburn Valley, but because of opposition from irrigation interests this proved politically impossible. Instead the Thompson River, which flows southeast to Gippsland, was tapped at greater cost (Johnson, 1973a).

Until after the Second World War Adelaide's water supply came from local streams, stored in catchments in the nearby ranges. Once these sources were exhausted it was forced to build a pipeline to bring water from the Murray River. Adelaide competes with irrigation demands further up the river. Much of the water used for irrigation eventually drains back into the river, but in the process becomes increasingly saline. River water is now being treated to reduce its salinity.

Perth also faces a shortage of water. Only a limited number of catchments in its vicinity are suitable for tapping, and the nearest available alternative source of supply—Western Australia's Murray River, south of the city—is also sufficiently saline that it will have to be treated. Among the state capitals only Brisbane and Hobart, with quite large, relatively high rainfall catchments in their hinterlands, appear to be free of the constraints of high-cost water.

Telephones

Telegraphy was introduced in Australia in 1854 with a line linking Melbourne and Williamstown. By 1858 Sydney, Melbourne and Adelaide were linked, and by 1911 there were 4041 telegraph stations in Australia. Telephone services were introduced in Sydney and Melbourne in 1880. The first exchange in Melbourne was operated by a private company and by 1887, when it was bought out by the Government, it had 1121 subscribers in Melbourne, Ballarat and Bendigo. In 1901 telecommunication functions were taken over by the Commonwealth Government and Sydney and Melbourne were linked by telephone in 1907. The telephone network developed earlier in the metropolitan areas than elsewhere. For example, in 1892 there were 1509 subscribers in Sydney and only 185 in country areas of New South Wales. Telephones were mainly a service for businesses in the early years. Of the 1509 Sydney subscribers only 332 were described as 'private'.

The remarkably steady growth of telephone services in Australia is shown in Table 2.6. It reflects trends in investment in telegraph and telephone facilities in

TABLE 2.6   *Telephone Services per thousand population; Australia: 1892–1971*

1892	2	1941	74
1901	6	1951	101
1911	18	1961	155
1921	33	1971	224
1931	57		

Sources: T.A. Coghlan, *The Wealth and Progress of N.S.W.*, *1893*; *Australian Year Books.*

Australia. From 1860 to 1911 it only twice exceeded 5 per cent of total public investment, and was more commonly between 1 and 3 per cent (Butlin, 1962, 26–27). In
the second decade of the century it usually ran between 4 and 6 per cent and in the
1920s climbed to 10 to 12 per cent. It fell in the 1930s, but not as dramatically as investment in housing or motor vehicles, and after the Second World War it became
important again, keeping pace with the general level of public investment in the
1950s and 1960s (*Australian National Accounts*).

Separate statistics for residential and business services are available only for recent
years. Data from the Australian Post Office for New South Wales and the Australian
Capital Territory shows that use of telephones by residents is at a significantly higher
level in the metropolitan area than in other parts of the state.

TABLE 2.7   *Residential Telephone Services in New South Wales: 1971*

	Population	Residential Telephone Services Per person	Per dwelling
Sydney Inner Zone	2 397 215	0.218	0.702
Other N.S.W. including A.C.T.	2 348 028	0.155	0.552
Total	4 745 243	0.187	0.632

Source: Australian Post Office.
Note: These figures include an allowance for the business services which are connected to a dwelling
associated with a business.

Gas

Town gas was distributed in Australian cities at an early stage in their development. It
was produced first in Sydney in 1841 and in Melbourne in 1849. Brisbane's first gas
supply appeared in 1865 and Adelaide's in 1863. In the early stage of the industry's
development gas was used exclusively for lighting, both within buildings and in the
streets. In the 1870s the use of gas in radiators began to become popular and in the
1880s gas for cooking. With the increasing availability of electricity the use of gas for
lighting was eventually replaced but in 1922 it was recorded that 'the use of gas for
purposes of illumination, power and cooking is extending also' (*N.S.W. Year Book*,
1922, 408).

Private companies have taken most of the responsibility for provision of gas in the
main cities, for example, the Australian Gas Light Co. and the North Shore Gas Co. in
Sydney, and the South Australian Gas Co. in Adelaide. In Melbourne the major supplier is a public corporation, which took over the functions of a number of private
companies in 1950. One private company, the Colonial Gas Association, also supplies
part of the urban area. Outside the large cities gas supply was quite frequently initiated
by local governments, usually with the prime aim of providing street lighting. Most of
these have been taken over by private companies, or the Gas and Fuel Corporation in
Victoria. Municipal gas undertakings are now found only in New South Wales

where, in 1971, some 22 local authorities supplied gas; they account for only a small fraction of the total gas consumed in the state.

The availability of gas to individual homes has never been as widespread as electricity has become in recent years. Apart from the gas produced in the La Trobe Valley, and piped to Melbourne from 1956 to 1969, coal gas was always produced and distributed locally. It has not been a rapidly growing industry. The first data available showing the number of dwellings supplied with gas were collected in the 1947 Census. These are compared in Table 2.8 with subsequent census results to show the changes in the penetration of the domestic market by gas suppliers.

TABLE 2.8   *Percentage of Houses and Flats with Gas Supply: 1947–1971*

	Metropolitan	Other Urban	Rural	Total
1947	84.6	37.4	3.6	49.6
1961	64.8	34.4	5.2	44.2
1966	60.3	27.3	14.2	44.9
1971	50.8	23.9	18.8	41.0

Source: Censuses

Conversion from coal gas has been occurring over a number of years as products from oil refineries gradually replaced coal as a fuel source. More recently the introduction of natural gas, piped directly from gas fields, opens the way for a possible revival in the use of gas as an industrial as well as a domestic fuel.

The decline in the proportion of metropolitan houses and flats supplied with gas has been quite dramatic. It appears to be largely a result of the reduction in the use of gas for cooking. In 1947, when nearly 85 per cent of metropolitan houses and flats had gas supply, nearly 75 per cent used gas as the main method of cooking. By comparison, in only 7 per cent of houses and flats was electricity the main means of cooking, even though over 98 per cent of houses were supplied with electricity. The increased use of gas in rural areas resulted from the more ready availability of bottled gas.

Electricity

The earliest use of electricity in Australia was for lighting, and especially for street lighting. Electricity was first generated in Australia quite soon after the invention of the incandescent lamp in 1879. Melbourne was probably the first city to have a power station, built in 1880. During the 1880s most of the electricity was generated by private companies, and used to light private and public buildings. In 1888 Tamworth became the first town in Australia to light its streets by electricity. In order to provide street lighting a number of other municipalities began to generate and distribute electricity, especially in New South Wales, but private companies remained the main source of supply for many years in most states. The Melbourne City Council began to generate electricity in 1894, and Sydney City Council in 1904.

From a relatively early stage there was a trend for private companies to be replaced by municipal, state or special-purpose governmental authorities. Sydney City Council established its supply system by taking over private companies in 1904. Private companies supplied almost all of the electricity in South Australia until the formation of the Electricity Trust in 1947. In Brisbane, however, the city purchased bulk electricity from private companies to distribute within its own boundaries and to surrounding municipalities, and after consolidation in 1925, to power its trams. In Perth the state government took over a private and a City Council supply system in 1913. It was not until 1957 that the last private companies generating electricity for sale in the Sydney region were taken over by the Electricity Commission.

Prest (1963), in describing the organisation of electricity supply, divides the Australian states into two groups. The State Electricity Commission of Victoria, formed in 1919, the Hydro-Electric Commission of Tasmania, which took over from a government department in 1930, the Electricity Trust of South Australia and the State Electricity Commission of Western Australia (both formed in 1946) produce and distribute nearly all of the electricity in their respective states. There are still small, independent local producers in the remote areas, especially in Western and South Australia, and the Victorian Commission sells some of its power to eleven local authorities in the metropolitan area and elsewhere for distribution.

In Queensland and New South Wales the Electricity Commissions, established in 1938 and 1950 respectively, play no role in distribution, which is in the hands of local and special-purpose regional authorities. The New South Wales Commission generates almost all of the electricity produced in New South Wales (outside the Snowy Mountains Scheme) and sells wholesale to thirty-four Electricity County Councils whose sole function is its distribution. The Queensland Commission, while involved in the development of the industry, does not generate power itself. Regional and some local authorities generate and distribute electric power. Brisbane is served partly by the City Council, and partly by the Southern Electric Authority. Electricity is distributed in Sydney by four County Councils, of which the largest, Sydney County Council, took over the City Council's electricity undertaking in 1936.

Because of the mixture of government and private undertakings involved, there is little data about the spread of the use of electricity in Australia before the Second World War. In particular it is difficult to discover when electricity became generally

TABLE 2.9   *Percentage of Houses and Flats with Electricity Supply: 1947–1971*

	Metropolitan urban	Other urban	Rural	Total
1947	98	92	47	80
1961	100	99	82	97
1966	100	99	94	99
1971	100	100	99	100

Source: Censuses

available for use in homes. The first reliable information comes from the 1947 Census (see Table 2.9). By that time electricity was connected to almost all houses and flats in metropolitan areas, to over 90 per cent in other urban areas, but to less than half of those in rural areas. Rural electrification, subsidised by the states in various ways, was pursued energetically after the Second World War and as a result, by 1971 almost all houses and flats in Australia had electric power.

Guy Allbut (1958, 31) notes that, in New South Wales at least,

> Growth was most rapid in the years between 1915 and 1929 when electricity was displacing other forms of energy for light, heat and power for tractions, industrial, commercial and domestic purposes. New service areas too, were rapidly being opened up and over those years the average rate of increase was no less than 15 per cent per annum ...

The first available data about the number of consumers in a state relates to Victoria in 1929 (Table 2.10). Its 13 consumers per 100 population was already more than one-third of today's level. Data for the parts of Sydney and Melbourne supplied by Sydney City Council and Melbourne Electric Supply Co. show that by 1927 they supplied 20 consumers per 100 population (*Tait's Electoral Directory*, 1929). Butlin (1962) shows that investment in electric power supply was high throughout the 1920s and after a fall at the beginning of the Depression continued in the late 1930s. Most houses in metropolitan areas probably had electricity by about 1930, and the sustained high rate of increase in the number of consumers has been accounted for by new dwellings and the spread of supply to smaller towns and rural areas.

TABLE 2.10 *Numbers of Ultimate Consumers of Electricity*

			No. of Consumers '000	Consumers (per 100 pop.)
All Consumers:	Victoria*	1929	230	13
	"	1939–40	398	21
	Australia	1939–40	1332	19
	"	1949–50	1929	24
Residential consumers: †	Australia	1949–50	1609	20
	"	1960	2608	25
	"	1970	3695	29

Sources: Allbut (1958); *Australian Year Book*, 1953; *Statistics of the Electricity Supply Association of Australia*, Annual.
* Data refer to electricity generated by the State Electricity Commission. Therefore it omits some small undertakings.
† Number of dwellings.

Synopsis and Prospects

This chapter has described some of the features of urban development in Australia, from its inception until the post-war period. It has emphasised the physical development of the cities—their geographic spread at relatively low density, the development of the transport system, the provision of utilities and housing. These particular aspects of development are measurable. Some of the other important aspects are much more difficult to assess in the same way; for example, where people work and the conditions under which they work, the kinds of education and health services and the availability of parks and recreation facilities.[2]

Urban expansion in Australia can usefully be divided into a number of phases. Within each phase the rate of expansion has usually been greatest in one or two decades. The first phase, from 1788 to the middle of the nineteenth century, has been given little attention in this chapter, apart from the choice of sites for capital cities. The early colonial towns and cities fixed to a degree the layout of the present centres of the major cities, but few buildings survive. These small centres had piped water, but few other services, and horses powered the only transport vehicles available. Most journeys were made on foot.

In the second half of the nineteenth century the first suburbs were established in what are now the inner suburbs. The 1880s was the decade of most rapid expansion, especially in Melbourne. The nineteenth century suburbs were of two kinds. The suburbs of the wealthy occupied the more attractive areas and had large houses. The working class suburbs comprised small houses, often terraced and often with factories scattered among them. Despite the rapid expansion of public transport services in the last two decades, their use was quite limited until the early years of the twentieth century. Drainage and waste disposal was a problem in most of the inner suburbs until late in the century. Streets were lit by gas, if they were lit at all.

The first half of the twentieth century included a period of steady expansion before the First World War, the boom decade of the 1920s and periods of very slow development in the thirties and forties. This period was dominated by public transport. Tramways, suburban railways and then buses became increasingly important in serving suburban areas that were spreading at increasing distances from the city centres. Roads were also improved during this period, and the twenties saw the first significant spread in the use of private cars. Employment remained concentrated in the city centres and the inner industrial suburbs. Housing in the suburbs of the 1920s was more generous than in the nineteenth century and built at much lower density. Both trams and suburban trains were electrified during this period, and electricity became widely available, being used for street lighting and lighting inside houses and commercial buildings. Gas was gradually replaced for lighting but retained an important role in heating and cooking. Telephones, which at the beginning of the century were mainly used by businesses, had reached the homes of the upper and middle classes by the end of the 1920s. This was a period of consolidation and improvement in sanitary drainage. Partly through the use of relief funds, in the 1930s sewerage was extended to most of the new suburbs, especially in Melbourne.

[2] Spearritt (1976) describes conditions in Sydney from 1920 to 1950.

By the end of the Second World War Australian cities had grown into very different kinds of urban centres from the small colonial capitals of a century before. They were sizable cities and can be seen as products of the demands, incomes and technologies of the previous century. Their previous development constrained them in a number of ways in adapting to post-war changes in the urban growth environment.

The third main period of urban expansion began in the early 1950s, once post-war shortages of materials were relieved. This period will be examined in more detail in following chapters. It continued many of the trends that have been observed in earlier periods. The public transport system was well suited to moving people between compact residential areas and high job concentrations, but could not easily be adapted to serving the new low density suburbs that developed in the inter-war years. Planners saw the need for additional road capacity and began to reserve routes for future freeways soon after the Second World War, but Australian cities were not well adapted to deal with the great increase in the use of private cars. Road improvement proved slow and expensive and was strongly resisted by those who stood to lose their houses.

Public transport patronage declined as more people used cars. One reason was that increased car ownership and use of road transport encouraged employers and retailers to locate in suburban areas, and in turn many of the jobs and more of the shops were not readily accessible by public transport. Trams disappeared, except in Melbourne. Telephones became much more widely used, and electricity progressively replaced gas for cooking. Sewerage, however, remained a problem. A backlog of un-sewered houses appeared in Melbourne, expanded in Sydney and continued in Perth. Only Brisbane markedly improved its situation.

Suburban expansion in the interwar period had pre-empted much of the land along the railway lines. As a result, when manufacturers, wholesalers and shopping centre developers began to look for sites they were forced to locate away from rail lines, forcing their workers and customers to use road transport and increasing the burden of freight on the roads, rather than using the railways. The new housing areas were at even lower density—60-foot rather than 40-foot frontages—and almost all were detached houses. The 1960s also saw a revival of flat building on a larger scale than in the previous flat-building booms of the 1920s and 1930s. Brick became increasingly the dominant building material.

Given the growth of the cities a modest increase in housing densities might have been expected in the inner and middle suburbs after the Second World War, but the inherited pattern of subdivision and the inherited stock of single family houses meant that only a quite significant increase in density could justify demolition and rebuilding. As a result redevelopment was limited, and mainly consisted of building small blocks of flats on one or two house sites.

The unsewered areas in a number of cities posed financial and planning problems for urban governments. Large amounts of resources were needed to keep up with demand, even without catching up with the backlog. As environmental awareness increased there was a demand that all new housing be sewered and this began to constrain the release of land for development. Attempts to control the scattering of development around the urban fringes that had been a feature of growth in the 1920s also led to tighter controls over the release of land, but even in the 1970s some of the scattered subdivisions of fifty years previously were still causing difficulties for planning and servicing authorities.

Governments had become firmly established as important participants in urban development. They were responsible for nearly all of the investment in utility services as well as in roads and public transport. In the post-war period they were to move further into housing and urban planning. Continuing the long-established habit, people living in the cities held 'the government'—in this case the state government—mainly responsible for dealing with problems that threatened their amenity.

3 Where People Live

This chapter supplements the broad historical outline of development given in the previous chapter with a more detailed examination of the period since the Second World War and of the present-day characteristics of Australian cities. The three main aspects of the growth and distribution of urban development are population, employment and land use. This chapter deals with population, Chapter 4 with employment and Chapter 5 with land use. As in the previous chapter we will be examining the distribution of growth, both between cities and between different parts of cities. There is little data about the location of population within cities that lends itself to an analysis of variations in population density. The 1971 Sydney Area Transportation Study provides more data than is available for most other cities and this chapter will use Sydney as an example in many instances. In this chapter and in Chapter 4 the analysis of the growth of different cities uses demographic and economic measures to distinguish different components of growth to throw some light on the extent to which cities are able to attract residents and jobs. In the analysis of features of the pattern of growth within cities, some of the data will be presented in tables and graphs showing the features of annular rings of the city at varying distance from its centre—the best single dimension along which to analyse urban spatial structure.

Australians have been concerned about the size of Sydney and Melbourne relative to other centres for a long time, and policies to decentralise population to smaller centres have a long history. This chapter examines the reasons for the continued concentration of population growth in the state capitals and shows the powerful forces of inertia, supplemented by the effects of immigration, which would have to be offset to reduce the concentration of population.

Australian cities are also remarkable for the extent to which they spread over large areas at relatively low densities. Reformers have suggested more high density development in inner suburbs. In the last part of the chapter the evidence from the post-war period on the distribution of population within cities is presented. It shows that it would be very difficult to dramatically increase the population of inner suburban areas.

Distribution Between Cities

Chapter 2 described how the capital cities became the dominant urban centres in the early stages of the development of each of the colonies, and how their dominance increased over time. The five mainland state capitals were firmly established as the

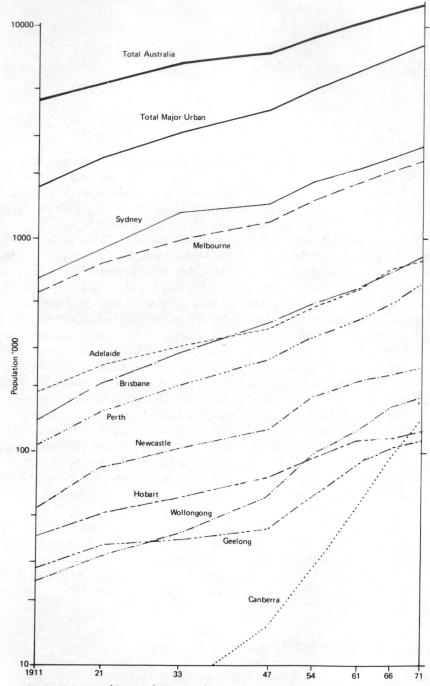

Figure 3.1 Population of major urban areas: 1911–1971.
Source: Censuses.

largest centres in Australia by the turn of the century, and have never been challenged. Among them the only change in position in the ranking since Sydney's population exceeded Melbourne's about the turn of the century was the alternation of Brisbane and Adelaide since the 1930s (Figure 3.1). Hobart's population, however, had been passed by Newcastle's even before the establishment of the steel industry in Newcastle in 1915. The other towns, among what are now regarded as the major urban centres, were all smaller than Hobart up to 1954. The rapid expansion of the steel industry in Wollongong in the 1950s and 1960s resulted in its population passing Hobart's by 1961, and the latest city to do so was Canberra, between 1966 and 1971.

Table 3.1, showing the percentage rate of growth of each of the ten major urban areas from 1947 to 1971, demonstrates the very considerable variation in growth rates from year to year among the individual centres. As a group, the ten major urban centres have usually grown about a third faster than the national population. Each of the major urban centres has also grown faster than the national average rate of growth in every intercensal period, with the exceptions of Hobart since 1954 and Newcastle since 1961. These growth rates suggest that the major centres are more attractive than the smaller centres, but when the components of population growth are examined later in the chapter this conclusion is questioned, especially for Sydney and Melbourne.

TABLE 3.1.   *Annual Growth Rates of Larger Urban Areas: 1947–1971*
(per cent per year)

	1947-54	1954-61	1961-66	1966-71	1947-71	1961-71
Sydney	3.3	2.4	2.2	2.2	2.6	2.2
Melbourne	3.2	2.9	2.6	2.6	2.8	2.6
Adelaide	3.4	2.7	4.7	2.2	3.2	3.4
Brisbane	3.2	2.3	4.0	2.7	3.0	3.4
Perth	3.6	2.8	3.4	5.1	3.6	4.2
Hobart	3.2	2.1	1.6	1.7	2.2	1.7
Canberra	9.3	10.2	10.6	8.8	9.7	9.7
Newcastle	5.2	2.8	1.3	1.4	2.9	1.3
Wollongong	5.4	5.1	4.8	2.8	4.6	3.8
Geelong	7.2	2.8	3.6	1.9	4.0	2.7
Total	3.6	2.7	2.9	2.6	3.0	2.8
Others > 10 000 in 1966*	—	—	2.5	2.4	—	2.5
All Australia	2.5	2.3	2.0	1.9	2.2	2.0

Source: Census Reports and Year Books.
Notes: No uniform boundary definition was used prior to 1961.
   * Excludes two centres which became part of metropolitan urban areas in 1971. No data is available for these urban centres > 10 000 before 1961.

Between 1961 and 1971 the other 54 centres included in Table 3.1 also grew faster than the national average. The growth rate of the ten major urban centres (populations >60 000 in 1966) is compared with three size-classes of smaller urban centres between 1961 and 1971 in Table 3.2. Although the largest centres grew most rapidly between 1961 and 1966, and over the whole period, the other size-classes over 20 000 (in 1966) kept in step with them. Only those centres which were less than 20 000 in 1966 showed significantly slower growth rates.

TABLE 3.2   *Growth of Urban Areas, 1961–71, by size in 1966*
(percentage over the period)

	1961-66	1966-71	1961-71	No. of Centres
Population in 1966				
60 000 +	14.9	13.3	30.1	10
30 000 — 59 999	12.2	12.4	26.1	6
20 000 — 29 999	12.9	13.5	28.1	13
10 000 — 19 999	10.0	9.3	20.2	32

Source: Censuses.

Most urban growth in Australia has been attracted to a few large cities. The ten major urban areas increased their share of the national population from 53.5 per cent in 1947 to 64.4 per cent in 1971. Moreover the five mainland capital statistical divisions, as defined for the 1966 and 1971 Censuses, accounted for some 70.6 per cent of the national population increase over this period; the statistical divisions of Sydney and Melbourne alone accounted for 44.9 per cent. If we define city development as the growth of urban centres which had populations in excess of 10 000 in 1966, Sydney and Melbourne together accounted for 49.5 per cent of the total between 1966 and 1971, the five mainland capitals for 77.6 per cent and the ten major urban areas for 8 8.4 per cent of urban population growth.

Population estimates for June 1975 suggest that there has been something of a change in the distribution of population growth since 1971. The share of Sydney and Melbourne in national population growth fell from 45 per cent in 1966–71 to 36 per cent between 1971 and 1975. However, because of quite rapid growth in Perth and Brisbane the share of the three smaller mainland capitals grew from 25 per cent to 31 per cent. The share of the other major urban areas increased from 10 to 12 per cent, mainly because of the growth of Canberra. The major urban areas in total accounted for only 0.7 per cent less of the national growth in 1971–75 than in the previous five years. If the growing share of national growth in the Outer Sydney Statistical Division is regarded as an overspill from Sydney, the proportion would increase. These data suggest that Sydney, and perhaps Melbourne, might be losing some of their dominance over urban growth to the smaller capitals, though the period is too short to draw firm conclusions.

The population shown as living in rural areas (settlements with less than 1000 population) increased up to 1961 but has declined since then. Part of this decline was due to internal migration offsetting natural increase, and part to changes in the classification of areas from rural to urban.

Of course, urban development provides for more than population growth. Much of it provides more and better housing, services and business facilities for the population and firms established in a city. As long as living standards are increasing at a similar rate in all cities, and technology and consumer tastes are changing in similar ways, this 'deepening' urban development would be expected to be distributed between cities roughly in proportion to their total population and workforce. The main focus of our attention in the following chapters will be, as it was in Chapter 2, on the mainland capitals, and particularly on Sydney and Melbourne.

Components of Population Growth

In analysing whether a city has attracted more or less than its share of population growth it is useful to distinguish three main components of growth: natural increase (births minus deaths), internal migration and overseas migration. Cities which simply retained the natural increase in their population can be said to have no more than held their own. Information about internal migration is not available before 1966 to 1971, but by using birthplace data, growth due to migration can be separated into migration of the Australian-born (mainly internal migration) and migration of the foreign-born (mainly overseas migration). Analyses of these three components of growth were carried out for the National Population Inquiry, and the results are summarised in Table 3.3 for the centres that had populations of over 10 000 in 1966. For this kind of analysis it is necessary to use areas with constant boundaries and for which vital statistics are available. Therefore the data refers to local government areas in the case of the smaller cities, and statistical divisions for the capital cities. Because the necessary vital statistics were not collected for local government areas in Victoria and Western Australia prior to 1966, it is not possible to analyse the growth of the smaller centres in those states before that date.

The percentage growth by natural increase between two censuses is affected by three main factors. Firstly, the level of fertility varies between cities. In particular the average completed family is smaller in metropolitan areas than in 'other urban' areas, tends to increase as urban size decreases, and to be largest in rural areas (National Population Inquiry, 1975, 158). Secondly, age composition affects both fertility and mortality. Areas with a preponderance of older people will have a lower rate of natural increase. This is evident in the low rates in Gosford and the Blue Mountains in both periods shown in the table. Thirdly, areas which have attracted many migrants over the period will have a high percentage growth from natural increase, since the percentage is calculated on the population at the beginning of the period; children born to those who moved into the area after the initial date also contribute to the natural increase.

Migration has been by far the most important direct determinant of differences in population growth rates. Most of the cities which grew rapidly attracted both Australian-born and foreign-born migrants, but there are some important exceptions.

TABLE 3.3   *Components of Population Change in Australian Cities: 1947-1971 (percentage change)*

Cities Ranked by 1966 Population	1966 Population	1946-1966				1966-1971			
		Natural Increase	Net Migration Aust. Born	For. Born	Total Growth	Natural Increase	Net Migration Aust. Born	For. Born	Total Growth
Over 2 000 000									
Sydney	2 541 307	22.2	b20.0	27.3	49.6	5.0	-0.8	6.3	10.5
Melbourne	2 230 580	27.3	0.1	39.0	66.3	6.4	-0.1	6.0	12.2
500 000 — 1 000 000									
Brisbane	777 674	27.0	19.2	23.8	70.0	5.4	2.6	3.6	11.5
Adelaide	771 175	25.4	12.8	49.7	88.0	4.7	0.2	4.3	9.2
Perth	558 821	34.3	12.4	37.8	84.5	7.4	4.4	13.9	25.8
90 000 — 500 000									
Newcastle	329 239	25.7	6.1	8.5	40.3	4.7	0.6	1.7	7.0
Wollongong	177 456	55.3	39.2	62.2	159.7	6.8	0.8	6.1	12.2
Hobart	141 311	34.1	11.8	21.7	67.6	5.7	0.4	2.3	8.4
Geelong	120 168	—	—	—	101.8	6.2	0.9	3.4	10.5
Canberra	96 013	212.0	247.2	293.0	752.2	15.0	23.4	11.4	50.0
40 000 — 60 000									
Townsville	59 031	36.2	26.5	9.9	72.5	7.7	10.0	3.1	20.7
Ballarat	58 873	—	—	—	32.4	3.5	-2.2	0.4	1.0
Launceston	58 718	28.6	-7.4	11.5	32.6	4.7	-4.0	0.7	1.4
Toowoomba	55 805	39.0	22.2	6.4	67.6	4.1	1.7	0.9	6.7
La Trobe Valley	50 679	—	—	—	133.5	7.9	-7.5	-1.9	-1.6
Gold Coast	49 485	50.1	190.2	56.9	297.2	4.1	23.2	7.5	34.8
Bendigo	49 227	—	—	—	27.5	4.0	0.9	0.8	5.7
Rockhampton	46 119	27.7	2.6	1.4	31.7	3.6	2.2	0.8	6.6
Gosford	42 807	20.3	127.9	32.2	180.4	1.3	24.7	5.7	31.7
20 000 — 40 000									
Mackay-Pioneer	35 586	41.7	6.2	5.8	53.6	7.8	-1.8	2.1	8.1
Blue Mountains	30 733	18.4	11.5	14.3	44.2	2.0	12.0	5.6	19.5
Broken Hill	30 043	36.7	-27.8	2.1	11.0	5.3	-5.8	-0.3	-0.8
Burnie-Somerset	28 175	36.0	25.2	10.5	71.7	9.4	-2.5	1.5	8.4
Cairns	26 802	50.3	-2.7	12.7	60.4	5.4	4.2	3.2	12.8
Wagga Wagga	25 850	46.4	12.6	9.3	68.3	7.6	2.7	1.6	11.8
Bundaberg	25 444	35.6	19.4	4.5	59.5	6.2	1.0	0.2	7.4
Albury	25 112	59.2	10.9	4.1	74.2	9.2	1.6	2.4	13.2
Whyalla	22 131	65.9	9.9	106.2	182.0	14.2	5.7	22.8	42.7
Tamworth	21 683	42.2	30.7	6.7	79.6	6.9	3.4	0.9	11.1

TABLE 3.3 continued

Cities Ranked by 1966 Population	1966 Population	1946-1966				1966-1971			
		Natural Increase	Net Migration Aust. Born	Net Migration For. Born	Total Growth	Natural Increase	Net Migration Aust. Born	Net Migration For. Born	Total Growth
Kalgoorlie	21 386	—	—	—	21.5	7.5	-6.4	2.4	3.5
Mt Isa	21 307	86.6	64.1	62.7	213.4	15.2	17.7	8.5	41.4
Orange	20 996	43.6	-1.7	10.5	52.4	6.7	2.5	1.1	10.4
Goulburn	20 871	33.2	-7.5	4.8	30.5	4.0	-0.9	0.5	3.5
15 000 — 20 000									
Lismore	19 757	34.2	-6.9	2.3	29.7	4.2	0.8	0.9	5.8
Maryborough	19 670	29.4	5.9	1.3	36.6	2.9	-5.0	-0.02	-2.1
Warrnambool	17 500	—	—	—	75.1	5.7	1.3	-0.2	6.8
Shepparton	17 488	—	—	—	121.0	8.2	1.1	1.6	11.0
Mt Gambier	17 261	78.8	35.3	40.6	154.8	8.5	-7.5	-0.3	0.7
Bathurst	17 230	29.0	9.4	6.7	45.1	4.1	-5.5	1.2	-0.2
Devonport	16 758	46.9	24.1	13.1	84.1	7.9	7.7	2.5	18.2
Grafton	15 987	34.4	-3.8	2.0	32.7	4.0	-1.7	0.2	2.5
Dubbo	15 629	49.2	7.4	6.5	63.0	7.7	5.4	0.8	14.0
Bunbury	15 467	—	—	—	147.7	7.7	2.6	4.6	15.0
Armidale	15 360	41.0	34.4	16.5	91.9	6.9	8.9	2.4	18.2
Wangaratta	15 268	—	—	—	127.5	6.9	-4.0	-0.8	2.1
10 000 — 15 000									
Traralgon	14 080	—	—	—	161.0	8.9	-4.9	0.2	4.2
Port Pirie	13 965	34.5	-23.5	5.1	16.2	5.9	-10.6	-0.6	-5.3
Mildura	12 934	—	—	—	85.7	6.0	-4.1	0.2	2.0
Lithgow	12 911	28.4	-38.3	-1.4	-11.4	3.1	-4.0	0.3	-0.7
Queanbeyan	12 515	48.2	27.9	72.6	148.7	12.3	9.8	6.4	28.3
Gladstone	12 470	42.7	59.1	35.1	137.0	10.3	12.1	-0.8	21.6
Geraldton	12 196	—	—	—	103.0	10.9	8.1	4.9	24.0
Wodonga	11 878	—	—	—	178.0	8.4	0.03	1.7	10.0
Albany	11 440	—	—	—	140.0	8.2	-1.1	2.0	9.1
Gympie	11 286	30.7	2.9	0.5	34.1	4.1	-6.0	0.2	1.7
Taree	10 563	44.8	44.5	5.4	94.7	4.7	3.1	1.1	8.8
Horsham	10 562	—	—	—	69.3	6.6	-1.4	-0.6	4.5
Warwick	10 075	33.1	5.8	2.3	41.2	5.6	-13.6	0.3	-7.7
Hamilton	10 062	—	—	—	40.0	4.7	-8.4	-0.1	-3.9

Source: *National Population Inquiry* 1975, Ch. 4, and C.Y. Choi, "Components of Population Changes in Non-Metropolitan Urban Areas, 1947-1971", *Working Paper No. 9, National Population Inquiry.*

Sydney and Melbourne grew during the whole of this period almost entirely by natural increase and migration of the foreign-born. Between 1947 and 1966 both of these cities lost about as many Australian-born people to the rest of Australia as they gained. According to estimates by Choi and Burnley (1974), however, the net effect of this migration has varied greatly between the different intercensal periods. Between 1947 and 1954 both lost heavily, (Sydney 43 000 and Melbourne 21 000) but this was reversed in the next period, from 1954 to 1961, when Sydney gained 42 000 and Melbourne 36 000. From 1961 to 1966 Sydney was close to balance, gaining 1000, while Melbourne lost 13 000. Finally, between 1966 and 1971 Sydney lost 20 000 and Melbourne 2000.

By contrast with migration of the Australian-born, migration of the foreign-born has contributed significantly and consistently to these cities' growth. Between 1947 and 1971 this source contributed some 620 000 to the growth of Sydney and over 650 000 to the growth of Melbourne. In each intercensal period migration of the foreign-born contributed much more to their growth than natural increase. The ports of Sydney and Melbourne are the major points of entry for overseas migrants. They also have foreign-born communities which are likely to receive new migrants and help them to become established in their new country. These cities also have the largest concentrations of jobs in the manufacturing, construction and service industries, in which many migrants have found employment.

The analysis of components of growth shows that much of the growth of Sydney and Melbourne in the post-war period has been through increases in 'captive population'—people who were either born there or migrated there from overseas. By contrast, those cities have gained very little from the movement of people within Australia. This suggests that the largest cities are not overwhelmingly attractive to those who have experience of living elsewhere in Australia and make a choice about where to live. On the other hand, those born there or who arrive there from overseas have not moved away in large numbers—or at least not prior to 1971.

Brisbane, Adelaide and Perth, however, have attracted a significant amount of growth from net migration of the Australian-born in most periods. Those flows have varied with economic conditions in each city in the different periods. This is illustrated by the small gain in Australian-born migrants in Adelaide between 1966 and 1971, when its economy grew less rapidly than in earlier periods, while Perth, whose economy was booming in the late 1960s as a result of mineral exploitation in the north of the State, was able to attract many more. Throughout the post-war period Brisbane has tended to attract more internal migrants than the other two, probably because it can draw on the relatively large population in its hinterland: between 1966 and 1971 three-quarters of its net gain was from other parts of Queensland. Migration of the foreign-born, however, contributed more to the growth of Adelaide and Perth than to Brisbane. Like internal migration it has been sensitive to economic conditions, but has tended to be less volatile. Unlike Sydney and Melbourne, these three centres appear to attract many more through internal migration than they lose. To the extent that attractiveness is a function of size, this suggests that Sydney and Melbourne may have reached a size at which they are proving less attractive, at least to those who are free to make a move.

Among the next group of centres, Canberra has attracted a great deal of migration of the Australian-born, whereas overseas-born have been more important in the growth of the industrial centres of Newcastle, Wollongong and Geelong. In fact, as the National Population Inquiry, (1975, 162) points out, between 1966 and 1971 Canberra gained nearly as much from migration of the Australian-born as all six state capital cities combined.

Regional centres, tourist and holiday resorts which experienced large population gains from migration received mostly Australian-born migrants. Gosford, Armidale and Taree in New South Wales, Townsville, Toowoomba and the Gold Coast in Queensland, Geraldton in Western Australia and Devonport in Tasmania are examples. Another group of centres, whose growth was much more closely associated with mining and manufacturing, has tended to attract more migrants from overseas. The outstanding examples are Wollongong, Mt Isa, Gladstone and Whyalla. It is of interest that Queanbeyan, which functions partly as a relatively low income dormitory, and partly as a manufacturing centre, for Canberra, has attracted a high proportion of its migrants from among the foreign-born, Canberra's proportion is much lower. Despite these differences between cities, most of the fast-growing centres gained from net migration of both Australian and foreign-born.

Among the centres distinguished in the table relatively few were unable to at least keep their natural increase, and not many more registered net losses from migration of the Australian-born. Between 1947 and 1966 Broken Hill, Goulburn, Lismore and Lithgow in New South Wales and Port Pirie in South Australia were the only ones to lose through the overall effect of migration. Orange and Cairns lost by migration of the Australian-born, but more than made it up from migration of the foreign-born. Between 1966 and 1971, when data is also available for Victorian and Western Australian towns, a rather larger number were unable to hold their natural increase.

Internal Migration

In the 1971 Census a question about the place of residence at the previous census was asked for the first time, so that it is possible to observe gross migration flows. The data can be used to describe the extent to which Australians move both within and between urban areas, and between rural and urban areas. Since the smallest geographical areas for which origins and destinations are recorded is the rural and urban parts of statistical divisions, it is not possible to analyse the pattern of moves within cities. The following analysis is based on an unpublished matrix produced by the Bureau of Statistics which shows the total number of moves between major urban, other urban, and rural parts of each state and territory.

The census results give one indication of the frequency with which people change their place of residence. Unfortunately it did not ask whether more than one change of residence had occurred in the five years since the previous census. The Bureau of Statistics has, however, included a question about movements annually, since 1970, in its population survey of persons aged 15 or over, though excluding those in institutions (Ref. No.4.26). On average, in each of the years ending 30 April 1970 and 1971, 15.35 per cent of the population surveyed changed their place of residence.

Had this rate of movement continued throughout the five years from 1966, 56.5 per cent of the population would have moved between the two censuses. In fact only 39.4 per cent of the 1966 residents who were still in Australia in 1971 had changed their place of residence.

Some of the difference might be due to the exclusion of those aged 5 to 14 from the population survey. However, the *Report of the National Population Inquiry* shows (Table IV.9) that 5–9 year olds are slightly over-represented among those migrating between capital cities between 1966 and 1971, and 10–14 year olds somewhat under-represented. The exclusion of those who were overseas in 1966, and those who were away from their usual residence in 1971, may also reduce the apparent frequency of movement from the Census, but the main reason is that people do not have an equal probability of movement. Many of those who moved between the two censuses moved more than once. Even within the one year (1969–70) when the survey asked about numbers of moves, no less than 11.6 per cent of those who moved, moved twice, and 5.7 per cent moved three or more times. These survey figures suggest that in a five-year period there are nearly 95 moves for every hundred adults. The census figures show that these moves are made by less than 40 out of every hundred, so that on average each person who moved did so more than twice in the five-year period. Most of the moves are made by a minority of the population, and that minority tends to move quite frequently.

Several attempts have been made to explain patterns of internal migration in Australia. For example, an econometric model using the 1966–71 data found that the number of job vacancies was the most important explanation of variations in in-migration, though there was also more in-migration into the large city statistical divisons (Cities Commission, 1975). Out-migration is approximately proportional to population, though divisions with high unemployment experienced somewhat more out-migration. This is consistent with results of overseas studies that show that out-migration occurs fairly indiscriminately, but in-migration is more selective.

One way to analyse internal migration is to see how frequently people living in different areas in 1966 moved, and how far they moved. This is shown in Table 3.4. Of those living in the major urban areas in 1966 who were also living in Australia in 1971, 38 per cent had moved between the two dates. The proportion was about the same in rural areas, but higher (45 per cent) in other urban areas. A low frequency of movement in rural areas would be expected, but the lower frequency in major urban areas than in smaller centres is more surprising. The best explanation is that a change in job is more likely to require people living in small towns to move to a different town than to require people living in a major urban area to move. The population survey asked the reason for moving during the year ended 30 April 1970. The reason given for 27 per cent of all moves was 'employment', but for those who moved either into or out of a capital city this reason accounted for over 55 per cent of all moves, and was by far the most important reason. The other major reason, 'housing', is most important for moves within capital cities and, one suspects, moves within other urban areas.

Internal migration between 1966 and 1971 appeared to be mainly individuals changing places with one another rather than part of a significant change in internal population distribution. A high proportion of the moves were within a statistical divi-

TABLE 3.4   *Mobility of the 1966 Population Between 1966 and 1971*
(percentages)

1966 Location		Never moved	Moved within urban or rural section of stat. div.*	Moved between urban and rural sections of stat. div.	Moved to another stat. div. same state	Moved to another state
NSW	Major urban	61.5	29.3	0.8	4.9	3.5
	Other urban	57.5	20.5	3.2	13.7	5.1
	Rural	61.7	10.1	12.5	11.7	4.1
Vic.	Major urban	62.3	29.9	1.0	2.7	4.1
	Other urban	57.6	19.2	3.6	14.8	4.8
	Rural	65.8	8.5	10.3	11.5	4.0
Qld.	Major urban	61.5	25.6	1.4	5.8	5.7
	Other urban	52.1	20.2	4.4	17.6	5.8
	Rural	60.2	10.3	10.0	15.8	3.7
SA	Major urban	64.7	25.9	0.7	3.0	5.7
	Other urban	55.7	16.8	3.5	16.7	7.3
	Rural	65.1	8.7	6.3	15.6	4.4
WA	Major urban	61.4	28.1	1.6	4.7	4.2
	Other urban	46.7	22.1	4.5	23.4	3.3
	Rural	54.1	17.3	9.7	21.1	2.8
Tas.	Major urban	61.0	24.7	1.3	4.8	8.3
	Other urban	55.0	16.3	2.7	13.7	6.6
	Rural	61.3	11.0	8.1	15.1	4.1
ACT	Major urban	57.1	25.5	0.3	—	17.1
	Rural	45.3	4.3	22.5	—	27.9
NT	Other urban	36.3	20.5	2.1	5.2	35.8
	Rural	66.9	12.8	3.6	7.2	9.5
AUST	Major urban	62.0	28.6	1.0	4.1	4.4
	Other urban	55.4	19.8	3.6	15.5	5.7
	Rural	62.0	9.9	10.2	13.9	4.0
	TOTAL	60.6	23.9	2.9	8.0	4.6

Source: 1971 Census, unpublished tabulation.
*   Those who neither crossed a statistical division boundary *nor* changed from urban to rural or vice versa.

sion. Since there are 68 divisions in Australia these could be classed as short distance moves, though outside the metropolitan areas they are not necessarily moves within a single labour market area. These short distance moves are more important among those living in the major urban areas in 1966, where three out of four moves were within the division, reflecting the wide range of job opportunities and living conditions available within the larger cities. By contrast, nearly half of the moves of those living outside the major urban areas were moves to a different statistical division. And since the non-metropolitan statistical divisions are larger, their moves were, on average, significantly longer. Only about one person in twenty moved interstate, or one in eight of those who moved. The table also gives a measure of the frequency of short distance moves between rural and urban areas. One-tenth of those living in rural areas in 1966 had moved to urban areas in the same statistical division by 1971, but only 1 per cent of those in major urban areas and 3.6 per cent of those in other urban areas in 1966 moved in the opposite direction. Because of the much smaller numbers of people living in rural and other urban areas the actual numbers of migrants were, as we see later, much closer to being in balance.

It has often been observed in studies of internal migration that regions whose population is growing rapidly experience a higher rate of out-migration as well as a higher rate of in-migration. This is reflected in Table 3.4, where the highest rate of mobility among the major urban areas is in Canberra and the lowest in Adelaide. Rural and 'other urban' residents in the boom state of Western Australia appear to have moved more frequently than elsewhere.

In many countries, migration of population from rural to urban centres often proceeds in a series of steps; first to a relatively close town and then to a larger centre. Table 3.5 shows that there was a large number of moves from rural areas to local urban centres. In Australia, where there is a high level of mobility and relatively few sizeable regional centres, it might be expected that many more rural-to-urban migrants would move directly to the major urban centres. In 1966 those centres housed about five-eighths of the Australian population, and at least as great a percentage of the jobs, as against a little less than one-fifth in the other urban centres. Despite their having over three out of four urban jobs, the major urban centres attracted less than half of the gross migration from rural to urban centres in Australia between 1966 and 1971 (Table 3.5). Potential rural migrants are more likely to know about job opportunities in nearby smaller centres and be able to move there without breaking too

TABLE 3.5   *Percentage of Rural to Urban Migrants Moving to Major Urban and Other Urban Centres: 1966–1971*

	Destination of Migration	
Source of Rural Migration	Major urban	Other urban
New South Wales	40.5	59.5
Victoria	49.2	50.8
Queensland	35.0	65.0
South Australia	54.4	45.6
Western Australia	58.3	41.8
Tasmania	38.2	61.9
Australian Capital Territory	82.2	17.8
Northern Territory	27.6	72.4
Total: Rural Australia	44.5	55.5

Source: 1971 Census, unpublished tables.

many ties or changing their lifestyle very much. As a result the smaller centres have attracted a relatively high proportion of those moving from rural areas.

Differences between the states in the proportion of their rural migrants going to major urban centres reflect the relative importance of major urban and other urban centres in each state. The capitals are very dominant in South and Western Australia, but much less so in Queensland and Tasmania. In both New South Wales and Victoria the major urban centres account for a high proportion of the urban population, but were unable to attract as much as half of those moving from rural areas.

So far internal migration has been examined from its origin—where people lived in 1966. The alternative is to ask where those living in different areas in 1971 came from. Table 3.6 shows the sources of migration from within Australia into the major

TABLE 3.6   *Sources of Migration to Urban Areas: 1971*
(*percentage of total to each destination*)

Destination		Major urban	Other urban	Rural
			Source of Migration	
N.S.W	Major urban	43.7	36.0	20.3
	Other urban	43.9	21.7	34.4
	Total urban	43.8	29.2	27.0
Vic.	Major urban	34.6	39.7	25.7
	Other urban	34.6	25.1	40.3
	Total urban	34.6	34.2	31.2
Qld.	Major urban	28.2	47.3	24.5
	Other urban	35.8	31.5	32.8
	Total urban	32.7	37.9	29.4
S.A.	Major urban	28.0	41.6	30.4
	Other urban	40.7	20.1	39.2
	Total urban	32.7	33.6	33.7
W.A.	Major urban	30.1	35.1	34.8
	Other urban	41.7	22.6	35.8
	Total urban	34.9	29.9	35.2
Tas.	Major urban	28.6	29.2	42.2
	Other urban	22.6	37.2	40.2
	Total urban	24.5	34.7	40.8
A.C.T.	Major urban	59.5	28.4	12.1
N.T.	Other urban	54.1	26.4	19.5
Australia	Major urban	36.7	38.5	24.8
	Other urban	38.9	25.8	35.2
	Total	37.8	32.6	29.7

Source: 1971 Census, unpublished table.

urban and other urban areas.[1] Considering that other urban and rural residents account for only about 21 and 17 per cent respectively of the 1966 population, they provided a high proportion of the gross flow of migrants to both larger and smaller cities. This is not because those who live outside the major urban areas move more frequently but because a higher proportion of their moves were to another urban area. It is noticeable that Canberra in particular, but also Sydney and Melbourne, draw more people from other major urban areas than do the smaller state capitals and other urban centres.

Table 3.7 summarises the gross flows of people who were in Australia on the two dates. It shows that many of the flows in opposite directions were quite close to balance: net migration is small relative to gross migration flows. There is a large volume of movement between urban areas of each class, and smaller flows between rural areas in different statistical divisions. Major urban areas received 241 000 people moving from other urban areas, but also lost 213 000 to them. From rural areas the flows were even closer to balance—gains of 155 000 being more than offset by losses of 160 000. By contrast other urban areas gained 193 000 from rural areas, and lost only 132 000 to them.

TABLE 3.7   *Summary of Gross Internal Migration: 1966–1971*
('000)

| | | 1966 Location | | |
		Major urban	Other urban	Rural	Total
	Major urban	230	241	155	627
1971	Other urban	213	141	193	547
Location	Rural	160	132	76	367
	Total	603	514	424	1541

Source: 1971 Census, unpublished tables.
Note: Only migrants who crossed a statistical division boundary, or who moved between rural and urban parts of a statistical division are included.

The discussion so far has described gross flows of people within Australia. It has also shown that there are large flows in opposite directions. In order to trace in more detail the effects of internal migration on the growth of cities, it is necessary to focus attention on net migration as in Table 3.8.[2] Internal migration contributed significantly to the growth of Brisbane, Perth and Canberra but very little to the growth of the major urban areas in Victoria (Melbourne and Geelong). Adelaide, Hobart and New South Wales' major urban areas (Sydney, Newcastle and Wollongong) lost popula-

[1] The table understates the amount of movement between other urban centres, since the data does not distinguish between those who moved within an 'other urban' centre and those who moved between centres in the same statistical division.
[2] The data in this table are not comparable with the earlier data on migration of the Australian-born as a component of growth (Table 3.3), for a number of reasons. Perhaps the most important is that Table 3.8 includes those born outside Australia who were living in Australia at both the 1966 and 1971 Censuses, and excludes those who were away from their normal place of residence in 1971.

tion by internal migration. Canberra, Perth and Brisbane were clear gainers from migration between major urban areas. But apart from the New South Wales group all gained from net migration from 'other urban' areas.

TABLE 3.8   *Net Internal Migration to Urban Areas, 1966–1971*

Destination	Source of Internal Migration			Total net gain	Total growth 1966-71	Net gain from internal migration as a % of total growth
	Other m.u.	Other urban	Rural			
Major urban						
N.S.W.	−3 863	−15 132	−13 297	−32 292	318 151	−10.1
Vic.	−7 135	13 866	−5 013	1 718	295 837	0.5
Qld.	1 373	10 502	1 755	13 630	104 741	13.0
S.A.	−7 680	3 476	989	−3 215	81 203	−4.0
W.A.	6 791	7 541	6 559	20 891	141 554	14.8
Tas.	−2 646	38	1 967	−641	10 459	−6.1
A.C.T.	13 160	7 649	2 733	23 542	48 553	48.5
Total	0	27 940	−4 307	23 633	1 000 498	2.4
Other urban						
N.S.W	3 010	−195	25 068	27 883	81 041	34.4
Vic.	−22 692	−3 474	7 231	−18 935	23 479	−80.6
Qld.	−1 802	1 634	6 671	6 503	73 744	8.8
S.A.	−7 875	−1 685	3 317	−6 243	8 223	−76.0
W.A.	−661	2 928	6 489	8 756	56 284	15.6
Tas.	−2 349	−735	−1 374	−4 458	18 139	−24.6
N.T.	4 429	1 527	1 441	7 397	25 245	29.3
Total	−27 940	0	48 843	20 903	286 155	3.7

Source.   1971 Census, unpublished table.

It is sometimes difficult to distinguish migration between urban and rural areas from migration to suburban fringes and ex-urban areas around growing cities. The distinction depends on how urban boundaries are defined. In Australia areas that exceed the relatively low density of 200 persons per square kilometre are regarded as urban and at least some of the intra-urban migration is to areas on the urban fringe which are quite thinly settled. However, a good deal of the migration from the major urban areas is to rural areas and other urban areas in the near vicinity. Some of it is to outer suburbs and ex-urban areas. An attempt is made in Table 3.9 to show its relative importance for the mainland state capitals. The table shows the movements of people between the urban parts of the metropolitan statistical divisions and (a) the rural parts of the same divisions, and (b) other divisions in the near vicinity. Because of the way statistical division boundaries are drawn the data are only broadly comparable between states—for example, no other statistical division lies wholly within 200 kilometres of Perth.

TABLE 3.9   *Migration Between Major Metropolitan Urban Areas and
Nearby Statistical Divisions: 1966–1971*

Between:	Into Metrop. Urban	Out of Metrop. Urban	Net gain
1. Sydney urban and:			
(a) Sydney (rural)	8 518	15 169	−6 651
(b) Outer Sydney	8 060	24 249	−16 189
(c) Illawarra	10 634	12 135	−1 501
Total	27 212	51 553	−24 341
(d) All of Australia	160 552	176 775	−16 223
(a)+(b)+(c) as a percentage of (d)	17.0	29.2	150.0
2. Melbourne urban and:			
(a) Melbourne (rural)	13 491	17 141	−3 650
(b) West Central	7 633	6 702	931
(c) East Central	3 147	3 534	−387
Total	24 271	27 377	−3 106
(d) All of Australia	145 601	137 432	8 169
(a)+(b)+(c) as a percentage of (d)	16.7	19.9	−38.0
3. Brisbane urban and:			
(a) Brisbane rural	5 703	8 824	−3 121
(b) Moreton	10 278	11 827	−1 549
Total	15 981	20 651	−4 670
(c) All of Australia	97 868	82 293	15 575
(a)+(b) as a percentage of (c)	16.3	25.1	−30.0
4. Adelaide urban and:			
(a) Adelaide rural	3 134	4 507	−1 373
(b) Mount Lofty ranges	4 825	3 721	1 104
Total	7 959	8 228	−269
(c) All of Australia	56 569	61 419	−4 850
(a)+(b) as a percentage of (c)	14.1	13.4	5.6
5. Perth urban and:			
(a) Perth rural	5 978	7 333	−1 355
(b) All of Australia	71 954	47 655	24 299
(a) as a percentage of (b)	8.3	15.4	−5.6

Source: 1971 Census, unpublished tabulations.

The table shows a considerable, though very variable, volume of movement
between the capitals and ex-urban areas. There was a net loss of population from the
urban part of every mainland state capital statistical division to its rural part. In Sydney
in particular, but also in Brisbane, there was a substantial net loss of population to adjacent statistical divisions. In fact that net loss in Sydney was greater than the whole of

the net loss of urban Sydney; the Sydney and outer Sydney divisions together experienced a net gain from internal migration of over 6000 compared with a net loss to
urban Sydney of 16 000. The net effect of ex-urban migration in Sydney is much
greater than for any other capital, perhaps because of the high cost of land in the
Sydney urban area.

A quite high proportion of the gross migration from the state capitals was to nearby areas in every case. The statistical divisions included in the table contain the large
urban areas of Wollongong (Illawarra), Gosford-Wyong (Outer Sydney), Geelong
(West Central) and Gold Coast (Moreton). Some of the movement to, those cities
themselves could be regarded as ex-urban, because there is some commuting to the
capital, but some is clearly inter-urban.

Migration to and from state capital city statistical divisions in the three and a half
years following the 1971 Census shows that the patterns established in the previous
five years were continuing (Table 3.10). Since the 1971 to 1974 data refer only to
those 15 years of age and over they could be expected to understate in-migration and
out-migration, as well as both net gains and losses. Sydney's losses had accelerated
significantly and both Melbourne and Brisbane had made gains at a more rapid rate
than in the previous five years. Perth, on the other hand, was making much less rapid
gains than in the late 1960s, and in both Adelaide and Hobart net gains had increased
slightly. In the state capital statistical divisions as a group there had been a significant
change from net gain to net loss. Outside the state capitals Canberra has made consistently large gains—about 23 000 in both 1966–71 and 1971–74. Non-
metropolitan Queensland and Western Australia have gained while Victoria and
South Australia have lost.

TABLE 3.10   *Internal Migration to and from State Capital City*
Statistical Divisions* ('000): June 1966–Dec. 1974

	June 1966 to June 1971	June 1971 to December 1974		
	Net gain	Gains	Losses	Net gain
Sydney	−10.3	159.3	222.5	−63.2
Melbourne	9.7	150.5	136.8	13.7
Brisbane	17.5	120.9	99.5	21.4
Adelaide	−1.6	66.8	65.4	1.4
Perth	22.7	80.5	71.2	9.3
Hobart	0.3	15.7	13.9	1.8
Total	43.4			−15.6

Source: Estimated from ABS, *Internal Migration* (Ref. No. 4.26), and 1971 Census.
*   Persons aged 15 years and over.

Although internal migration has occurred at quite a rapid rate in the period
between 1966 and 1974, especially in the larger urban areas, much of the movement
is within urban areas and a great deal of the migration in one direction is offset by
flows in the opposite direction. Some trends appear to be well established, such as
Sydney's losses and Brisbane's and Canberra's gains, while others appear to be very

closely related to current economic conditions. Recently Perth has been doing well and Adelaide poorly, while Hobart has lost nearly as many as it has gained. Internal migration is not redistributing Australia's population rapidly, and is certainly not dominated by a drift to the biggest cities.

Distribution Within Cities

In this part of the chapter a good deal of the data will be presented in terms of density: persons per unit area. In all cases the data is confined to areas within the urban boundary. All of the data in the previous chapter, and most of the data used in overseas studies, shows the number of people living in a municipality or census tract divided by the *total* area of that municipality or tract. This measure will be referred to as the 'population density'. Two other measures are also used. 'Residential density' is the number of persons per unit area *used for residential purposes*. Unfortunately the area used for residential purposes in some land use classifications includes streets in residential areas and often includes local parks, businesses and other activities commonly found in residential areas (see Chapter 5). Residential density will vary between the cities studied later depending on the definition of residential land use, but it will generally be higher than population density because it excludes land used for non-residential purposes from the denominator. The third density measure is 'urban density'. Its denominator is all land *used for urban purposes*; it excludes vacant land and land used for non-urban purposes within the urban area.

In the previous chapter the long-term trends in the population distribution within Sydney and Melbourne were described using graphs which showed the fall in gross population density with distance from the city centre. These graphs showed a tendency to flatten over time, both because of decreases in density in the inner suburbs and because of increasing densities in the middle and outer suburbs. In this chapter we concentrate mainly on the period between 1947 and 1971 and analyse in more detail changes in population distribution over the period of very rapid post-war growth, and the distribution in 1971.

This chapter concentrates on the distribution of the total population—it does not describe the distribution of particular groups within the population within cities. This feature of cities—the extent to which particular groups are segregated—has been explored extensively by sociologists and geographers. One technique that has been used is social area analysis, first applied in Australia by Jones (1969) in Melbourne. The various social and economic characteristics of individual areas can be expressed by a number of dimensions—usually socio-economic status, ethnicity and familism. In general it has been found that outer suburbs contain high proportions of families with children. Migrants concentrate in inner suburbs and low-status outer suburbs, and high income groups locate mainly in middle and outer suburbs in particular sectors of cities. A less formal approach is to map a number of characteristics of people living in different parts of cities. Computer mapping techniques have been used by Davis and Spearritt (1974) for Sydney, and Cities Commission and Davis (1975) for Melbourne.

Two main explanations have been advanced for the tendency for population density to decline with distance from the city centre. The first concentrates on competition for space near the city centre, which forces up its price and encourages a higher density of development. Because it assumes that densities can adjust quickly to changes in prices, this can be called an equilibrium explanation. The second points out that cities grow over long time periods, and that the optimum density varies over time as transport costs, living standards and tastes change. The older inner suburbs have higher densities. Both explanations help us to understand the distribution of population within cities. Since much of this part of the chapter will be examining Australian data to compare the relative power of these two explanations it is worth examining them in more detail (Richardson, 1969).

The equilibrium explanation was first advanced by Wingo (1961), though concurrent work by Alonso (1964) and Muth (1969) extended his findings. Using a simple model of an urban area in which all jobs are at the centre and residents attempt to maximise utility by choosing where to live and how much housing to buy, they pointed out that everyone would prefer to live close to the centre to minimise commuting costs, in both time and money. As a result there will be competition for space close to the centre. One way to economise on its use is to build housing at a higher density, though as Evans (1973) points out, this will be more expensive in construction costs. People choose where to live, in relation to the centre, by trading off the lower cost of housing further from the centre, with the higher cost of access to the centre.

Alonso derives 'bid rent' curves, showing how the rent a household will be prepared to pay diminishes with distance from the centre. A further factor which influences density is people's preference for living at a high or low density. Among the interesting implications drawn from the theory by Evans are that families with more than one worker will prefer to be close to the centre, whereas if there are a lot of children it will be better to live further away where rents and housing densities are lower.

The main criticism of the theory is that it assumes that all jobs are located at the centre, an assumption which was never strictly valid and is becoming less valid. Partly to meet this criticism, Mills (1967) has adapted the model so that local service employment is scattered throughout the suburban area in proportion to population. Other jobs and a wide range of services are now located outside the city centre, as we shall see in the next chapter, and the assumption that the journey to work dominates a household's location decision has been questioned by empirical research (see Chapter 9). Nevertheless, as long as the city centre remains the largest employment centre and has the widest variety of services, and especially when most public transport routes run radially from the centre, it will remain the peak location for accessibility for many purposes.

Another criticism is that the model assumes that density can be readily changed as conditions change, and in the previous chapter it was shown that gross densities do change over time. Many of the changes in density have been changes in gross population, rather than net residential density. In the inner areas housing is replaced by factories, commercial buildings and institutions, while in the middle and outer suburbs houses and flats fill in the gaps that remain after the first wave of development.

The historical explanation (Burgess, 1925; Harrison and Kain, 1974) emphasises the tendency for the new housing to be built at lower densities as transport speeds increase and costs fall, as incomes rise and preferences for low density living increase. Since cities grow from the centre outwards this leaves higher density housing near the centre. Although some is demolished much remains as the new, lower density housing is built further from the city centre. Housing density in the areas of expansion need not continue to fall over time, since it will also be influenced by subdivision regulations, by decentralisation of jobs and services and by tastes.

There are two ways in which the relative power of these two theories can be tested. The first is by examining the density at which people actually live: net rather than gross densities. The equilibrium theory predicts that this density increases with closeness to the city centre as people are prepared to forgo the amenities of a garden and accept a higher cost of housing to gain the advantages of access to the centre. The historical theory is less clear in its predicitions. It depends on transport, incomes, tastes and the location of workplaces at the time the area was first developed, though in the older inner suburbs density would be expected to be higher. Secondly, the equilibrium theory predicts that density in any part of an urban area will increase with city expansion while the historical theory implies relative stability or even a decline once an area is fully developed.

The three density measures defined above can be used to evaluate the alternative explanations of the gradient in population density. The equilibrium explanation implies that *residential* densities will always decline with distance from the city centre. Because data about land use is scarce in Australia, graphs showing *residential* and *urban* density can only be derived for a few cities at particular dates. Figure 3.2 shows the variation in density with distance from the centre of Adelaide in 1965, using the three measures of density. Adelaide is a smaller city than Sydney, with a good road system, therefore the competition for the most accessible space is likely to be less. The figure shows densities in seven rings, aggregated from some 60 zones. There are two distorting features of the Adelaide data. Firstly, it does not include the City of Adelaide, which had a population of 18 000 in 1965. Secondly, the ring furthest from the city centre, which housed only 6.3 per cent of the urban population, is very largely composed of developments by the South Australian Housing Trust in the 'new town' of Elizabeth, and nearby Salisbury. Since the urban area does not extend so far from the centre in other directions there are no significant areas of the more scattered private development usually found around the fringe to balance these compact developments by the Trust. The relatively high population density in Trust developments also reflects higher than average numbers of persons per dwelling.

From the figure it can be seen that, outside the City of Adelaide, there is no observable fall in *residential* density with distance from the city centre, despite the very large fall in *population* density. The fall in *urban* density is smaller than in population density. The fall in population density is due to two factors (see Chapter 5); firstly, the proportion of vacant and rural land increases with distance from the city centre, and secondly, the proportion of urban land used for non-residential purposes is greater further from the centre. A third possible explanation—that people in inner areas actually live at a higher residential density—must be rejected on this evidence, at least for the suburban areas outside the city of Adelaide.

Similar data for Perth in 1966 and for Sydney in 1971 are shown in Figures 3.3

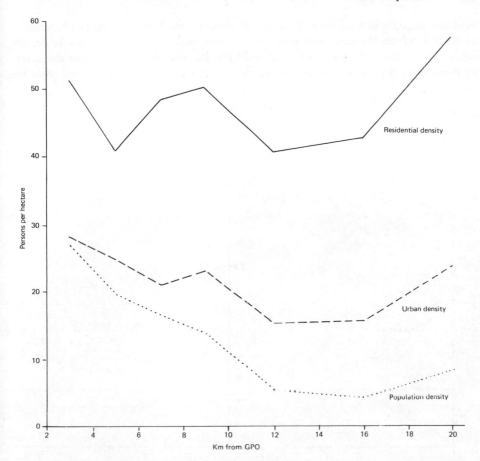

Figure 3.2 Population, urban and residential density and distance from the city centre: Adelaide 1965.
Source: MATS (1966).

and 3.4. The Perth data does not include population density because many of the zones for which the data is available overlap the boundaries of the urban area. It is consistent, though not directly comparable, with the Adelaide data since commercial and community land is included with residential land outside the two CBDs of Perth and Fremantle.[3] Since the Perth data includes the central business districts there is more

---

[3] Comparisons of residential densities in the three cities are not possible because residential areas in Adelaide include roads and footpaths, but do not in Perth. On the other hand, residential areas in Perth include 'many other uses such as local shopping centres and their parking areas, schools ... churches, halls, libraries, theatres, hotels and small open spaces ... In the Central Business Districts of Perth and Fremantle a further classification has been made to distinguish between residential acreage and the land used for administrative, professional, business and community activities.' The *urban* density data for Perth is not entirely satisfactory as 'special reserves', which include such obviously urban land use as railway land, port installations, high schools and technical colleges also include pine plantations, lakes, reservoirs and state forests. They have been treated as non-urban (*Perth Region Data Book 1966*, 13).

evidence of peaks in residential density, and of course the business centre of Fremantle, some 29 km from the main central business district, makes a uniform decline in density with distance from the centre of Perth unlikely. Beyond about 4 km from the centre of Perth there is no evidence of any fall in residential density with distance from the city centre.

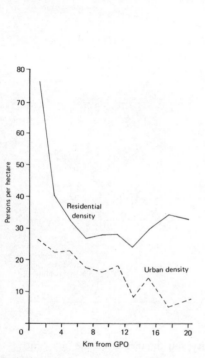

Figure 3.3 Urban and residential density and distance from the city centre: Perth 1966.

Source: MRPA (1969), based on data for 55 zones aggregated into rings.

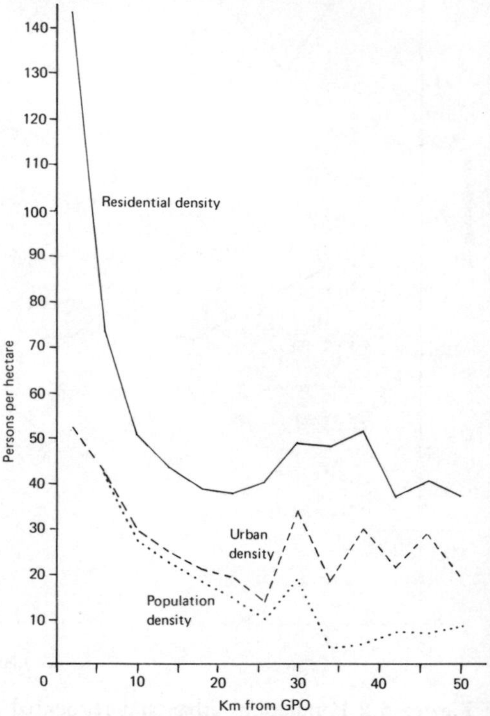

Figure 3.4 Population, urban and residential density and distance from the city centre: Sydney 1971.

Source: SATS (1974).

While there are no large areas of high residential density near the centres of Adelaide and Perth, there are in central Sydney. However, even in Sydney, the *residential* density profile takes quite a different form from the *population* density profile. *Residential* density falls sharply up to about 10 km from the city centre and then becomes nearly horizontal, while population density falls more or less continuously. Urban densities fall less sharply and less regularly. Very broadly the 10 km ring includes the great majority of the areas that were developed before the First World War. Another feature of Sydney is that urban densities are higher south of the harbour than to the north. The reasons, canvassed in the previous chapter, include broken topography to the north, the barrier to expansion posed by the harbour, and the higher socio-economic status of areas in the north which have tended to attract people who wanted 'house-and-garden'. In addition many of the northern suburbs have restrictions on high density development. Thus by far the lowest municipal residential density in Sydney is found in the richest local government area, Ku-ring-gai. The highest residential density in any outer municipality is in Liverpool, where about one-third of the 1971 population was housed in the large Housing Commission estate of Green Valley. Like the data from Adelaide relating to Elizabeth, and evidence from large housing commission estates in Melbourne, this shows that large planned residential developments can have relatively high population densities even without a high proportion of flats. This occurs because of the number of large families and because large scale site planning allows efficient use of land, minimises the waste of unusable areas, and avoids scattered development interspersed with undeveloped land.

There are a number of possible reasons why suburban areas built during the last twenty to thirty years have rather similar residential densities, irrespective of their distance from the city centre. One is that the advantages of living close to the centre have declined, and most people are no longer willing to pay a premium either in price or higher density to live closer to it. As we shall see later, the proportion of the metropolitan jobs and shopping facilities in the city centre has fallen, although it retains by far the largest concentration of jobs and of a number of other facilities. Another reason might be that subdivision regulations have become so important and uniform that they preclude large differences in density. However, the proportion of flats varies between inner and outer suburbs, at least in part reflecting market demands. A third reason is the historical one. All suburbs are on the fringe of development when they are first developed. After they 'fill up' only relatively minor changes in population density occur, unless there is a massive amount of flat construction. Controls over flat redevelopment are part of the reason for the relative stability in population after initial development. Even where flats were built they often housed smaller households, before or after child-rearing, and therefore population density increased less than dwelling density. On this reasoning large differences in residential densities would only occur if parts of the city were originally developed at different densities.

As a city grows the population in any suburb would be expected to follow something like the growth curve shown in Figure 3.5. The horizontal axis measures the time from the commencement of urban development. When it is beyond the urbanised area its population will be at a rural level, though it could grow gradually if it attracts ex-urban dwellers. When areas closer to the city centre are becoming fully developed, growth will begin to spill over into the new area, and its growth will accelerate as more accessible sites are used up. Growth will begin to tail off as sites in the area itself become scarce. Once it is fully developed its population may fall as some houses are replaced by factories, shopping centres or other non-residential land uses. The initial development often houses families with growing numbers of children and later, as the children leave home, dwelling occupancy falls. Alternatively, if flat redevelopment is important the population could continue to increase, though the rate of increase is likely to be small relative to the rates achieved when the area was first urbanised.

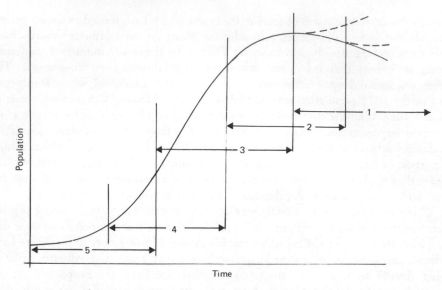

Figure 3.5 Schematic representation of population in an urban sub-area over time.

In the following sections local government areas are classified according to their post-war growth experience from 1947 to 1971. Starting from the oldest central areas, any sub-areas of a growing city can be classified as:

1. Central city areas which experienced population decline. In some cases decline was continuous, but in others it was arrested to some degree, or even reversed, by flat redevelopment (shown by the broken lines).
2. Inner suburban areas with roughly constant, or slowly growing, population. In some cases the rate of growth fell due to filling up. In other cases the rate of growth accelerated due to flat development.
3. Middle suburbs that experienced substantial growth, but where the rate of growth fell over the period.
4. Outer suburbs which grew substantially and where the rate of growth tended to accelerate over the period.
5. Remote outer suburbs which experienced modest growth (up to 150 per cent) on a small base, and usually at an accelerating rate.

The shape of the curve can vary between different areas depending on the speed with which the 'filling up' occurs. This in turn depends on the size of the areas and the rate of growth of the whole city. Figure 3.6 shows the population of a number of local government areas in Melbourne whose boundaries have remained the same over a long period. They range from the inner suburb of Collingwood, which was substantially developed by 1861 and fully developed by the end of the boom period of the 1880s, to the middle suburbs of Coburg and Camberwell whose development occurred in the 50 years from 1911 to 1961. Brunswick and Kew are intermediate. Kew's development has occurred over a long period, and it has not suffered any significant loss in population.

A number of general features of the growth of Melbourne are reflected in the growth curves. The boom of the 1880s was followed by very slow growth in the 1890s, and rapid growth in the 1920s by slow growth in the 1930s. In the early post-war period a number of the inner and middle suburbs lost population as the crowding that occurred during the war years was reduced.

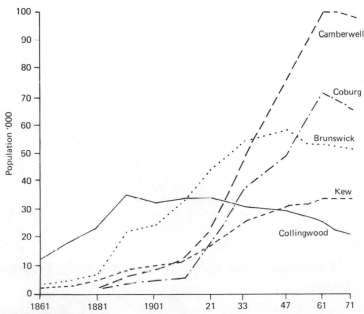

Figure 3.6 Population of Melbourne local government areas: 1861–1971.

Source: Censuses.

Similar curves can be drawn for a number of Sydney municipalities, though the extensive amalgamations of 1948 make it difficult to trace populations of others. Figure 3.7 shows the populations of two municipalities which are at a middle distance from the city centre. Bankstown was the great boom suburb of the early post-war period: there were more houses built there in the late 1940s and early 1950s than in any other suburban municipality in Australia. Its boom had started in the 1920s, and by the end of that decade it had more vacant blocks than any other suburban municipality (Spearritt, 1976). Its growth was slowed by the depression and the war, but was virtually completed by 1961. By contrast Hurstville's growth has been less spectacular and has continued over a longer period.

Municipalities can usefully be classified according to stage of growth, in a way similar to the classification of Melbourne municipalities by Paterson (1970). The main criteria are the absolute amount of growth between 1947 and 1971 and the rate of

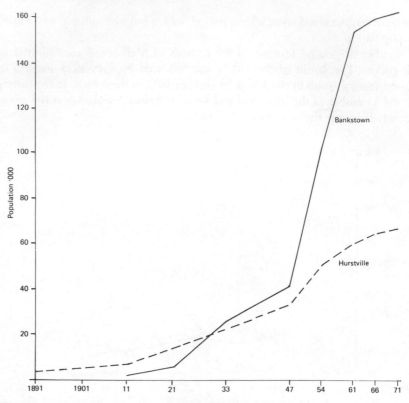

Figure 3.7 Population of Bankstown and Hurstville: 1891–1971.
Source: Censuses.

change in the rate of growth. Because data are available for 1947 to 1971 for
municipalities, adjusted for boundary changes, in Sydney, and there have been few
significant changes in Adelaide, the following analysis concentrates on those two cities
(Figures 3.8 and 3.10.) Wherever they are available for the same areas, 1975 population estimates have been plotted. Vertical scales vary between parts of both figures.

Table 3.11 shows the importance of flat construction in each of the inner and
middle suburbs between 1958, when post-war flat building began to become significant, and 1971. The table can be used to help to understand the changes in the population of each LGA. Sutherland and Warringah have been included in the table since
their coastal areas attracted a good deal of flat development despite their distance from
the city centre. Because flat building has occurred mainly in the 1960s and early
1970s it accounts for the upward curves.

The City of Sydney (1949–68 boundaries), which is not shown in Figure 3.8,
was the only local authority in the Sydney area to lose more than one-fifth of its population between 1947 and 1971, despite significant volumes of high density flat
redevelopment by the Housing Commission and private developers. The expansion of
commercial and industrial activities has replaced some old houses, some others are now

used for business purposes, and dwelling occupancy has fallen. The populations of the ring of suburbs immediately surrounding the City are shown in Part 1 of Figure 3.8 and are identified in the map (Figure 3.9). They all lost population quite heavily between 1947 and 1954, and most continued to do so up to 1961. However, from 1961 onwards, in Mosman, Ashfield, Marrickville and Drummoyne, there was a distinct upturn in population, reflecting a relatively high level of flat building. Despite its high level of flat building North Sydney's population declined until 1966. Its housing has suffered from the same kind of commercial intrusion as the City, and it also lost housing to make way for the Warringah Expressway. Woollahra's population has continued to fall, despite a high level of flat building. The first ring of suburbs extends further west from the centre than in any other direction, reflecting the early development of Sydney towards Parramatta.

TABLE 3.11   *Flats Completed 1958–1971 as a Percentage of Houses and Flats in 1971: Inner and Middle Suburban LGAs in Sydney*

Ashfield	28.6	Manly	21.1
Auburn	12.6	Marrickville*	15.8
Bankstown	2.0	Mosman	34.0
Botany	38.3	North Sydney	39.2
Burwood	13.0	Paramatta	11.9
Canterbury	27.6	Randwick	28.4
Concord	5.3	Rockdale	15.3
Drummoyne	18.1	Ryde	17.8
Hunters Hill	20.9	Strathfield	15.9
Hurstville	9.2	Sutherland	9.1
Kogarah	9.6	Sydney*	20.1
Ku-ring-gai	5.2	Warringah	19.0
Lane Cove	34.1	Waverley	23.8
Leichhardt*	11.8	Willoughby	8.5
		Woollahra*	20.9

Source: N.S.W. Statistical Register and 1971 Census.
* The proportions for these LGAs have been estimated for their pre-1968 boundaries.

The next ring of suburbs (Parts 2a and 2b in Figure 3.8)[4] were mostly still growing after the war, though in both Randwick and Manly the growth due to new housing was more than offset by the fall in occupancy of existing housing. All of these suburbs still had some vacant land for housing. In Randwick, for example, it was in the south; the north of the municipality was much like neighbouring areas of Waverley and Woollahra. Willoughby, like Randwick and Manly, is at the margin between the first and second rings of suburbs. Its population has increased very little in the post-war period. The adjacent suburb of Lane Cove is at the opposite extreme, growing in population by nearly 50 per cent. At least some of the difference between the two is due to the much greater amount of flat building in Lane Cove. The extent to which flat

[4] These two parts, Parts 4a and 4b and some parts of Figure 3.10, have been separated to prevent congestion of space.

building revived the growth of a number of these suburbs can be seen by comparing Kogarah, which still had some space for new houses after the war, with neighbouring Rockdale which had very little. Despite this Rockdale, through flat redevelopment, grew faster during the 1960s. Most of the growth during the 1960s in this ring of suburbs has been due to redevelopment, and the rate of growth is closely related to the extent of flat building.

The next ring (Part 3 of Figure 3.8) comprises four suburbs which grew very rapidly between 1947 and 1961, but whose growth slowed during the 1960s. In this case the extent of slowing varies, partly with the extent to which they were fully

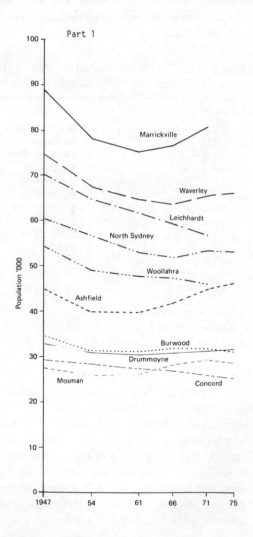

Figure 3.8 Population in Sydney LGAs: 1947–1975.
Source: Censuses.

developed by 1961, and partly with the volume of redevelopment they experienced. At one extreme Bankstown was close to fully developed by the end of the 1950s and

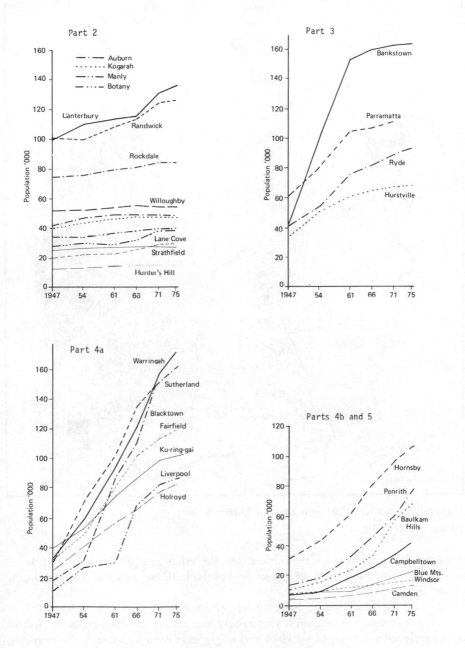

Figure 3.8 (contd.)

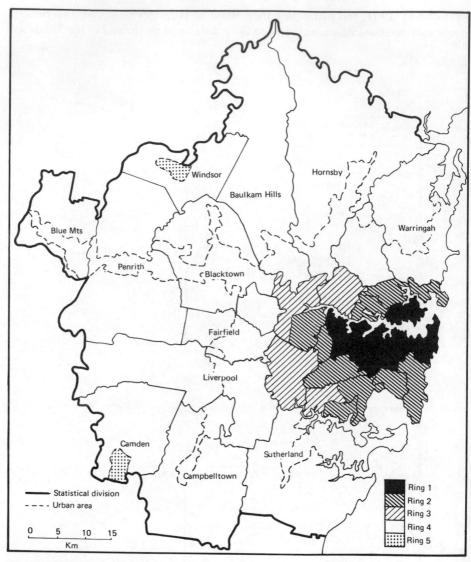

Figure 3.9 Location of growth rings of LGAs: Sydney.
Source: Figure 3.8.

permitted very little flat redevelopment. At the other extreme Ryde maintained its growth rate partly as a result of a great deal of flat building, much of it on previously vacant sites.

Among the large ring of outer suburbs (Parts 4a and 4b, Figure 3.8) which experienced increasing urbanisation throughout the period, Ku-ring-gai and Holroyd were nearly fully developed by 1971 and might have been included in the next inner ring. In Warringah and Sutherland also, the land available for further development is limited by the reservations of Ku-ring-gai Chase National Park in the north and the Royal National Park in the south. In none of these LGAs had growth slowed down by 1971 and in Warringah in particular this was partly because of the popularity of the beachside suburbs for flats, despite the distance from the city centre.

Finally, three local government areas. Windsor, Blue Mountains and Camden (Part 5, Figure 3.8), are only at the early stages of development in a metropolitan sense. No part of either Windsor or Camden is in the Sydney urban area as defined at the 1971 Census.

In one respect Sydney municipal population data is not good for testing the hypothesis of simple geographic spread of urban areas. Because many of them cover large areas, different parts of local government areas can be at different stages of urban development at the same time. This has become increasingly true in the post-war period when the urban area has spread into large shires which radiate out from the developed area. Quite rapid urbanisation could continue in Hornsby, Baulkham Hills, Blacktown, Penrith, Fairfield, Liverpool and Campbelltown for several decades if areas currently zoned as non-urban were to be rezoned.

Adelaide is a good deal smaller than Sydney. Its LGAs are also quite small, and therefore tend to 'fill up' over a shorter time period. In addition development controls have limited the scattering of development around the urban fringe to a greater extent than in other Australian cities: the urban boundary has been kept more distinct. The effects of changes in the overall rate of growth of Adelaide can be seen in the population growth in individual LGAs shown in Figure 3.10; in particular the rapid growth between 1961 and 1966 which was followed by a much slower rate between 1966 and 1971. As in other cities a central group of suburbs has experienced population decline over most if not all of the post-war period (Part 1 of Figure 3.10, also shown in the map, Figure 3.11). Only in Walkerville is there any evidence of a resurgence of growth like that produced by flat redevelopment in many inner and middle suburbs in Sydney—but, as Table 3.12 shows, not many new flats were built in Walkerville.

Only three suburban LGAs are in the next stage of modest growth, and in two of those, Port Adelaide and Burnside, the growth was concentrated into the earlier periods. The third, Glenelg, developed early as a somewhat separate seaside suburb and has recently experienced some flat redevelopment (see Table 3.12). Unlike Sydney, this group does not form a ring round the declining suburbs.

A much larger third group of LGAs experienced strong growth over the whole period, but a decline in growth rate in the last intercensal period (Part 3, Figure 3.10). Some of this is due to the fact that Adelaide, as a whole grew more rapidly in the earlier post-war period. Without a slackening of general growth, areas like Marion could have expected a continuation of quite rapid growth. The actual growth of these areas from 1947 to 1971 varied from 80 per cent in Payneham to over 700 per cent in Campbelltown. Campbelltown could have been classified in Group 4 because it maintained quite a strong growth rate, but since all of its territory is in the urban area as defined in 1971 it cannot be expected to continue rapid growth. The slackening in its growth rate during 1966 to 1975 marks the end of its period of rapid growth. The continued growth of Henley and Grange derives in large part from flat redevelopment.

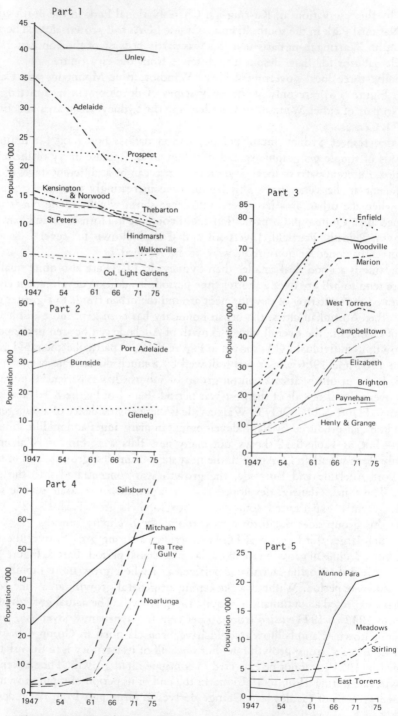

Figure 3.10 Population growth in Adelaide LGAs: 1947–1975.
Source: Censuses.

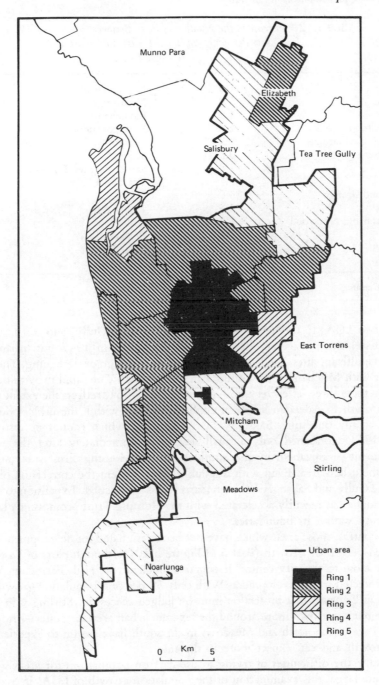

Figure 3.11 Location of growth rings of LGAs: Adelaide.
Source: Figure 3.10.

TABLE 3.12   *Increase in the Number of Flats Between 1954 and 1971*
as a Percentage of Total Houses and Flats in 1971
Adelaide LGAs

Adelaide	11.3	Munno Para	0.2
Brighton	5.0	Noarlunga	1.4
Burnside	4.9	Payneham	8.2
Campbelltown	2.0	Port Adelaide	3.1
Colonel Light Gardens	2.2	Prospect	4.3
East Torrens	0.6	St Peters	4.2
Enfield	1.8	Salisbury (incl. Elizabeth)	1.1
Glenelg	10.4	Tea Tree Gully	0.4
Henley and Grange	13.0	Stirling	0.5
Hindmarsh	3.3	Thebarton	2.9
Kensington and Norwood	7.8	Unley	7.6
Marion	2.5	Walkerville	4.8
Meadows	0.9	West Torrens	9.0
Mitcham	3.4	Woodville	3.2

Source: Censuses

In two LGAs to the north (Salisbury and Tea Tree Gully) and one in the south (Noarlunga) there was very little urban development in 1947 but urban growth became significant after 1961, and the rate showed no sign of slackening. These three, together with Mitcham, form Group 4 in Figure 3.10. The rapid growth during the 1960s in these three, after very slow growth up to 1961, reflects the extent to which urban growth in Adelaide has been confined to land within the urban boundary as defined at any one time. Salisbury (and Elizabeth, which cannot be distinguished before 1961) contained only a small settlement immediately after the war. The development of Elizabeth by the South Australian Housing Trust substantially extended the urban area. Even with less public development the conversion of parts of Tea Tree Gully and Salisbury has been scarcely less spectacular. Expansion to the south in Noarlunga has recently accelerated with the Housing Trust promoting a large new community within its boundaries.

By contrast those areas which have not been designated for development have experienced very little growth (Part 5 of Figure 3.10), although parts of East Torrens are very close to the city centre. It contains much of the Hills Face Zone which is being protected from development. With only 50 per cent population growth in East Torrens in 28 years that protection must be judged successful. Stirling is in a similar situation but has grown more around the separate urban area at Crafers-Bridgewater. Munno Para in the north and Meadows in the south have begun to experience quite rapid growth and can expect more in the future.

Despite the difficulties of trying to use data on populations for areas which are often quite large, this examination of the population growth of LGAs in Sydney and Adelaide has generally confirmed that most population growth is accommodated by spreading of the fringe from the centre. The major qualification is that significant population increases in a number of inner and middle suburbs in Sydney have resulted from flat redevelopment. The period during which any locality becomes fully developed varies considerably; it is shorter for smaller areas and in rapidly growing cities.

To a very considerable extent differences in density in residential areas are determined by the type of dwellings and the density at which they are built at the time of first development. Consequently *residential* densities are higher in a small ring of inner suburbs that were built before the First World War, and relatively uniform outside that ring. *Population* density in the urban area, which also varies with the proportion of land used for non-residential purposes, declined fairly continuously with distance from the centre, mainly because more land in the middle and outer suburbs was either vacant or used for open space, institutions and the like. After the Second World War there was a widespread trend towards flattening of the *population* density gradient as the inner areas lost population and nearly all growth occurred near the fringe. The flat building boom of the 1960s reversed the decline in some inner suburbs, especially in Sydney.

This examination of population distribution in Adelaide (1965), Perth (1966) and Sydney (1971) shows that, beyond the inner suburbs, densities in residential areas did not decline significantly with distance from the city centre. The equilibrium explanation of the density-distance relationship is not sustained by this Australian data.

Summary

The increasing concentration of Australia's population in the mainland state capitals has often been used as evidence that they are the most attractive places for most people to live. The first part of this chapter showed that the situation is actually much more complex. Since most of their growth has resulted from natural increase and migration from overseas, it is more captive growth than growth resulting from a conscious choice. This is especially true of Sydney and Melbourne, where internal migration figures show a net loss in most intercensal periods since the war. There is more evidence that Perth, Brisbane and Adelaide are attractive places to live since they have made considerable gains from internal migration.

Many smaller centres have also grown quite rapidly, though their growth is disguised when population growth is simply allocated between the capital cities and the rest. Canberra is the outstanding growth centre among the smaller centres, but Wollongong, the Gold Coast, Darwin and a number of smaller centres have also grown rapidly. Size may have been a less important determinant of growth than other more special factors such as mineral developments, tourism and government decisions. Even on average there is not much difference in growth rates between size groups of centres over 20 000 population.

Within cities the outstanding feature has been the spread of suburbs at a relatively uniform density outside a quite small core of older, higher density inner suburbs. The public transport suburbs that grew in the first three decades of the century were mostly at quite low density, spread along rail or train lines, rather than producing large areas of compact high density housing. Development since the Second World War has been almost entirely through filling in between suburbs at the fringe. The alternative way to accommodate population growth would have been to increase density in the area which was already developed. Up to about 1960, rather than increasing, the population of most fully developed suburbs actually fell as war-time housing shortages and crowding were relieved. Since 1960 there has been quite a high volume of flat building, which has caused the population to increase in some inner and middle suburbs, especially in Sydney. The volume of redevelopment has been too small, and most of it has been at too low a density, to absorb more than a small proportion of the population growth of the large urban areas.

As the larger cities have grown they have become less oriented to the city centres. It is not surprising, then, that the equilibrium or 'trade-off' theory of urban development does not provide a good explanation of residential densities. Indeed it appears that urban densities that are established at the time of first development usually only change gradually and to a minor extent with subsequent redevelopment. The initial subdivision, and even the initial housing stock, have a powerful and long-term influence.

4 Where People Work

Most people work in the towns where they live so that there is relatively little commuting between urban centres, except for a few which are close together. The proportion of the population in the workforce also varies between cities, because of differences in age composition or availability of jobs. Within urban areas jobs are usually much more concentrated in the central areas than the resident population and workers often travel considerable distances from home to work.

The most important, and perhaps the most difficult, part of a policy of a decentralisation or promotion of growth centres is getting the jobs into the non-metropolitan centres. This chapter reports recent trends in the growth in employment in the major urban centres which do not suggest that large centres are the most attractive for the growth of business.

If people worked and lived in the same part of a city journeys to work would absorb less resources and use less time. One of the objectives in planning the post-war development of Australian cities has been to encourage the growth of surburban employment centres. Data on the location of jobs show that there is already a lot of employment in the suburban area, and central business districts are becoming increasingly specialised in the kinds of jobs they offer. The kinds of jobs moved to the suburbs are not often attracted to large suburban *centres* but often dispersed throughout the suburbs.

Different towns and cities have concentrations of different kinds of industries and therefore offer different kinds of jobs. Even within a city some kinds of jobs are found mainly in the central business district, others in the inner suburbs and still others in some of the middle and outer suburbs. Still others are relatively evenly distributed throughout the urban area.

The location of workplaces can be analysed either by industry, which tells us something about the employer's preferences (in what kinds of industries do employers choose small or large cities, city centres or suburbs) or by occupation, which describes the location of job opportunities available to different kinds of workers. This chapter examines the distribution of employment in urban areas from each of these points of view.

Distribution Between Urban Areas

Some kinds of industries are highly concentrated in the large cities, others in rural areas, and others are quite widely distributed throughout the country. One way to make comparisons between industrial structures is to compare the percentages of the workforce employed in different industries in different cities. Table 4.1 does this for 1971 for the ten major urban areas, for other urban areas as a group, and for rural areas. Although the industry classification is broad, the extent to which different industries are concentrated in the major urban areas can be seen.[1] In particular the three major manufacturing cities of Sydney, Melbourne and Adelaide contain 63 per cent of the national employment in manufacturing. The percentage of employment in particular industrial groups varies considerably more among the smaller than among the larger cities, reflecting the greater likelihood of industrial specialisation in a small centre. Had the table been continued to include individual smaller centres, even higher degrees of specialisation would be found in mining centres like Broken Hill and Mt Isa, manufacturing centres like Whyalla and tourist centres such as the Gold Coast (Linge, Rimmer and Lance, 1976).

The table shows the main differences between the industrial structures of Australian cities. Melbourne and Sydney are very similar except that manufacturing is somewhat more important in Melbourne and various commercial activities, especially finance and real estate, more important in Sydney. In the smaller state capitals wholesale and retail trade and community services are more important than in the two largest. Manufacturing, on the other hand, is important in Adelaide but much less important in Brisbane, Perth and Hobart. These three are much more commercial and administrative centres for their hinterlands, and less centres for production of exports to other parts of Australia.

There are three more specialised production centres, though they vary in their level of specialisation. Newcastle is important both as a production centre and a regional centre. The proportion of its workforce in manufacturing and mining (36.1 per cent) is only a little higher than Melbourne's. Geelong serves as both a regional centre and a manufacturing centre. Wollongong is the most specialised, with 48.3 per cent of its workforce in mining and manufacturing. Its regional functions are very limited.

While these three centres have few employed in public administration and defence, since they are not capital cities, Canberra's employment in this industry is very high. Public administration is Canberra's 'export industry' just as mining and manufacturing are the export industries of Newcastle and Wollongong. Alternatively, Canberra can be seen as the government centre—at least for national government functions—for the whole of Australia. Community service employment, much of which is in government, is also high in Canberra.

Other urban centres in Australia are very varied. Not many of them depend heavily on manufacturing or mining. Most are commercial centres for the local region with strong employment in retailing and local services.

Table 4.1 is based on where people live rather than where they work. Many of those living in the rural areas who work in urban kinds of industries commute to jobs in urban areas. Others work in small country centres which are too small to be included among the urban areas (less than 1000 population).

---

[1] F.J.B. Stilwell (1974, 38–48) describes the extent of concentration in more detail.

TABLE 4.1 *Industrial Distribution of the Workforce in Major Urban Areas: 1971 (per cent of total workforce)*

	Sydney	Melbourne	Brisbane	Adelaide	Perth	Newcastle	Wollongong	Canberra	Hobart	Geelong	Other urban	Rural	Total Australian
Agriculture	0.4	0.4	0.7	0.7	1.0	0.5	0.4	0.4	0.8	0.8	4.2	45.5	7.4
Mining	0.3	0.3	0.8	0.4	1.1	3.4	6.3	0.2	0.2	0.3	3.9	2.2	1.5
Manufacturing	28.5	31.8	20.8	27.9	18.1	32.7	42.0	5.6	19.1	38.3	17.0	9.2	23.5
Electricity, gas, water	1.8	1.5	1.5	1.9	1.2	2.6	2.1	0.7	3.6	1.4	2.6	1.0	1.7
Construction	6.8	6.5	8.4	7.2	9.5	7.1	7.7	10.3	8.2	7.6	10.4	7.4	7.9
Wholesale & retail	19.6	19.5	23.0	21.5	23.3	18.9	14.0	13.0	20.0	18.6	21.0	10.0	19.1
Transport & storage	5.7	5.0	5.9	4.6	6.3	6.1	4.9	2.5	4.8	4.3	5.8	3.2	4.6
Communication	2.1	2.0	2.3	1.9	2.2	1.3	1.1	1.6	2.8	1.4	2.3	1.4	2.0
Finance, real estate	9.6	8.1	8.4	7.3	8.8	5.5	4.6	6.1	8.0	5.0	5.3	2.2	7.0
Public administration, Defence	5.3	4.9	7.5	4.8	6.0	3.4	1.9	32.7	8.3	2.4	5.0	3.8	5.3
Community Service	10.2	10.5	12.1	18.9	18.3	10.7	7.9	17.8	14.8	11.8	12.0	6.9	10.8
Entertainment	5.3	4.5	5.0	5.0	5.7	5.2	4.3	6.2	6.3	4.2	6.7	3.3	5.1
Other	4.5	5.1	8.7	8.0	3.6	2.8	2.8	3.0	3.2	3.9	4.0	4.0	4.1
Total Number ('000)	1218	1082	330	332	264	105	74	62	52	45	1008	717	5240

Source: 1971 Census

Table 4.2 shows the occupational distribution of the workforce in each of the major centres, and in other urban and rural areas. The occupations of people living in Canberra and the rural areas are often quite different from those in other urban areas. The most notable feature of the table however, is the similarity of the proportions in different occupations in the different cities. Even the larger and smaller urban centres have similar shares of most urban-type occupations. If the farmers are excluded, even rural areas have a similar occupational structure. In part this similarity results from the coarseness of the occupational subdivision in the table. If, for example, sales workers were subdivided into those working in shops and those working in warehouses or as sales representatives, the latter would be much more concentrated in the larger centres. The differences that can be seen in the table reflect to some degree the industrial distribution shown in Table 4.1. For example, the high proportion of Newcastle, Wollongong and Geelong residents who work in manufacturing industries is reflected in the high proportions of their workforce in the 'tradesmen, process workers, labourers' occupation group. Correspondingly these three centres, particularly Wollongong, have relatively small numbers in administrative, managerial and clerical occupations. Each of these occupations is to some extent concentrated in the administrative centres of the various states and in Canberra.

The first four occupation groups comprise the white collar workers. They constitute as much as 62 per cent of the workforce in Canberra, compared with around half in the state capitals, less than 40 per cent in Geelong and Newcastle and only 32 per cent in Wollongong. This difference is probably the most important between Canberra, a city dominated by white collar jobs, at one extreme and Wollongong, a mainly blue collar city, at the other. The "other urban" centres as a group fit into this continuum just above Newcastle and Geelong.

The table also gives some indication of the level of workforce participation of females, as indicated by the proportion of total jobs they hold. As a general rule the higher the proportion of white collar jobs the higher the proportion of all jobs that are held by women. This is partly a direct result of the fact that females hold relatively few of the jobs in the largest blue collar occupation group. Furthermore, two of the cities with a high proportion of blue collar jobs—Newcastle and Wollongong—specialise in heavy industry in which there are very few jobs for women. The result is a serious shortage of jobs for women in the smaller urban centres, with the exception of Canberra. Wollongong again stands out, having three men employed for every woman.

The industrial distribution of a city's jobs can have a very significant impact on its growth since different industries grow or decline at very different rates. The growth of employment in a city can be analysed to separate the effect of its industrial structure from other influences on its growth. The technique is known as 'shift and share analysis'. It has been applied to Australia by Stilwell (1974) and Kerr (1970). The following summary draws on those sources. The technique separates growth into three components:

1. Growth which would have occurred if the city had just maintained its share of the nation's employment ('regional share' component);

TABLE 4.2 *Occupational Distribution of the Workforce in Major Urban Areas: 1971 (per cent of total workforce)*

		Sydney	Melbourne	Brisbane	Adelaide	Perth	Newcastle	Wollongong	A.C.T	Hobart	Geelong	Other urban	Rural	Total Australian
Professional and technical	M	6.6	6.8	6.2	6.5	6.8	6.0	5.5	11.5	8.1	6.5	5.3	2.8	5.9
	F	4.5	4.5	4.6	5.2	4.9	4.2	3.5	6.4	6.1	4.5	4.6	2.6	4.3
Administrative and managerial	M	6.6	6.4	5.9	6.1	6.6	4.6	3.7	5.9	5.8	4.8	6.4	3.2	5.9
	F	0.9	0.8	0.8	0.9	0.9	0.7	0.6	0.7	0.8	0.6	0.9	0.5	0.8
Clerical	M	6.9	6.8	7.7	6.4	7.0	5.0	4.7	13.5	9.1	4.9	4.5	1.7	5.7
	F	18.2	11.6	12.2	10.7	12.3	8.5	7.0	17.4	11.6	7.6	7.8	3.9	10.1
Sales	M	4.4	4.6	4.9	4.5	4.6	4.0	2.8	3.2	4.5	4.1	4.7	2.0	4.2
	F	3.6	3.6	4.2	4.6	4.9	4.7	4.0	3.1	4.5	4.1	4.9	2.5	3.9
Farming etc.	M	0.6	0.7	0.9	1.0	1.5	0.9	0.6	1.2	0.9	1.3	4.2	37.7	6.5
	F	0.1	0.1	0.2	0.2	0.2	0.1	0.1	0.1	0.1	0.2	0.5	7.5	1.2
Mining etc.	M	0.1	0.1	0.3	0.1	0.2	1.9	4.2	0.1	0.2	0.2	1.7	1.2	0.6
	F	0.0	0.0	0.0	0.0	0.0	0.0	0.0	0.0	0.0	0.0	0.0	0.0	0.0
Transport and communication	M	4.6	4.2	5.2	4.3	4.8	5.8	5.1	2.8	4.4	4.4	6.1	3.9	4.8
	F	0.8	0.7	0.7	0.7	1.0	0.6	0.6	0.8	0.5	0.6	0.7	0.8	0.8
Tradesmen, process workers, labourers	M	28.2	28.8	28.5	31.5	28.1	37.7	43.8	17.6	27.3	37.9	30.3	17.6	27.8
	F	5.8	7.3	3.8	4.6	2.5	2.7	4.0	0.7	2.7	5.8	2.4	1.3	4.3
Service, recreation	M	3.2	2.8	3.1	2.7	2.8	2.6	2.1	3.1	3.3	2.5	3.0	1.5	2.8
	F	4.1	3.9	4.9	5.8	6.0	5.7	4.2	4.3	6.1	4.8	6.1	3.4	4.6
Armed Services	M	1.1	0.8	1.7	0.7	0.8	1.1	0.2	4.1	0.4	0.3	1.2	1.7	1.2
	F	0.0	0.0	1.1	0.0	0.0	0.0	0.0	0.4	0.0	0.0	0.1	0.1	0.0
Not stated	M	3.1	3.4	2.7	2.2	2.6	2.2	2.4	2.2	2.3	3.3	3.6	3.0	3.1
	F	1.6	2.1	1.4	1.3	1.5	1.0	0.9	1.1	1.3	1.6	1.3	1.1	1.5
Total	M	65.4	65.4	67.2	66.0	65.8	71.8	74.9	65.1	66.5	70.1	70.8	76.3	68.4
	F	34.6	34.6	32.8	34.0	34.2	28.2	25.1	34.9	33.5	29.9	29.2	23.7	31.6
Total Number ('000)		1218	1032	380	332	264	105	74	62	52	45	1003	717	5240

Source: 1971 Census.

2. Growth above or below this rate which can be attributed to the city's industrial structure; whether its employment is mostly in fast or slow growing industries ('industrial mix' component); and

3. Growth above or below the regional share which is due to individual industries in the city growing more or less rapidly than the national average for the industry ('differential' component).

Because of the changes in industrial classification between the 1966 and 1971 Censuses this analysis can only be applied between 1954 and 1966, and only the metropolitan, other urban and rural parts of each state can be distinguished. The level of disaggregation is into 23 industrial sectors. The main interest in the results is the relative importance of the industrial mix component and the differential component in accounting for the more rapid growth of employment in the metropolitan areas. Are the metropolitan areas growing more rapidly because they have more of the fast-growing industries or because they provide better environments for employment growth in each industry? The differential component is an indicator of the competitive success of different cities in attracting employment, including the effect which the presence of some industries might have in attracting employment in other linked industries. Stilwell's Table 5.1 is reproduced below in Table 4.3. Rural areas are included for completeness. It is interesting that the slow growth of employment in rural areas, though due mainly to the slow growth of employment in rural industries, is also partly due to the fact that secondary and tertiary employment in rural areas grew less quickly than in urban areas.[2]

The actual growth in employment in urban sectors over this twelve-year period was fastest in Canberra and Darwin/Alice Springs, followed by 'other urban' in South Australia, Adelaide, Brisbane and Perth. In both Tasmania and South Australia employment grew faster in other urban areas than in the capital, and it was not much slower in Western Australia and Victoria. Over this particular period, then, there was not a rapid and widespread drain of employment from the smaller centres to the state capitals, except in New South Wales and Queensland. And even though they grew slightly less rapidly, or not much faster in percentage terms, most of the metropolitan areas were already so dominant in 1954 that they accounted for three-quarters of the absolute growth in employment.

In every state the industrial mix was much more favourable to growth of the metropolitan than the other urban areas. Because the rapidly growing industries are more concentrated in the metropolitan areas, each industrial sector in the other urban areas has to grow faster than the national average for that sector, if the other urban areas are to maintain their share of the national employment. Only in South Australia, Tasmania and Western Australia did they achieve this, as shown by the higher percentage growth due to the differential component in their 'other urban' areas. In South Australia the rapid growth of Whyalla has been the main contributor. In Tasmania the north coast towns have grown faster than Hobart, and in Western Australia mining

---

[2] The differential growth, and therefore the total growth of employment in urban areas, will be high partly because of the outward shift of the boundaries of metropolitan and other urban areas. To this extent the rate of differential growth will overstate growth performance relative to rural areas.

TABLE 4.3 Components of Employment Growth: 1954–1966

State or Territory	Area Type	Actual Growth (000's)	%	Regional Share (000's)	%	Industrial Mix Effect (000's)	%	Differential Effect (000's)	%
New South Wales:	Metropolitan	+308.3	+38.3	+253.1	+31.4	+52.0	+6.5	+3.2	+0.4
	Other Urban	+93.9	+25.3	+116.9	+31.4	+8.8	+2.4	−31.8	−8.6
	Rural	+37.7	+1.7	+70.3	+31.4	−43.7	−19.6	−22.8	−10.2
Victoria:	Metropolitan	+268.5	+39.6	+213.3	+31.4	+36.3	+5.4	+18.9	+2.8
	Other Urban	+62.4	+34.3	−57.3	+31.4	+5.0	+2.7	+0.2	+0.1
	Rural	+5.4	+3.0	+56.0	+31.4	−31.2	−17.5	−19.4	−10.9
Queensland:	Metropolitan	+88.3	+43.5	+63.9	+31.4	+13.7	+6.7	+10.8	+5.3
	Other Urban	+36.9	+20.9	+55.4	+31.4	+1.1	+0.6	−19.6	−11.1
	Rural	+10.8	+7.3	+46.4	+31.4	−34.3	−23.2	−1.4	−1.0
South Australia:	Metropolitan	+103.8	+52.4	+62.3	+31.4	+12.2	+6.2	+29.3	+14.8
	Other Urban	+26.1	+61.5	+13.3	+31.4	+0.6	+1.4	+12.1	+28.7
	Rural	−0.4	−0.5	+24.9	+31.4	−14.3	−18.1	−11.0	−13.8
Western Australia:	Metropolitan	+58.6	+41.4	+44.5	+31.4	+8.9	+6.3	+5.1	+3.6
	Other Urban	+14.7	+37.0	+12.5	+31.4	−2.0	−4.9	+4.2	+10.4
	Rural	+7.5	+10.1	+23.6	+31.4	−31.4	−17.9	−2.6	−3.5
Tasmania:	Metropolitan	+10.4	+27.1	+12.0	+31.4	+3.5	+9.2	−5.2	−13.6
	Other Urban	+14.8	+35.5	+13.1	+31.4	+0.7	+1.6	+1.0	+2.4
	Rural	+3.9	+10.5	+11.9	+31.4	−6.7	−17.6	−1.3	−3.3
Northern Territory:	Other Urban	+8.1	+144.5	+1.8	+31.4	+0.6	+11.2	+5.7	+101.8
	Rural	+1.9	+56.6	+1.1	+31.4	−0.5	−14.0	+1.3	+39.1
A.C.T.:	Metropolitan	+29.8	+232.9	+4.0	+31.4	+2.7	+20.8	+23.1	+180.6
	Rural	+0.5	+51.5	+0.3	+31.4	−0.04	−4.5	+0.2	+24.6
Total:	Metropolitan	+867.7	+41.8	+653.2	+31.4	+129.4	+6.2	+85.1	+4.1
	Other Urban	+256.8	+29.9	+270.3	+31.4	+14.8	+1.7	−28.2	−2.8
	Rural	+33.4	+4.5	+284.5	+31.4	−144.1	−19.3	−56.9	−8.0
Total: Australia		+1157.9	+31.4	+1157.9		0	0	0	0

Source: Stilwell (1974, 69). Derived from the 1954 and 1966 Censuses.

towns and Geraldton have grown very rapidly. However, the negative differential component of growth in other urban areas in New South Wales and Queensland, and a rate near zero in Victoria—the states which contain most of the other urban employment—were sufficient to make the national component negative.

Comparisons between the metropolitan areas give results similar to comparisons between their population growth rates. Apart from Canberra, Hobart has the most favourable industrial mix for growth, primarily because tertiary employment has been growing faster than secondary. This also accounts for Melbourne's less favourable mix—it has the highest proportion of its employment in manufacturing.

The favourable industrial mix accounted for some 94 per cent of the difference between growth in employment in Sydney and the national growth rate. Two-thirds of the excess of Melbourne's growth over the national average rate was due to its favourable industrial mix. In Adelaide, on the other hand, most was due to the differential component, showing Adelaide's success during this period in attracting industrial employment. If the differential component is regarded as an indicator of the power of a city to attract employment, Sydney is not significantly above the Australian average, and Melbourne and Perth very little higher.

The dangers of using data for this particular period to draw conclusions for the post-war period in general can be seen from our earlier discussion of population growth rates in the intercensal periods. For example, while Adelaide's employment grew 25 per cent more rapidly than Perth's between 1954 and 1966, its population and employment grew much less rapidly between 1966 and 1971, and slightly less rapidly between 1947 and 1954. Even within the 1954 to 1966 period there were significant differences, as Kerr (1970) shows, between 1954–61 and 1961–66. In particular Melbourne's differential component (which Kerr calls 'regional share') changed from 5.75 per cent in the first period to −2.87 per cent in the second. By contrast Perth registered −3.11 per cent in the first and 9.25 per cent in the second. In fact, apart from Hobart, all of the state capitals changed sign. The industrial mix effect was, of course, much more stable, and was positive for all cities in both years.

Our conclusions from this analysis must be limited. Employment in Sydney and Melbourne has grown more rapidly than the national average, mainly because they have fast-growing industries. However, more of the rapid growth that has occurred, especially in particular periods, in Perth, Adelaide and Brisbane has been due to industries in those centres growing more rapidly than comparable industries elsewhere. Furthermore, relative growth rates have varied greatly from one period to another, and similar variations can be expected in the future.

There are some parallels between this analysis of the components of growth in employment and the analysis of components of population growth in the previous chapter. Although they apply to slightly different periods, both show that the two largest cities have grown through having a fast growing mix of industries, through being the points of entry of overseas migrants into Australia, and through the natural increase of their populations. If they were good places to produce, employment in their industries would have grown faster than in the same industries elsewhere, and they would have made net gains from internal migration. In fact they did neither.

Canberra did well, and Hobart poorly on both criteria, but the performance of the other state capitals varied between periods. Adelaide's industries prospered between 1954 and 1966, but Perth's boom period was the late 1960s and early 1970s. Brisbane has been the most consistent in attracting internal migration and in rapid employment growth.

Distribution Within Urban Areas

Where people work within urban areas is known much less precisely than where they live. There is very little published data on workplaces, though the Census of Population question on 'where do you work' was tabulated as an origin-destination matrix for a 10 per cent sample of returns for Sydney and Melbourne only in 1961, and all returns in a wider range of urban areas were tabulated in 1966 and 1971. Apart from brief summaries most of the data is unpublished. In particular data on the characteristics of the workforce by where people work, comparable to data about the workforce by where people live, can only be extracted from large data files on magnetic tape.[3] Prior to 1961 some information was available from regular factory returns and from special censuses on the location of jobs in manufacturing and retailing, and some data of doubtful quality on the location of other jobs from special surveys for planning studies, for example for Sydney in 1945 and Melbourne in 1951. The following analysis concentrates on Sydney in the years 1961 and 1971 with some attention to Melbourne and Perth. First we examine the location of all jobs, and then look at the location of jobs in particular industries and particular occupations.

Figure 4.1 shows the total number of jobs per hectare in the Census journey-to-work zones in Sydney in 1971. There is a clear, though by no means uniform, decline in job density with increasing distance from the centre. Apart from a series of zones following the North Shore line from Milsons Point to Chatswood, the job density north of the harbour is lower than in areas a similar distance from the city centre south of the harbour. On the other hand, the suburbs between Sydney and Parramatta, and south to Bankstown and Rockdale, have high job densities. These suburbs have good access to transport services by rail, road and in some cases by water. The suburbs from Sydney to Parramatta developed at a very early stage in the growth of Sydney. Apart from Parramatta and industrial areas to the south and west, the map also picks up a number of other suburban centres of employment, for example at Brookvale, Manly, Sutherland, Penrith, St Marys and Blacktown. The map divides zones into four groups of equal number. The zones having the highest job densities cover a very wide range from 18 to 3502 jobs per hectare, and have a high proportion of all jobs. Because of this it does not show the extent to which the city centre zones have very high densities.

Figure 4.2 shows the number of jobs per hectare in annular 4 km rings from the city centre. This figure, like the map, shows gross job density, comparable to the gross population densities of the previous chapter. It shows the very great difference between the central city area and other areas. However, density in the 8 to 12 km ring

---

[3] Dr I.G. Manning of the Urban Research Unit has analysed some of the data for Sydney in 1971. Maps and some tables will be published.

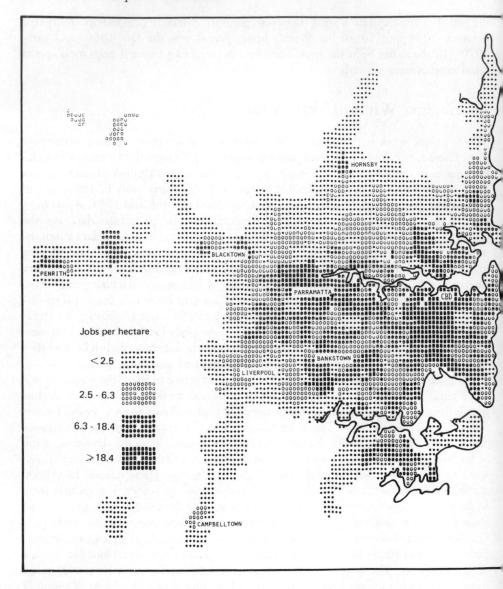

Figure 4.1 Gross employment density: Sydney 1971.
Source: 1971 Census journey-to-work tapes.)

is only about half that in the 4 to 8 km ring, and it nearly halves again in the 12 to 16 km ring. Despite its high density the central 0 to 4 km ring employs only a little over a quarter of the total workforce.

Another interesting feature, which does not show up very clearly on the scale of

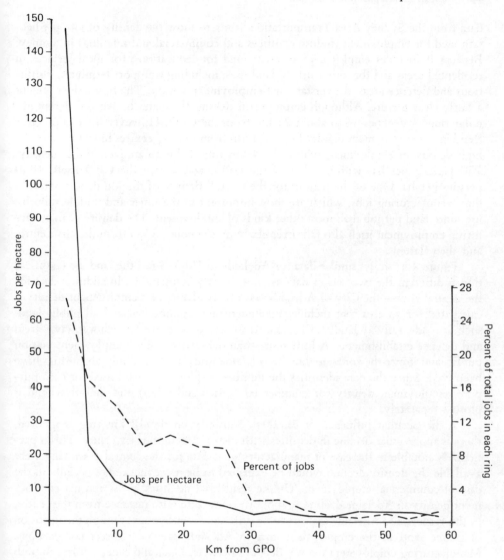

Figure 4.2 Gross employment density and distance from the city centre: Sydney 1971. *Source*: 1971 Census journey-to-work tapes.

Figure 4.2, is a rise in employment density beyond 48 km from the city centre. This occurs because towns like Penrith and Campbelltown are both service and employment centres for the rural areas that almost surround them, and suburban communities.

One of the reasons for high job densities in the centre is that a high proportion of the land is used for activities that provide jobs. Another is that the density of jobs per hectare of land used for employment is much higher in the city centre. Figure 4.3 uses data from the Sydney Area Transportation Study to show the density of jobs per hectare used for employment (industry, offices and commercial and retailing) in Sydney. Because it includes employment in areas used for 'education', for local services in residential areas and for 'other urban' land uses, including transport terminals, institutions and defence areas, it overstates net employment density. The figure does present a fairly clear picture. Although employment density fluctuates between different annular rings it declines up to about 25 km from the GPO. However there is no clear trend in net employment density beyond 4 km from the city centre. In fact most of the high density of employment within the 4 km ring is due to an even higher density, 750 persons per ha, within 2 km of the GPO, and within the CBD itself, 1050 persons per ha. One of the reasons for the overall flatness of the job density curve is that manufacturing jobs, which are most important in the inner and middle suburbs, use more land per job than most other kinds of employment. The density of manufacturing employment itself also falls irregularly up to about 25 km from the city centre, and then flattens.

Figure 4.4. shows similar data for Adelaide in 1965. Since the land use classification is different the two sets of data are not directly comparable. In addition data for the central zone—the City of Adelaide—is not available. Net employment density is calculated for an area that includes manufacturing, commercial and all public land, such as roads, railway land and sewage treatment areas as well as schools, civic areas and defence establishments. A little more than one-quarter of all employment was on public land. Since the zones used in the Adelaide study are large, only seven rings have been used. Since the data identifies the number employed on land used for each purpose, employment density for commercial (office and retail) and industrial land is plotted separately.

If the peculiar influence of Elizabeth-Salisbury on the 18 km ring is ignored, there is an irregular decline in densities with distance from the city centre. This is particularly notable in the case of manufacturing. If data for the central 2 km ring were available the density decline would be expected to be more marked, especially in the case of commercial employment. Unlike residential densities, gross and net employment density in Adelaide decline at about the same rate with distance from the centre. In this respect also Adelaide appears to be different from Sydney, though the inclusion of public land in the employment area in Adelaide precludes direct comparisons. Manufacturing employment density declines between inner and outer suburbs in both cities.

Businesses deciding where to locate within an urban area are concerned about access to transport, to a labour force and to business services as well as access to their customers (see Chapter 9 for a more detailed analysis). Some kinds of business find great advantages in locating in the city centre and are willing to pay a significant premium in terms of higher rents for a central location. Like residents, they attempt to economise on land by having their employees in high-rise offices or multi-storey shops and warehouses. Other kinds of business do not value closeness to the centre highly and are scattered through the urban area at fairly uniform density. Because they are handling, and often processing, goods, they need more space per worker. Some manufacturing and warehousing premises remain in the

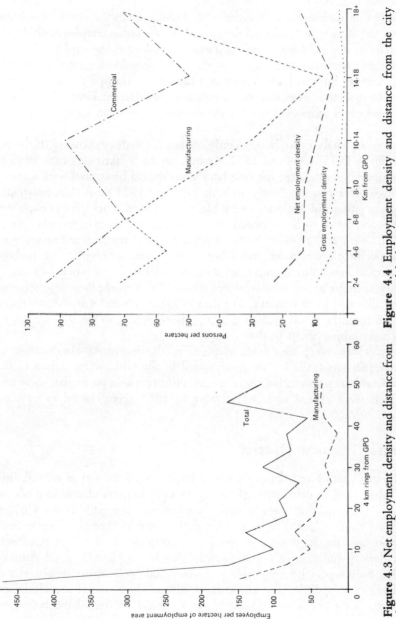

Figure 4.3 Net employment density and distance from the city centre: Sydney 1971.
Source: SATS; RTZ data file.

Figure 4.4 Employment density and distance from the city centre: Adelaide 1965.
Source: MATS (1966).

inner suburbs from the period before the advent of the motor truck, when closeness to transport terminals was sufficiently important to warrant building multi-storey warehouses and factories.

The decline in employment densities with distance from the city centre is more marked than the decline in residential densities. Like the latter, employment densities tend to flatten out beyond a quite short distance. In both cases the explanation for the variation is partly competition for space in the most accessible locations and partly a heritage of premises built at high density at a time when transport costs were much higher. The next section examines the distribution of different kinds of jobs within urban areas and gives some evidence for the distinction between industries described above.

The following analyses are based mainly on data for Sydney showing the location of employment in 1945, 1961 and 1971. Apart from the weaknesses of the 1945 data already mentioned, the data for the two later years should be treated with some care for at least two other reasons. Firstly, in both 1961 and 1971 more than one-tenth of the respondents either did not nominate a place of work, did not give enough detail about its location for it to be tabulated, or did not have a fixed or regular place of work. In 1961 very few workers in the building and construction industry were allocated to a specific place of work, and in both years significant numbers of workers in both the transport and building industries were not allocated to a workplace zone. In 1971 the largest single group who were not allocated to a workplace were those who could not be allocated to an industry. The data in Tables 4.8 and 4.9 allocates the 'not stated' in each industry or occupation group proportionately to the various rings according to their employment in that group.

Secondly, there were significant changes in the industrial classification system between 1961 and 1971. The groups used in the table were chosen to be as closely comparable as possible, but there are still differences. In particular, some repair services which were classed as manufacturing in 1961 were classed as services in 1971.

The Central Business District

The CBD is that part of an urban area which has the highest level of accessibility to the whole urban area, to other parts of the region in its hinterland, and to other cities and countries. Consequently there is strong competition for space in the CBD and only those activities which derive large benefits from a central location find it worthwhile to pay the high price of space. One response to the high price is that more high density buildings are constructed. This has happened in all Australian cities and has been especially noticeable in Sydney and Melbourne; despite this employment has increased little, if at all, in the CBDs of these two cities. Those activities which do not place a high premium on a central location have been forced out.

Although varying boundaries have been used to define the Sydney Central Business District, the boundaries used for census purposes enclose a gross area of some 454 ha. If parklands, railway yards and wharf areas are excluded the area is 300 ha. A very rough estimate of its employment in 1945 was 200 000. In 1954, the gross floor area in the part of the CBD with the largest employment, north of Goulburn Street, was 3.86 million square metres. The first census estimate of employment was made in 1961, when a 10 per cent sample of census returns showed 217 000 employed in the CBD. By that time the estimated floor space had grown to about 4.04m sq.m. However, 11 per cent of the workers in the Sydney statistical division in 1961 were not allocated to a workplace zone (60 per cent of these were in the building industry). If an adjustment is made for these workers, employment in the CBD in 1961 is estimated at 240 000 to 244 000. In 1971 all census returns were analysed for workplace. The CBD accounted for only 205 000 workers, though allowance for the 11 per cent who could not be allocated to a workplace would bring that figure up to between 225 000 and 229 000.

On any calculation it appears that there were some 15 000 fewer workers in the CBD in 1971 than in 1961. This is surprising in the light of the large number of new office buildings completed during this period—approximately 1.16m sq.m. There are no data available about the amount of floor space demolished to make way for the new buildings, but a reasonable estimate might be 20 per cent of the space provided in the new buildings. Those completed between 1961 and 1971 would then represent a net addition of 0.93m sq.m., or about a 23 per cent increase on the 1961 area. On the face of it 23 per cent more floor space, accommodating 10 per cent fewer workers, implies a large increase in space standards per worker. The report of the Sydney Area Transportation Study (1974, Vol. 1, p.11–27) comments:

> The change in the role of the CBD from ordinary and everyday functions to more specialised functions has been accompanied by a doubling in floor space consumption per employee. All indications suggest that this situation will continue. It is staggering indeed to realise that the unprecedented growth in floor space and the dramatic changes in the skyline in Sydney have served only to rehouse office workers and replace the migrating industrial and commercial establishments.

This interpretation was based on an estimate, before the 1971 Census results were available, that the CBD employment was 232 000 in 1971.

Another interpretation of the data suggests slightly different conclusions. As Paterson (1972) pointed out, when a decision is made to increase floor space on a site by redevelopment, the first effect is a reduction in floor space when the existing building is demolished. In mid-1971 some 39 buildings were under construction, planned to add 0.8m sq.m. to the city's floor space. Demolitions to provide sites for these buildings might have removed, say 0.16m sq.m., in which case the net increase over the decade would be reduced to 0.77m sq.m. or 19 per cent. On this basis floor space per worker increased by a little less than one-third between 1961 and 1971. Between mid-1971 and the end of 1974 a further 0.50m sq.m. of floor space was built, and another 40 buildings with a total floor space of approximately 1.14m sq.m. were under construction at the end of 1974.

A study of the central business district in Melbourne by Paterson (1972) used data from surveys of floor space and employment in 1951, 1961 and 1966. The results were:

	Total employment	Total floor space	Floor space per worker
1951	142 600	3.42m sq.m.	24.0 sq.m.
1961	135 247	3.78m sq.m.	27.9 sq.m.
1966	137 706	4.00m sq.m.	29.1 sq.m.

These data show a 21 per cent increase in floor space per employee in the 15-year period—a much slower increase than appears to have occurred in Sydney. However, our estimates put the actual level in Sydney at only about 22.4 sq.m. per employee in 1961, and even in 1971 at only 24.6 sq.m. It appears then that central Sydney workers still had less generous work space than those in central Melbourne.

One possible explanation is that Sydney CBD has a higher proportion of its jobs in those kinds of activities which need little space per employee. The data needed to compare space used by workers in different industries are not available for Sydney, but in Melbourne offices used 20.2 sq.m. per employee in 1966 compared with 42.8 sq.m. in other activities. Table 4.4 summarises the floor space per employee for major activities in Melbourne CBD in 1966. Unfortunately the classes used in the table are land use rather than industry classes, and cannot be compared directly with census data for Sydney. It is of interest that manufacturing in the CBD does not use significantly more space per employee than offices, reflecting the importance in the city centre of industries such as printing, clothing and footwear, and jewellery, which are labour intensive and need little space.

Retailing uses somewhat more space per employee than offices, but the extensive users of space are the showroom-office-storage facilities of the wholesaler who keeps stocks on the premises. The two different kinds of wholesaling distinguished in the table show the difficulty of using simple industry classifications to explain differences in space use. The table does nothing to help explain increases in space use per head over time. On the whole the industries that have grown use less space than those which have declined.

Data on the kinds of jobs found in central business districts from 1961 to 1971 show that they are becoming increasingly specialised in office activities. As a result, even when total employment is falling in Sydney and Melbourne CBDs the number of office jobs is increasing. The CBDs of the two largest cities are more specialised than the CBDs of smaller cities which can carry out many functions which would be found more frequently in suburban employment centres in the larger cities.

The industrial distributions of the workforce in Sydney and Melbourne CBDs are remarkably similar, as shown in Table 4.5. In making comparisons it should be noted that Melbourne's CBD is more confined, as shown by its smaller proportion of the total metropolitan employment. Sydney's higher rate of central city redevelopment in 1966 is reflected in the greater importance of the building industry. The higher proportion of Sydney's CBD workforce in transport and storage probably reflects the fact that the CBD takes in a large area of wharves, whereas Melbourne's wharves are just outside the CBD. The headquarters of the Australian Postmaster-General's

TABLE 4.4   *Space Used in Different Activities: Melbourne CBD 1966*

Activity	Per cent of total floor space	Per cent of total employment	Floor space per employee (sq.m.)
Retail	14.8	17.3	25.8
Banking	3.4	5.2	19.8
Insurance	4.1	7.1	17.6
Finance & property	2.1	3.2	19.6
Wholesale (without stocks)	2.1	2.7	23.3
Community & business services	5.5	8.0	20.6
Offices of manufacturing enterprises	2.6	3.9	20.2
Transport & communications	1.9	3.1	18.5
Non-profit organisations	1.5	1.6	28.5
Miscellaneous commerce	0.7	0.9	24.4
Showroom-office-storage (wholesale with stocks)	12.1	8.0	45.2
Manufacturing	7.5	10.5	21.6
Public authorities (part)	13.7	20.5	20.2
Education	1.9	1.8	32.6
Health & medical	1.3	1.7	22.2
Religion	0.6	0.1	134.2
Miscellaneous public & non-profit	0.1	0.1	31.4
Dwelling (hotels etc.)	4.0	1.0	124.3
Entertainment	1.5	0.5	96.3
Places of assembly	1.9	0.8	67.0
Passenger & freight terminals	0.4	0.4	82.0
Services to occupants of buildings	1.0	0.3	93.9
Building, construction & vacant space, etc.	8.2	0.6	395.8
Parking	6.5	0.3	661.0
Other	0.4	0.3	38.3
Total*	100.0	100.0	30.1

Source: Paterson (1972)

Department was in Melbourne CBD. The greater importance of finance and property and the lesser importance of public authority employment confirm the popular view of Melbourne as a more 'private enterprise' city (Stretton, 1975).

Perth is a much smaller city than either Sydney or Melbourne. Its CBD, as defined in the various editions of the *Perth Region Data Book*, employed 34 per cent of the metropolitan workforce in 1966, a much higher proportion than the areas usually included in the CBDs of Sydney and Melbourne. Table 4.5 includes data relating to only the central part of the CBD—zone 132 in the *Data Books*.[4] Although the percen-

[4] The whole CBD also covered a large area (637 ha) compared with Sydney (454 ha). In the Perth Data Book's Zone 132, the gross employment density in 1971 was 474 per ha, and in Zones 130–4, 126 persons per ha. This compares with 485 persons per ha over the whole Sydney CBD in 1971. If parks, railway yards and wharves are excluded the Sydney density rises to 733 and the Perth Zone 132 density to 517.

TABLE 4.5   *Industrial Composition of CBD Workforce:*
Sydney, Melbourne, Perth (per cent of total)

	Sydney 1961	Sydney 1966	Melbourne 1966	Perth* 1966
Primary production, mining & quarrrying	0.4	0.4	0.5	0.5
Manufacturing	15.3	12.9	13.3	9.3
Electricity, gas & water	5.7	4.4	4.5	2.0
Building & construction	1.0†	4.2	2.6	2.2
Transport & storage	6.5	7.3	5.7	5.9
Communication	4.2	3.8	5.4	5.4
Finance & property	14.0	15.1	16.2	14.1
Commerce	24.4	21.6	22.0	30.8
Public authority & defence	9.1	10.1	8.8	11.3
Community & business services	12.7	13.7	13.8	10.3
Amusements, hotels, etc.	6.3	6.0	6.9	7.3
Other & not stated	0.5	0.4	0.3	0.9
CBD as a per cent of metropolitan employment	25.6	21.5	16.8	21.8

Sources: Sydney: State Planning Authority of N.S.W. (1965 and 1972).
Melbourne: Paterson (1972).
Perth: MRPA (1969).
*   Zone 132 only.
†   Most building jobs were not allocated to a zone in Sydney in 1961.

tage of the metropolitan region's employment in the CBD has fallen, for both CBD
definitions, the actual number employed has increased quite significantly (Table 4.6).
Perth CBD is both less congested and more accessible to growing suburban areas than
the CBDs of either Melbourne or Sydney, therefore there has been less pressure to
force out activities that do not need to be in the city centre.

TABLE 4.6   *CBD Employment in Perth: 1961–1971*

	Number Employed Zone 132	Number Employed Zones 130-4	Percentage of Total in Perth Region Zone 132	Percentage of Total in Perth Region Zones 130-4
1961	41 703	61 893	25.1	37.3
1966	46 124	70 382	22.1	33.7
1971	51 676	80 539	18.2	28.3

Source: MRPA (1975)

Table 4.5 can also be used to compare the industries found in the CBDs of
Sydney and Melbourne with Perth. It was noted early in the chapter that Perth as a
whole has a much smaller manufacturing sector: it accounted for only 23 per cent of
jobs in the urban area of Perth in 1966 compared with 38 per cent in Melbourne and
35 per cent in Sydney. Since the pressures on central area space in Perth are smaller it

is not yet as specialised as the CBDs of Sydney and Melbourne. This is especially evident in the greater importance of commerce (wholesale and retail trade) as a central city employer in Perth. Since the Perth metropolitan area is smaller, access to the city centre for shopping is much easier than in the larger cities. Offsetting the high proportions in commerce are lower proportions in manufacturing, community and business services. The Perth CBD still had a slightly higher proportion of metropolitan manufacturing employment (8.2 per cent) than either Sydney (7.7 per cent) or Melbourne (5.9 per cent).

Changes in the Sydney CBD over the five-year period from 1961 to 1966 show a clear trend towards increasing specialisation. Even if an allowance is made for the understatement of construction jobs in 1961, there was still an increase in the three primarily office industries (finance and property, public authority and defence, and community and business services) and a decrease in manufacturing, wholesaling and retailing. These trends are demonstrated even more starkly in the 1961 to 1971 changes shown in Table 4.8 for the selected industrial groupings, which appear to provide reasonable comparability between the 1961 and 1971 classifications. Finance and property is combined with community and business services in Table 4.8.

Although the industrial classification of the workforce is useful in describing the kinds of firms and government authorities providing jobs in the CBD, it does not give a good description of the kinds of jobs that are available, and how these are changing. For example, many of the CBD workers in electricity, gas and water, and in the transport industry, are office workers. Similarly, some of the workers in manufacturing are in head offices of manufacturing firms.

The occupational composition of the CBD workforce in Sydney in 1961 and 1971, Melbourne in 1971 and Perth in 1966 and 1971 are shown in Table 4.7. Since many kinds of jobs are more commonly filled by either males or females the sexes are distinguished in the table. Several of the less important occupation groups have been amalgamated with 'other and not stated'. The following description of the occupational distribution is partly based on a more detailed occupational classification of jobs in Sydney and Melbourne CBDs in 1971 than is shown in this table.

By far the largest occupation group is 'clerical workers' which accounted for two-thirds of the female jobs and one-third of male jobs in 1971. Those proportions have been increasing over time, and are higher in Sydney and Melbourne than in Perth. Only a little over one-third of the female clerical jobs are for stenographers and typists, the rest being more general clerical jobs. Professional, technical and related workers are the only other group that have been increasing in relative importance in Sydney and Perth CBDs.

Among the declining number of sales workers in the CBD, nearly all of the females work in shops, but half the males are either 'insurance, real estate salesmen and valuers' or 'commercial travellers, manufacturers agents'. The declining numbers of administrative and managerial workers are nearly all employed in the private sector. The number of workers in this occupation in Sydney as a whole has declined, mainly as a result of the declining importance of small businesses. The CBD's transport and communications workers are mainly female telephone operators and male road transport drivers and postal workers. A part of the decline in the importance of this group

TABLE 4.7   *Occupational Composition of CBD Workforce: Sydney, Melbourne, Perth (percentage of total)*

		Sydney		Melbourne	Perth	
		1961	1971	1971	1966	1971
Professional, technical	M	8.2	10.5	11.4	7.7	7.8
& related	F	2.2	2.5	2.9	1.6	3.6
Administrative, executive	M	8.1	7.6	7.2	6.8	6.1
& managerial	F	1.1	0.9	0.9	0.9	0.9
Clerical	M	17.3	19.1	19.0	17.8	15.1
	F	21.9	27.2	26.0	20.9	23.6
Sales	M	6.3	4.6	5.3	7.2	6.1
	F	3.6	3.2	3.8	7.6	7.3
Transport and	M	4.1	2.4	2.9	4.6	3.1
communication	F	1.0	1.5	1.5	1.3	2.0
Craftsmen, process and	M	13.8	11.1	9.0	11.9	9.7
production workers	F	3.8	2.1	2.3	2.0	1.2
Service, sport &	M	4.4	3.4	3.1	3.2	3.2
recreation	F	3.3	2.9	3.2	5.4	5.7
Other and not stated	M	0.6	0.5	0.9	0.5	2.5
	F	0.2	0.3	0.6	0.6	1.9
All males		62.8	59.4	58.9	59.7	53.7
All females		37.2	40.6	41.1	40.3	46.3
		100	100	100	100	100

Source: As for Table 4.5 and Census Journey to Work Tapes.

in Sydney since 1961 resulted from a transfer of postal workers from the GPO with the establishment of the mail exchange in Redfern, south of the CBD.

Although 'craftsmen, process workers etc.' occupy only a small proportion of the CBD jobs, a few particular occupations are quite important. Two-thirds of the jobs for females in this class (though only 3 to 4 per cent of all jobs for females) were for 'tailors, cutters, furriers, etc.'. The male jobs were more widely spread with electricians, metal workers and mechanics, the printing trades, and storemen and freight handlers the most important. The service trade jobs in the CBD are also quite specialised. Most of the females are either housekeepers, cooks, maids or waitresses, or building cleaners or caretakers. Caretakers and cleaners also account for many of the jobs for males, along with fire brigade, police and protective workers.

The somewhat less specialised workforce in the CBD of a smaller centre such as Perth is shown in this table, though the similarities between Perth and the larger centres are more striking than the differences. The smaller proportions of workers in professional and administrative jobs are offset by a higher proportion in sales and service jobs. Another change, which occurred rapidly in Perth, has been the increase in the relative importance of females in the CBD workforce.

The following discussion is related almost solely to Sydney, and is based on Tables 4.8 and 4.9, which show the industrial and occupational distribution of the workforce among the five broad rings of local government areas used in the historical chapter (in Table 2.3). The discussion compares the extent to which particular industries and occupations are concentrated in the CBD and the inner suburbs, and shows changes in the extent of concentration over time—mainly during the 1960s. We use data from analyses of the 1971 Census journey to work data, for a larger number of occupations and industries than are shown in the table, in describing the distributions.

Trends in the CBD workforce show that jobs have decentralised within urban areas. From the changing composition of the CBD workforce it would be expected that jobs which involve handling of goods (manufacturing, wholesaling, retailing), or find advantages in being close to where consumers live (retailing and some services) would have decentralised most while office jobs decentralised least.

The extent of concentration or dispersal of jobs in an industry or occupation can often be summarised by a single statistic such as the percentage found in the CBD, or within the City of Sydney. However, some kinds of jobs, such as those in manufacturing, are heavily concentrated in the inner and middle suburbs, but are underrepresented in both the CBD and the outer suburbs. Table 4.8 can be read in conjunction with Table 2.3 to show that while suburbanisation of jobs has occurred rapidly during the 1960s, it still lags behind the suburbanisation of population. There is some evidence that when the suburbanisation of jobs got underway after the Second World War they by-passed the inner suburbs, which were already pretty much filled up with housing. To find space, manufacturers, wholesalers and regional shopping centre developers had to go to the middle ring of suburbs and many, seeking cheaper space and to be closer to where their workers live, have gone as far as the outer suburbs.

In 1961 the inner ring of suburbs had 23 per cent of the population and 19 per cent of the jobs. Despite the growth in total employment and the fall in CBD employment by 1971, its number of jobs per worker had changed little; they still had 20 per cent of the population and 18 per cent of the jobs. The middle ring, whose proportion of population fell from 39 to 35 per cent during the 1960s, while its proportion of jobs increased from 26 to 30 per cent, and the outer ring, whose share of population increased from 30 to 40 per cent, and of jobs from 12 to 19 per cent, accounted for most of the growth in employment. In 1961 there were 0.16 jobs per resident in the outer suburbs. By 1971 this had increased to 0.20, compared with 0.36 in the inner ring, 0.38 in the middle ring and a metropolitan average of 0.43. Because of their lower workforce participation, in 1971 the outer suburbs could have provided jobs for just over half of their resident workers if outer ring residents took all of the local jobs.

Employment in some industries has dispersed over this period much more rapidly than in others. It has been quite slow in transport and communication and in public administration, but very marked in manufacturing, retailing and wholesaling and also in finance, community and business services. There are quite large differences in the extent of central concentration between the components of the broad industry groups shown in Table 4.8.

The greatest concentrations of manufacturing jobs are found in the remainder of the City and in the western inner and middle suburbs—especially the middle suburbs

TABLE 4.8 Distribution of Employment in Sydney by Industry: 1945–1971

		Thousands of jobs*						Percentage of total				
		C.B.D.	Remainder of city	Inner Ring	Middle Ring	Outer Ring	Total	C.B.D.	Remainder of city	Inner Ring	Middle Ring	Outer Ring
Manufacturing	1945		138	61	43	7	249		55	24	17	3
	1961	34	88	68	115	31	337	10	26	20	34	9
	1971	18	67	63	135	60	343	5	20	18	39	18
Retailing	1961	27	12	18	32	16	105	25	11	17	32	16
	1971	20	13	26	51	37	146	14	9	18	35	25
Wholesaling	1961	28	13	9	11	2	64	44	21	14	18	4
	1971	20	17	16	27	10	90	23	19	17	30	11
Electricity, gas and water	1961	13	1	2	4	2	22	60	6	11	17	7
	1971	9	2	2	6	3	22	41	10	10	26	13
Transport and storage	1961	18	12	15	12	5	63	29	20	24	20	8
	1971	20	14	16	13	6	69	29	20	24	19	9
Communication	1961	10	2	3	3	2	20	48	9	16	17	10
	1971	9	5	3	5	3	25	36	21	11	21	12
Building & construction†	1971	10	8	16	27	25	86	12	9	18	32	30
Finance, community and business services	1961	53	5	9	10	6	83	64	6	11	13	7
	1971	69	9	22	24	18	142	49	6	15	17	13
Public administration	1961	20	3	2	2	2	29	67	12	8	6	7
	1971	27	4	4	4	4	42	63	9	10	10	8
Health services	1961	3	8	7	11	4	34	10	23	21	33	13
	1971	4	9	11	19	11	54	8	17	21	35	20
Education	1961	3	6	6	8	6	28	10	19	20	28	22
	1971	2	7	9	11	14	43	4	16	21	26	33
TOTAL	1945		345	119	123	38	626		55	19	20	6
	1961	244	178	171	251	110	953	26	19	18	26	12
	1971	228	178	213	359	227	1205	19	15	18	30	19

Source: 1945: The Planning Scheme for the County of Cumberland, The County Council, Sydney, 1948. 1961 and 1971 Census Journey to Work Tabulations.

Notes: * The numbers are adjusted for the proportion whose places of work were not stated in 1961 and 1971 in each industry.
† In 1961 most building workers were not allocated to a place of work.

where over 40 per cent of all jobs are in manufacturing, compared with a metropolitan average of less than 30 per cent. Manufacturing employment decentralised rapidly during the 1960s, with the proportion of jobs in the City of Sydney and the inner ring falling from 57 per cent to 43 per cent. The most decentralised of the manufacturing industries are 'fabricated metal products', the large 'other industrial machinery and equipment, and household appliances' industries, 'wood and wood products', 'chemical, petroleum and coal products' and 'non-metallic mineral products'. In each case over 60 per cent of the jobs are in the middle and outer ring of surburbs. By contrast 'clothing and footwear' and the paper and printing industry are found mainly in the inner suburbs.

Suburban decentralisation has probably been more marked in retailing than in any other industry. Only the outer suburbs, with 25 per cent of the retail workers serving 40 per cent of the population, now have less than their share of retail jobs. Wholesaling also moved out of the CBD at a rapid rate during the 1960s, although it remains much more centralised than retailing, especially in the areas close to the CBD.

Among the various types of transport, jobs in road transport are quite decentralised, rail transport concentrated in the city and the middle suburbs, air transport in the inner suburbs (Mascot Airport) and jobs in water transport are nearly all in the city or the inner ring. Communication is the one industry which has clearly spilled out of the CBD, mainly to the rest of the City, and mainly due to the opening of the Redfern Mail Exchange. In 1971 the construction industry was perhaps, less decentralised than might be expected. Its 62 per cent of jobs in the outer and middle ring was scarcely above retailing (60 per cent) education (59 per cent) and manufacturing (57 per cent).

The two most highly centralised industries shown in the table—public administration, and finance, community and business services—primarily employ office workers. They have been rapid growth industries and, although the proportion of their jobs found in the CBD has fallen during the 1960s, the actual numbers employed there increased. Alexander (1976) has shown that office jobs in office buildings are very highly centralised in the CBD and North Sydney, but many office jobs are attached to factories, shops, warehouses and the like and are dispersed in the suburbs. Insurance is the most highly centralised major industry, with 73 per cent of its jobs in the CBD. It is followed by public administration, and finance and investment. While business services are highly centralised, community services are much more decentralised though, like retailing, they are deficient in the outer suburbs.

Health and education are relatively unimportant in the CBD but a number of important hospitals, Sydney University, technical colleges and secondary schools are located in the remainder of the City of Sydney. Both of these services, especially hospitals, tend to be deficient in the outer suburbs.

Differences in degrees of concentration between industries show where the producers find it profitable (or decision-makers in public authorities find it convenient) to locate. Differences in concentration between occupations show where people with particular occupational skills are likely to be able to find a job. The location of jobs in an occupation can be compared with where people who work in those occupations live, though such comparisons are not made here.

Among the major occupation groups by far the most centralised are the clerical jobs for both men and women (Table 4.9). Although, like every other occupation group, they were less concentrated in the CBD in 1971 than in 1961, the absolute numbers of both male and female clerical workers increased even though the total CBD workforce fell. The greater concentration of male than of female clerical workers in the CBD might be expected to be because many females (but no males) are classed as stenographers and typists, and work in widely spread offices. Jobs for men are more centralised than those for women in both of the other two clerical occupations: 'bookkeepers and cashiers' and 'other clerical workers'. Typists and stenographers are in fact the most centralised of the female clerical groups. There are very few male clerical jobs in the outer suburbs, and not many female ones either, despite the fact that many female sales and clerical workers live in the outer suburbs (Davis and Spearritt, 1974).

The only other occupation class to increase numerically between 1961 and 1971 in Sydney CBD was 'professional, technical and related workers'. The males in this class are mostly either 'draftsmen, technicians, teachers' or 'other professional etc.' with significant numbers of 'architects, engineers, surveyors', 'law professionals' and 'artists, entertainers, writers'. Law professionals are the most centralised single occupation (77 per cent in the CBD). Among the other main groups, except for teachers, the CBD provides between one-quarter and one-half of the jobs. By contrast, two-thirds of the female professionals are either teachers or nurses, and very few of these work in the CBD. Within each sub-group there is little difference between the concentration of male and female jobs.

The administrative group is divided between those working for government and those in the private sector. Over 40 per cent of both males and females working for government in 1971 worked in the CBD, but less than 18 per cent in the private sector. Less than two per cent of administrative and managerial workers are employed by governments—apparently most public servants who are not technical or professional are classed as clerical.

Sales workers have decentralised rapidly with the movement of retailing and wholesaling to suburban locations. They are also a composite group. 'Insurance, real estate salesmen, valuers' is a small, mainly male occupation and over one-third work in the CBD. 'Commercial travellers, manufacturers agents' are also mainly male, but are, like the third sub-group, 'proprietors, shopkeepers, workers on own account, retail/wholesale trade salesmen, shop assistants', more widely dispersed. The last, which includes most shop workers, also accounts for nearly all of the female sales workers. Within this group, as we saw in the previous section, retail workers are less concentrated than wholesale workers, and are more likely to be females.

The transport and communication group is one of the very few where males are less concentrated in the CBD than females. The reason is found in the composition of the group. Two-thirds of the females are 'telephone, telegraph and telecommunication' workers whereas two-thirds of the males are 'drivers, road transport'. Over 40 per cent of the former group—male and female—are in the CBD, compared with less than 7 per cent of the latter.

Among the large group of 'craftsmen, production and process workers', few sub-

TABLE 4.9 Major Occupation Groups in Each Major Ring: Sydney 1961 and 1971

			Thousands of jobs					Percentage of metropolitan total				
		CBD	Remainder of city	Inner Ring	Middle Ring	Outer Ring	Total	CBD	Remainder of city	Inner Ring	Middle Ring	Outer Ring
Professional, technical	M 1961	18	9	9	13	6	55	33	16	17	23	11
	M 1971	22	12	14	19	12	80	28	14	17	25	15
	F 1961	5	7	7	9	6	35	15	21	19	29	17
	F 1971	5	8	11	16	14	54	10	15	20	30	26
Administrative, managerial	M 1961	19	9	11	17	8	63	30	14	17	26	12
	M 1971	16	10	15	24	14	80	20	13	19	30	18
	F 1961	3	1	2	2	2	10	25	14	22	24	15
	F 1971	2	1	2	3	2	10	18	11	21	28	22
Clerical	M 1961	38	11	8	11	8	70	55	15	11	15	5
	M 1971	40	12	11	15	7	84	48	14	13	18	8
	F 1961	48	14	12	17	6	97	50	15	12	17	6
	F 1971	58	19	23	38	21	159	36	12	15	24	13
Sales	M 1961	14	7	8	12	5	47	31	16	17	26	10
	M 1971	10	7	10	17	9	53	19	13	19	32	17
	F 1961	8	2	5	10	5	30	27	8	17	32	16
	F 1971	7	3	7	15	12	44	16	6	16	34	28
Transport and Communication	M 1961	12	10	10	14	6	52	23	19	19	27	12
	M 1971	6	12	11	17	10	57	11	21	20	30	18
	F 1961	2	1	1	1	0	5	45	17	12	17	8
	F 1971	3	2	1	2	1	10	32	17	15	23	13
Craftsmen, process workers, labourers	M 1961	38	79	69	110	33	329	12	24	21	33	10
	M 1971	26	61	64	126	67	344	7	18	19	37	20
	F 1961	9	15	12	9	6	60	14	25	20	31	10
	F 1971	5	12	13	26	14	69	7	17	19	37	21
Service, sport and recreation	M 1961	10	6	7	8	4	34	30	17	19	24	10
	M 1971	8	6	8	10	6	38	20	16	22	26	17
	F 1961	8	7	9	9	5	38	20	18	25	25	13
	F 1971	6	6	10	15	11	49	13	12	21	30	23
Other and not stated	M 1961	2	3	3	4	13	25	8	12	12	16	52
	M 1971	4	7	9	12	21	53	7	13	14	17	50
	F 1961	1	0	1	1	1	4	19	19	13	19	30
	F 1971	3	3	4	5	5	20	13	15	17	22	33
Total	M 1961	151	132	125	187	79	674	24	19	18	27	12
	M 1971	138	126	142	240	145	790	17	16	18	30	18
	F 1961	83	49	71	68	30	279	30	17	17	25	11
	F 1971	90	53	71	119	82	415	22	13	17	29	20
Total	1961	234	181	173	255	109	953	26	19	18	26	12
	1971	228	178	213	359	227	1205	19	15	18	30	19

Sources: 1961: The Commonwealth Statistician's Journey to Work Survey, 1964, State Planning Authority, Sydney.
1971: Journey to Work Computer tapes for 1971 Census.

Note: The absolute numbers have been adjusted for those who did not adequately define their place of work in each occupation, on the assumption that they were distributed between rings in proportion to those who did.

classes have many people working in the CBD. The two most concentrated are 'instrument makers, jewellers', and 'printing trades workers', followed by 'tailors, cutters, furriers', and male 'electricians'. Of these 'tailors etc' are by far the most important among females, and electricians among males.

Service, sport and recreation workers are a very diverse group. One-quarter of 'fire brigade, police and protective workers' (nearly all male) and of photographers work in the CBD. The largest female group, 'housekeepers, cooks, maids' is quite widely dispersed through the metropolitan area.

It is often stated that women, especially those that are married, have a stronger preference for working close to their homes than men. This would suggest that a smaller proportion of females would be employed in the CBD. Our data do not allow us to distinguish married women. In total a significantly *higher* proportion of women than men worked in the CBD in both 1961 and 1971, but Table 4.9 shows that, with few exceptions, a smaller proportion of the females than of the males in each occupation work in the CBD. Even those exceptions, mainly in 'transport and communication' and 'craftsmen etc'., mostly disappear when a finer occupational classification is used. Female workers are much more concentrated in those occupations, especially clerical (nearly 40 per cent of all female jobs), which are most highly concentrated in the CBD. Despite the relative decentralisation of the clerical workforce that occurred during the 1960s, there is still a large volume of commuting, and many of those that live in the middle and outer suburbs would probably prefer to work closer to home.

Summary

This chapter has described the distribution of different kinds of jobs between urban areas and within urban areas, concentrating on Sydney. The kinds of jobs available differ between cities, ranging from Canberra which has little manufacturing or mining, but many white collar jobs and jobs for women, through the state capitals, smaller urban areas, Newcastle and Geelong, to Wollongong which has a high proportion of its jobs in manufacturing and mining, a high proportion of blue collar jobs and few jobs for women. An analysis of growth of different cities shows that the large cities grew rapidly mainly because much of their employment is in industries that grew rapidly, rather than because each industry grew more rapidly in the large cities than elsewhere. The largest cities do not appear to be the most attractive places for growth in employment.

Within urban areas decentralisation of jobs has occurred very selectively, with manufacturing, retailing and wholesaling moving out quite rapidly. As a result central business districts are becoming increasingly specialised as centres of office employment. Another result is that, because such a high proportion of jobs for women are in clerical occupations, a higher proportion of female than male jobs are in the CBD, even though the female jobs in almost every occupation are more dispersed than the male jobs. Despite the post-war decentralisation, jobs remain much more concentrated in the inner parts of cities than population, and employment densities much higher in the city centre and the inner suburbs.

5 Land Use and Transport Within Cities

The two previous chapters have introduced some of the important features of the internal structure of the city by describing recent trends in the location of residences and jobs within cities. People live at varying densities in different suburbs, and some kinds of jobs need more space than others. The organisation of activities within cities involves allocation of land for different purposes. There is more competition for land in more accessible locations, and therefore activities that pay a high premium for accessibility are likely to be concentrated in the most central locations. Accessibility is gained not only by choosing the right location but also by providing transport links between locations. Accessibility is the link that causes transport and land use to be interdependent. In this chapter we examine the distribution of land use within cities and then the provision of links between the various land uses through the transport system.

Traffic costs and congestion, pollution from exhaust fumes, the time spent in the journey to work and the possibility of a growing scarcity of energy are all reasons why transport within cities should be reduced if possible. One way do to that is to make parts of cities more self-contained by distributing land uses that generate a lot of traffic to sub-centres, and away from the city centre. This chapter examines some features of the present distribution of land uses. It also describes the relative importance of the different kinds of transport flows and recent trends in the use of different modes of transport. It shows the size of the task involved in reducing the use of resources in transport within cities.

Land use can be studied as a way of examining economic and social activities that puts particular emphasis on their location, and on the way different activities are located relative to one another. When we study land use we see that shopping centres are located in accessible places in the market they serve, and that manufacturing tends to be clustered in industrial zones. As compared with other ways of studying location, such as dividing the city into zones, a study of land use can reveal location patterns at a whole range of scales. A study of urban land use can also show how much of a city is used for purposes that provided neither jobs (or not many) nor housing. Only some land use classifications reveal the one-fifth to one-quarter of urban land taken up by roads and footpaths, but most show how much is used for education, recreation, institutions, waste treatment and other public purposes. Furthermore, data about land use shows that a large proportion of land in urban areas is either vacant or used for rural purposes.

Although land use surveys provide information which is essential for urban planning, it is uncommon for the data collected to be made available in a form which lends itself to further analysis. Frequently the result is a map showing dominant land uses. Land use data is difficult to analyse because different classification systems are used in different cities and the classes often have more relevance for future planning than for analyses of the existing use of land. For example, residential land may include all land which is zoned for residential development, rather than land that is currently used for residential purposes. Residential land often includes small local shopping centres as well as services such as primary schools, local parks and churches normally found in residential areas.

A particular difficulty occurs in relation to the urban boundary. Since planning authorities are concerned with future development, land use surveys for planning purposes cannot stop at the urban boundary—the boundary of the built-up area—that is usually used for census purposes. The zones for which the data are collected often straddle the urban boundary. Such problems are manageable if the land use classification system distinguishes non-urban land, but if some land use classes include major urban and non-urban uses the boundary problem becomes more difficult. The distinction between the urban area—the area within the census urban boundary—and land used for urban uses needs to be kept in mind.

Urban Use of Land

Perhaps the most useful Australian land use data was produced for the *Report on the Metropolitan Area of Adelaide* (1962) relating to 1957, and revised to 1965 for the Metropolitan Adelaide Transportation Study (MATS) (1966). The *Report* contains a land use table for 1957 for the defined urban area, and the zone boundaries used in the 1965 data allow an approximate identification of the urban area used for census purposes. For the 1957 data, '120 square miles were considered to be within a specially defined urban area. The boundary of the urban area was drawn so as to include all the predominantly built-up areas, together with any open areas which were surrounded by urban development' (p.61). The land use composition of this area is shown in the *Report's* Table 18, which is reproduced below as Table 5.1, with the 4000 acres of the Weapons Research Establishment and its associated airfield omitted.

One of the common findings of studies of land use in urban areas is that a high proportion of the land is vacant or used for non-urban purposes. This is particularly true in the dispersed low density urban areas that are common in North America and Australia and New Zealand. Manvel (1968) found that, even within U.S. cities (administrative rather than urban boundaries) with more than 100 000 population, 22.3 per cent of the area was undeveloped. In more broadly defined urban areas the proportion is higher. Within a relatively tightly defined north-eastern urban complex stretching from Boston to Washington, Clawson (1971, 214–23) reports that only about 20 per cent of the area is used for residential, commercial, industrial and 'public and semi-public' areas. Because of the breadth of the last land use class it can safely be said that over 80 per cent of the land was non-urban. Similar data for the megalopolis in England (South Lancashire and Yorkshire to the south-east) in 1961 showed less than 18 per cent of land developed (Hall, *et al.* 1973, Vol. 1, Ch.6). Within the much

TABLE 5.1   *Land Use in Defined Urban Area: Adelaide 1957*

Class	Use	Hectares	Percentage
Industry	Light industry	60.7	0.2
	General industry	732.9	2.5
	Special industry	83.4	0.3
		877.0	3.0
Wholesaling and storage	Warehouses and storage	298.3	1.0
	Wharves and depots	55.0	0.2
		353.3	1.2
Business	Shopping	244.4	0.8
	Petrol stations	63.9	0.2
	Hotels	27.5	0.1
	Offices	38.4	0.1
		374.3	1.3
Public service facilities	Reserves and waterworks	25.5	0.1
	Sewerage and industrial waste	422.9	1.4
	Railway land	405.9	1.4
	Airfields	958.3	3.2
	Defence departments	203.6	0.7
		2 106.1	6.8
Recreation	Public open space	970.4	3.3
	Private playing fields	581.5	2.0
	Caravan parks	29.9	0.1
	Golf courses	400.2	1.4
		1 982.1	6.7
Education, social and cultural institutions	School buildings	238.4	0.8
	School playing fields	318.5	1.1
	Civic, cultural, social	648.3	2.2
	Cemeteries	66.8	0.2
		1 271.9	4.3
Residential	Residential	11 263.2	38.1
Other	Parking of vehicles	42.1	0.1
	Rivers	240.0	0.8
	Mineral workings	157.0	0.5
	Agricultural land	2 006.4	6.8
	Vacant allotments	1 738.9	5.9
	Other vacant land	2 242.0	7.6
		6 426.4	21.7
Roads*		5 006.8	16.9
Total		29 571.1	100.0

Source: Report on the Metropolitan Area of Adelaide, 1962.
*   No areas of roads are included in the various areas of land use; the separate item includes all land used for roads.

more tightly defined Adelaide urban area one-fifth was either vacant or used for agricultural purposes in 1957.

Residences occupy a little under two-fifths of the area, but 48 per cent of the land used for urban purposes. The next largest single land use is roads, which occupy 21 per cent. Of the land used for urban purposes about 40 per cent is in public ownership. Half of this is used for roads, and the other half for public open space, airfields, railways, schools and 'civic, cultural and social' purposes. Industry, wholesaling and storage, and business occupy quite small areas—only about 7 per cent of the land used for urban purposes.

The 1965 data is for a larger area and is less detailed in its land use classification, but it does include land use in individual zones. Zones that are mainly within the 1966 Census urban boundary cover 56 000 hectares or 215 square miles. The data does not include the City of Adelaide, therefore it excludes the CBD and immediately surrounding areas. The first 'ring' used in the following analysis is two to four kilometres from the GPO. The City occupies approximately 1525 ha, or about 5 per cent of the total urban land. The data includes a classification 'vacant and rural' which permits an analysis of land used for urban purposes. Much of the vacant land is near the urban fringe and appears in our data partly because, although only those zones were included which are mostly within the census urban area boundary, there is a large amount of non-urban land in some outer urban zones (see Figure 5.1). About one-fifth of the land as close as four to eight kilometres from the city centre, and 40 per cent between eight and ten kilometres, is vacant, even though most of those rings were well within the urban boundary. Although the following analysis will be focused on land used for urban purposes it should be remembered that there are substantial vacant areas within the urban boundary.

Figure 5.2 shows the distribution of urban land among the various annular rings of the urban area. Nearly 90 per cent of the urban land is within zones whose centroids are within 14 km of the city centre, and over 70 per cent in zones within 10 km.

Figure 5.3 shows the percentage of non-urban land within the urban boundary in 4 km annular rings from the centre of Sydney. The data were collected for the Sydney Area Transportation Study (SATS), (1974). It relates to 1971 and includes only zones which are mainly within the 1971 Census urban area. In this case the 'non-urban and vacant' land is less inclusive than in Adelaide since it excludes 'other committed' land: defence areas and institutions, many of which occupy non-urban land. The largest of these 'other committed' areas have been excluded from our data by choosing only zones which are mainly within the census urban area, but other areas remain.

Vacant land is probably underestimated in the SATS land use classification for another reason also. Some vacant land *reserved* for a particular use may have been classified as being *used* for that purpose. For example, in the whole study area SATS recorded 8100 ha of land used for industry in 1971. An independent study using air photographs found only 4200 ha of zoned industrial land used for industrial purposes in 1972 (Australian Institute of Urban Studies (AIUS), 1975). Although the AIUS study probably omitted some areas used for outdoor storage or other casual uses, the SATS data probably included areas that were not used. In addition the AIUS data ig-

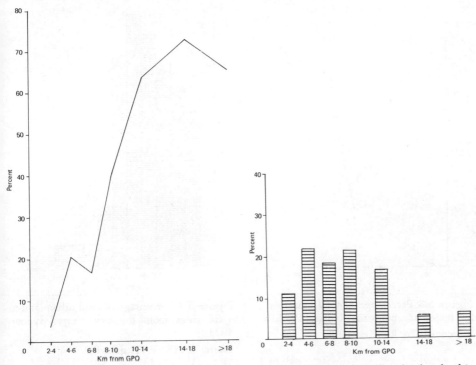

Figure 5.1 Percentage of all land rural or vacant by distance from the city centre: Adelaide 1965.

Source: MATS (1966).

Figure 5.2 Percentage of total urban land in each ring: Adelaide 1965.

Source: MATS (1966).

nored land used for industry in areas which are zoned for other purposes (non-conforming uses).

The extent of non-urban land in the zones chosen to coincide with the urban area is partly a reflection of our failure to follow the urban boundary precisely: the total area included in the SATS zones used in Figure 5.3 was 149 000 ha, compared with the census urban area of 143 000. It also shows that there is a large amount of vacant land within the urban area. Despite the suspected underestimation of the vacant area, over 20 per cent of the ring only 20 to 24 km from the city centre, and nearly 30 per cent of the ring from 24 to 28 km, are vacant. The five points on the right in Figure 5.3 should not be given too much weight. They represent zones in the west and south-west extensions of the urban area where, despite the attempt to follow the urban boundary, a significant amount of non-urban land was included. Of the total 149 000 ha some 28 per cent was vacant.

Figure 5.4 shows the distribution of urban land among the annular rings of the Sydney urban area. Nearly 90 per cent of it is within 28 km (17.4 miles) of the city centre, and only about 6 per cent more than 32 km away. Subsequent analyses of these data will refer only to the urban land. Beyond 28 km it applies only to the

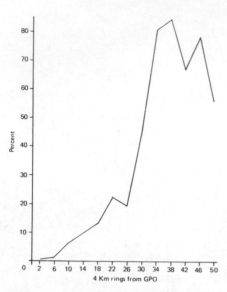

Figure 5.3 Percentage of total land used for non-urban purposes: Sydney 1971. *Source*: SATS; RTZ data file.

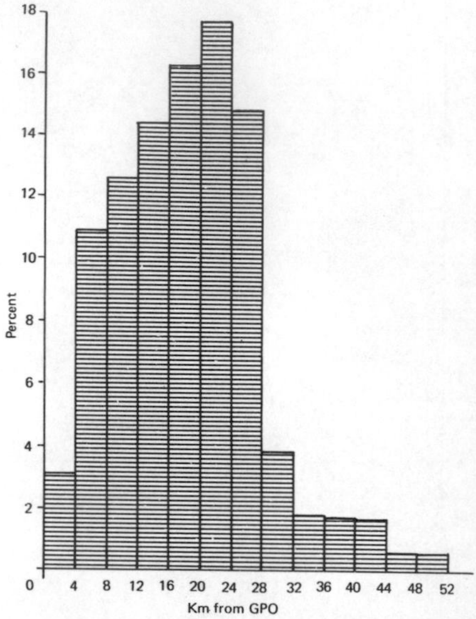

Figure 5.4 Percentage of total urban land in 4 km rings from the city centre: Sydney 1971.
Source: SATS; RTZ data file.

relatively small parts of the urban area extending to Campbelltown and the Blue Mountains and, as a result, land use composition sometimes fluctuates quite widely between 'rings'.

Identification of the land used for urban purposes in Perth is made difficult because the land use category 'special uses' includes not only railway land, port instal-lations, large hospitals, the university and high school grounds, which are clearly urban uses, but also pine plantations, state forest lands, lakes and reservoirs, which are just as clearly non-urban. Furthermore, the zones used are quite large and it is not easy to follow the census urban boundary at all closely (Metropolitan Region Planning Authority (MRPA), 1969). For these reasons the non-urban area is underestimated in Figure 5.5, probably to a greater extent than in the comparable figures for Sydney and Adelaide, but nevertheless the concentration of land used for urban purposes close to the city centre (Figure 5.6) is similar to that in Adelaide. Only a little over one-tenth of the land used for urban purposes in each region is more than 14 kilometres from the city centre. In Perth, as in Adelaide, an important sub-centre is quite remote from the city centre—although Fremantle, an old, established centre and port, is quite different from the new town of Elizabeth.

In all three cities the census urban areas exaggerate the area covered by urban development. Even though identifiable suburban development has taken place up to the census boundaries there remain large areas of vacant land within those boun-daries—up to 80 per cent in some places. Even in areas that would be regarded as middle suburbs it is common to find one-tenth to one-fifth of the land unused.

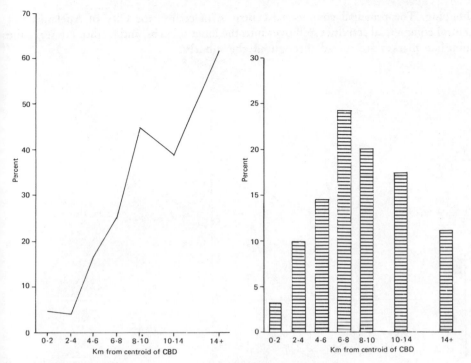

Figure 5.5 Percentage of total area in each ring which is 'rural plus balance of zone': Perth 1966.
Source: MRPA (1969).

Figure 5.6 Percentage of Perth's total urban land in each ring: 1966.
Source: MRPA (1969).

Distribution of Uses Within Cities

The main individual urban land uses in each annular ring in Adelaide in 1965 are shown in Figures 5.7 and 5.8. Unfortunately the data excludes the City of Adelaide. The distribution of urban land between different uses varies relatively little with distance from the city centre. The main difference is that residential land (which includes roads, local shopping centres, local open spaces and community buildings in residential areas) comprises a higher proportion of urban land in the inner suburbs. Nearly 80 per cent of the residential land is within 14 km of the city centre. Public uses, which include airfields, sewage treatment, railway land and secondary schools, are more important in outer suburbs. Commercial, and to a lesser extent industrial, land is concentrated in the innermost ring of suburbs, but in the next ring manufacturing appears to be under-represented. Manufacturing land is distributed widely throughout the urban area, although, as shown in Chapter 4, the industrial land in the inner suburbs is used more intensively. Commercial land is mainly used for wholesaling and suburban shopping. The principal commercial centre is, of course, the City of Adelaide, but central commercial activities spill over into the inner suburbs, and facilities to serve the suburban market are spread throughout the suburbs.

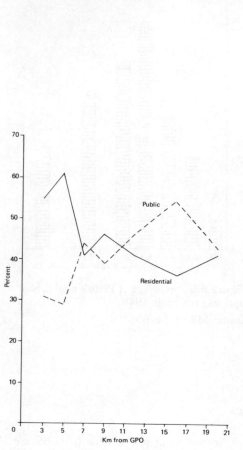

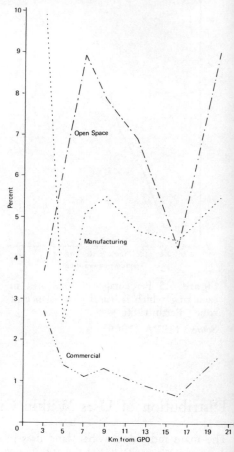

Figure 5.7 Percentage of urban land used for residential and public use: Adelaide 1965.

Source: MATS (1966).

Figure 5.8 Percentage of urban land used f commerce, manufacturing and open spac Adelaide 1965.

Source: MATS (1966).

Similar data for Sydney in 1971, which uses a similar definition of residential land, are plotted in Figures 5.9 and 5.10, and the total areas are shown in Table 5.2. Since this data includes the city centre there is much more variation in land use composition between the innermost and other rings. Land use has been averaged over all SATS zones within 4-km annular rings up to 24 km from the centre, and over 8-km rings beyond 24 km.

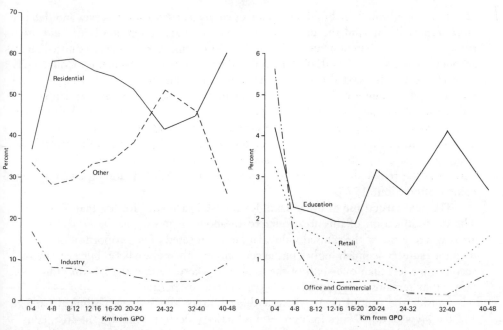

Figure 5.9 Percentage of urban land used for residential, industrial and other use: Sydney 1971.
Source: SATS; RTZ data file.

Figure 5.10 Percentage of urban land used for education, retailing and offices: Sydney 1971.
Source: SATS; RTZ data file.

TABLE 5.2   *Urban Uses of Land in Sydney Urban Areas: 1971*

Land Use Category	Hectares	Per cent of Total
Retail	1 311	1.2
Office and commercial	710	0.7
Education	2 684	2.5
Residential	55 513	51.8
Industrial	7 389	6.9
Other committed	39 561	36.9
Total urban uses	107 183	100.0

Source: SATS, RTZ data file. Land uses are defined in SATS (1974) Vol.1, pp.II-3 to II-15.

Residential land, which includes local roads, local open space and some local services, occupies between 35 and 60 per cent of the land used for urban purposes in each of the rings, and in total 52 per cent. Between 4 km and 24 km from the centre, in the 'fully developed' suburban rings which contain over 86 per cent of Sydney's urban land, it occupies between 50 and 60 per cent in every ring. Thereafter its proportion fluctuates, being lower where the proportion used for 'other committed' purposes is high. The latter class includes institutions, railway lands, major roads, airports, cemeteries, land unfit for building, major open areas, recreation reserves and defence areas. Especially around the urban fringe these areas are sometimes large, and often rural rather than urban in nature. Within the 24 km ring these 'other committed' areas account for between 25 and 40 per cent of the urban land in each ring. Collectively they are clearly the second most important uses of urban land in every ring up to 24 km. Thereafter they are the most important in some rings. Together residential and 'other committed' land account for 89 per cent of urban land in Sydney. An independent assessment of the open space within the urban boundary in Sydney shows that 12.8 per cent of the total area within the boundary, or 17 per cent of the urban land, is in open space. Of this just over a half is in 'municipal parks', a third in regional parks and the remainder golf courses (derived from N.S.W. Planning and Environment Commission, 1975).

The next largest use of urban land, for industry, accounts for less than 7 per cent. The over-estimation of this area, referred to above, is mostly in the outer suburban areas where most of the unused industrial land is located. The proportion of all land used for industry is much higher in the central zone than elsewhere, but even there it accounts for less than one-sixth of the total. Elsewhere, within the 24-km radius, the proportion remains between 5 and 8 per cent in each ring.

Outside the central ring, where Sydney University, Sydney Technical College and the New South Wales Institute of Technology occupy a significant area, education only accounts for around 2 to 3 per cent of the urban land in the inner and middle suburbs. In some of the outer suburbs there are educational institutions with larger grounds, though they never occupy more than 4.3 per cent of the urban land in any ring.

Retailing occupies a much higher proportion (3.3 per cent) of the land in the central ring than elsewhere—but retailing land in this ring accounted for only 8 per cent of the total retailing land in Sydney. The final land use class is 'office and commercial' which includes areas used for 'administrative, professional, business, cultural and civic purposes'. The only ring with more than 1.5 per cent of its urban land devoted to these uses is the central ring, which includes both the CBD and the North Sydney business district, and accounts for over a quarter of the land used for office and commercial purposes in Sydney. Other concentrations, though at lower employment density, occur in Parramatta, Bankstown and Chatswood.

In a broad band of suburban areas, between the city centre and about 24 km from it, there is a remarkably uniform distribution of urban land between different uses. In the central ring industry, offices, retailing and education all occupy more land and less is used for residential purposes. In the outer suburbs and fringe areas defence land and extensive institutions, including some educational institutions, are the main competitors with housing for land. In both inner and outer suburbs the broad class 'other committed' uses occupy most of the non-residential urban land. Most of this land, which includes most of Sydney's open space, is owned by public authorities or community organisations. It is often neglected in our thinking about urban land use, partly because it includes such a diverse group of uses. Finally, in outer suburban areas most of the land, even within the urban boundary, is vacant or used for non-urban purposes.

The three most important findings from this examination of land use are the large areas of unused land within the urban area, the importance of open space, transport routes and terminals, institutions and the like, and the relative uniformity of the distribution of land uses in successive rings of development. The vacant land within urban areas is not all available for use. Some is unusable and much is committed to particular uses by its owners. A significant amount is probably held by government and community groups, and much is in the process of conversion from one use to another. Some details about the kinds of areas of vacant land held within urban areas are described in studies of Redfern, Randwick and Bankstown in Sydney (Neutze, 1971a, 1971b, 1972a) and in North Melbourne (Johnson, 1973b).

Outside the central ring land use does not vary greatly with distance from the centre. A rather higher proportion of land in the inner suburbs is used for residential and for industrial and commercial purposes. But apart from the land used for housing, the largest use of urban land is for a rather amorphous group of mainly public and institutional activities, including major open space, institutions and transport. A higher proportion of urban land is used for these purposes closer to the urban fringe. One of the advantages of a very mixed pattern of land use is that the need for connection between activities can be served by transport movements that are very dispersed, and many may be quite short. In the next section we examine some features of the intra-urban transport system.

There are, of course, differences in land use composition that do not show up in comparisons between annular rings. For example, most of the industrial land in Sydney is found south and west of the CBD, and manufacturing workers often live in the sectors with a high proportion of industrial land. Generally, however, there do not appear to be very large differences between sectors in the main components of urban land use.

Costs of Transport

There are several ways to measure the relative significance of transport as a user of resources. Because of the limited amount of data available most of these measures can only be used for the whole of Australia rather than for urban areas as such. In Chapter 7, however, an attempt is made to estimate the level of investment in urban transport facilities in recent years, as part of an account of the level of investment in urban development.

Solomon (1974) made estimates of the level of expenditure on transport from 1955–56 to 1970–71, when the percentage of gross national expenditure devoted to transport varied only between 11.2 and 12.7. In the most recent year for which data was available, 1970–71, 12.1 per cent of GNE went on transport. Of this total some 70 per cent was spent on road transport, 6 to 9 per cent on rail transport and the remainder on air, sea and other forms of transport. A slightly different measure is personal expenditure on transport (about two-thirds of total expenditure on transport) as a percentage of all personal consumption expenditure. This percentage increased from 11.8 per cent in 1955–56 to 14.0 per cent in 1970–71. A third measure focuses on public capital expenditure. Transport has been responsible for about one-third of all capital expenditure by governments. Data drawn from the national accounts (Table 5.3) show again the high proportion of resources used by road transport.

TABLE 5.3   *Gross Fixed Capital Expenditure by Public Authorities on Transport: 1969–70 to 1973–74*

	Per cent of total
Rail	13.4
Sea	7.3
Road	67.7
Air	9.1
Pipelines	1.5
Other	1.1
Transport as a percent of GFC by public authorities	33.0

Source: Australian National Accounts.

Another way in which transport makes a large demand on the community's resources is that governments have to find revenue to meet the deficits typically incurred by public transport undertakings, especially in the main capital cities. Deficits on the operations of the state railway systems are not a recent phenomenon and can be attributed, at least in part, to the extension of rail services into rural areas which can no longer be economically served. Railway system costs cannot be accurately divided between suburban and other services, but it is widely believed that suburban services contribute significantly to the losses. In the case of bus and tram transport the deficits can be clearly attributed to city systems.

Most government bus services in Australia run at a loss, largely because the authorities concerned are required to provide services at times when they are only lightly used and therefore unprofitable. To some extent these services are providing a social welfare function by enabling people without access to cars to travel. In addition the high peak in demand for the journey to work and the high level of road congestion during those periods makes profitable operation more difficult. Public transport losses are quite large, as shown in Table 5.4, and have put a strain on state budgets. For example, in 1975–76 New South Wales budgeted for a deficit of $244 million for the Public Transport Commission (Railways $205 million, Sydney buses $34 mil-

TABLE 5.4   *Deficits in Public Transport Undertakings: 1973–1974 ($m)*

	NSW.	Victoria	Queensland	SA	WA
Railways	125.7	84.6	12.1	29.0	16.5
Capital city bus/tram*	20.5	5.8	n.a.	2.2	5.8

Source: Annual Reports of responsible authorities.
*   Operating deficit only, i.e. excludes interest costs.

lion, Newcastle buses $4 million) out of total budgeted expenditure by the state of $2 638 million—almost one-tenth of the total.

The Demand for Transport

The links between parts of a city are provided by its transport and communications networks. This section of the chapter describes some aspects of urban transport. It relies heavily on a few sources of data, in particular the results of the most recent study of transport in a major city—the 1971 Sydney Area Transportation Study (SATS).

Transport facilities in urban areas are needed for two main purposes: to provide for flows of goods and passengers within the urban areas and to provide for the flows into and out of the urban area which link it with other parts of the country and the world. Measured in terms of the number of passengers or tonnes of freight carried, the transport task is mainly one of moving goods and people within the urban area. For example, the Sydney Area Transportation Study (SATS, 1974, Vo.1, II–1) estimated that only 2 per cent of the person trips made in the Sydney study area either started or finished outside it. Commercial vehicle trips were even more frequently made wholly within the study area; only one per cent of such trips crossed its boundaries. On the other hand, estimates of freight movements by all modes of transport show that the volume of freight movement outside the region is important, though it accounts for less than 30 per cent of the tonnes of freight flows in the Sydney region (Table 5.5).

TABLE 5.5   *Freight Flows in the Sydney Region: 1971*
(thousand tonnes)

Mode	In Bound Domestic	In Bound Overseas	Out Bound Domestic	Out Bound Overseas	Total	Within the Region	Total
Rail	10 574	—	3 000	—	13 574	—	13 574
Road	3 758	—	3 535	—	7 293	107 600	114 893
Sea	7 132	6 592	2 072	6 226	22 021	—	22 021
Air	18	16	31	10	76	—	76
Total	21 482	6 608	8 638	6 236	42 965	107 600	150 563

Source: Commonwealth Bureau of Roads, 1975, 117.

Sea and air transport primarily bring passengers and freight into and take them out of urban areas. The terminal facilities are large in scale and involve quite massive trans-shipments. Like many other functions in urban areas, the terminals are changing in ways which require increasing areas of land to handle containers, bulk commodities and the road vehicles to move their passengers and cargoes. Most rail freight also requires trans-shipment at a terminal. The clearest features of Table 5.5 are that rail, sea and road traffic share the freight flows between the Sydney region and other parts of

Australia, in that order of importance. Road transport provides all of the freight transport within the Sydney region.

The remainder of this chapter concentrates on transport and travel within urban regions, and deals mainly with movements of people rather than goods.[1] Because cities are places where people and enterprises specialise in a narrow range of activities, it is necessary to move goods and people around within them. Workers have to travel between their homes and their jobs. The journey to work has been studied in more depth than other journeys, because it accounts for one-third of all trips and is largely responsible for the peak traffic flows that determine the capacity needed in transport systems. People also have to travel to get an education, to get services such as medical and dental treatment, to shop and to conduct business. Finally, people travel within the city to visit others, and for social and recreational purposes. Table 5.6 shows the purposes for which people made trips in Sydney in 1971 (Column 1).

TABLE 5.6   *The Purposes of Journeys by Residents: Sydney, 1971*

Journey purpose	Percentage of total number	Median journey length (km)		Median journey duration (minutes)	
		Public transport	Private vehicle driver	Public transport	Private vehicle driver
Home-based					
Work	33.4	10.8	9.8	46	28
School*	19.0	—	—	—	—
Shopping	10.1	4.5	3.2	29	12
Social/recreation	14.0	7.4	5.3	38	17
Personal business	10.8	6.6	3.4	36	13
Non home-based	12.7	6.3	4.7	34	18
Total	100.0	7.1	5.8	38	18

Source: SATS, 1974, Vol.1, p.IV-2, IV-12.
*   There were too few school trips by private vehicle for statistical significance. The median length of school trips by train and bus were 7.1 and 4.0 km respectively and their median duration 39 and 28 minutes.

The amount of travel and transport within urban areas is determined by two main factors. The first is the extent of spatial separation of different kinds of activities within cities. For example, if all jobs are in the city centre and everyone lives outside the city centre, all workers will have to commute to the centre. The extent of separation of shops, schools, hospitals, entertainment and recreation facilities from where people live similarly influences the amount of travel. Simple availability of jobs and shops near where people live reduces travel only to the extent that they meet the needs of people

[1] There is relatively little data on urban goods movement within cities. Most of the transportation studies have dealt with it in much less detail than passenger movement. Recent reviews have been published by the Bureau of Roads (Rimmer, 1975; Ogden and Hicks, 1975).

living in the area. Freight transport is minimised if factories, warehouses, docks and rail sidings are concentrated in limited parts of the urban area, though journeys to work and deliveries to shops may be longer.

The information in previous chapters about where people live and work, and in this chapter about the patterns of land use within cities, gives some indication of the extent of separation of activities and how it has changed over recent years. As population growth has spread away from the employment centre, separation between homes and workplaces has increased, but much of the growth in employment has also been away from the centre. There is not enough information available to be able to assess whether, on balance, separation between homes and workplaces has increased or decreased.

The second main determinant of the volume of travel and transport is the extent to which people choose the job, school, shop, or recreation opportunity closest to them, or take advantage of the wide choice offered in urban areas, and make use of opportunities further afield. Alternatively, do people choose to live as close as possible to where they work, shop and so on? Research seems to show that people choose to live where they can find a suitable house in an attractive physical and social environment, close to local facilities. They appear to be willing to travel considerable distances to work (Troy, 1972). We know very little about the extent to which the exercise of choice among the variety of places to live, work, shop and go to school influences the volume of travel. The kinds of trips where choice is exercised most are trips to visit friends while at the other extreme, many shopping trips are to the closest suitable shopping centre, and many children go to the closest school.

With increasing prosperity we indulge in a larger range of optional activities, which increase the number of trips we make. Between 1964 and 1972 the average number of home-based trips per household in Melbourne increased from 4.44 to 5.80 (BTE, 1975). This was the net effect of a *decrease* in the number of journeys to work from 2.28 to 2.13 (probably due to falling household size) and an increase in the number of trips for all other purposes from 2.16 to 3.67. In Sydney in 1971 the number of trips per household ranged from 3.47 per day for households with no cars to 10.71 for those with two or more vehicles.

Just as people live in cities partly because of the wide choice of opportunities for work, shopping and leisure activities, firms locate in cities partly because of the wide choice between suppliers and outlets for their products. Goods are not necessarily purchased from the nearest supplier or sold to the nearest customer or wholesale or retail outlet.

There are more journeys to work than journeys for any other single purpose, and they are longer than trips made for any other purpose. Journeys to and from work are usually more concentrated into short peak periods, in both the morning and the evening, than journeys for other purposes (Figure 5.11). The exception is journeys to school, most of which are much shorter and more dispersed throughout the urban area. It is the journey to work which determines the capacity needed on most intra-urban roads and passenger transport.

Because of its importance in determining peak capacity demand, the journey to work has been studied more closely than any other journey purpose. Australia-wide

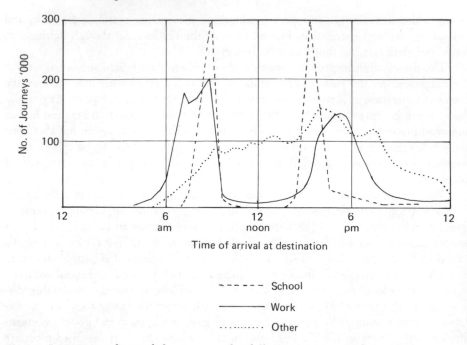

Figure 5.11 Time of arrival for journeys for different purposes: Sydney 1971.
Source: SATS (1974), Vol. 1, p. VI–5.

surveys by the Australian Bureau of Statistics in May 1970 and August 1974 collected data about the mode of travel to work. The only geographic breakdown of the
figures is between capital cities and the remainder of each state. The main results for
the state capitals are reproduced in Table 5.7.

In every state capital city the private car is used for at least 60 per cent of journeys
to work, and that proportion is increasing. Furthermore, most of those travelling by
car are driving rather than being driven to work. Outside the state capitals the motor
car is even more dominant. In the rest of Australia the proportion driving themselves
to work increased from 55.9 to 62.5 per cent between 1970 and 1974, and a further
15 per cent in each year were car passengers. Only 8.4 per cent (1970) and 5.5 per
cent (1974) used public transport.

The proportion travelling by public transport in every capital city declined over
the four-year period. The increasing proportion using trains in Adelaide was the only
case where a public transport mode increased its share. Sydney is the city where public
transport is most used for the journey to work, though even there it accounted for less
than one-third in 1974. The proportion using public transport is higher in the larger
cities, though the decline with city size is not regular. Thus a higher proportion use it
in Hobart than in Perth or Adelaide. In Canberra the proportions in the two years
(10.7 and 9.3 per cent) was lower than in any of the state capitals. Except in Sydney
and Melbourne suburban trains are less important than buses and trams. In some cities

there were minor increases in proportions walking or using other modes (bicycle, motor cycle, etc.).

Apart from being longer than journeys for other purposes, the journey to work is also one which most people have to make. Some can change jobs relatively easily but for others the destination is firmly fixed. For these reasons the cost of journeys and the time spent in journeys by different groups in the major cities have a significant effect on the welfare of workers.

While 8 per cent of all journeys to work in Australia in 1974 (excluding those who worked at home) took more than an hour, for some kinds of workers the proportion was much higher. In particular 15 per cent of male, and 11 per cent of female, clerical workers took longer than an hour to get to work. This is a result of the high proportion of clerical jobs that are found in central city areas.

TABLE 5.7   *Method of Travel to Work in State Capitals: 1970 and 1974 (percentage of total)*

		Train	Bus	Tram/ Ferry	Total Public Transport	Car Driver	Car Pass- enger	Total Car	Walk	Other	Total
Sydney	1970	19.8	15.7	1.2	36.7	43.4	9.9	53.4	7.9	2.0	100.0
	1974	16.3	12.6	0.7	29.7	51.7	10.1	61.8	6.3	2.2	100.0
Melbourne	1970	16.5	6.9	7.5	30.9	46.2	11.8	58.0	9.1	2.0	100.0
	1974	12.8	6.0	5.6	24.4	54.1	11.6	65.7	7.9	1.8	100.0
Brisbane	1970	11.3	17.0	*	28.5	49.2	14.4	63.6	5.7	2.2	100.0
	1974	9.2	11.4	*	20.8	55.5	13.6	69.1	6.4	3.7	100.0
Adelaide	1970	2.9	16.0	*	19.6	53.3	16.2	69.5	5.0	6.0	100.0
	1974	3.5	12.9	*	16.9	58.7	13.9	72.6	5.8	4.7	100.0
Perth	1970	4.3	16.5	*	21.0	56.3	13.5	69.8	6.6	2.6	100.0
	1974	2.5	12.5	*	15.1	61.6	13.7	75.3	5.3	4.2	100.0
Hobart	1970	*	18.3	*	19.7	51.6	12.6	64.2	14.4	*	100.0
	1974	*	18.6	*	19.5	58.3	12.9	71.2	7.9	*	100.0
Total	1970	14.5	13.1	3.0	30.6	47.1	12.0	59.1	7.8	2.5	100.0
	1974	11.7	10.5	2.1	24.3	54.5	11.7	66.2	6.7	2.8	100.0

Source: CBCS (1972) and ABS (1976) Ref. 17.5.
*   Too few observations for statistical accuracy.

If clerical workers are excluded, a smaller proportion of the other females (5.6 per cent) than of males (7.4 per cent) took over 60 minutes to get to work. Two other groups might be expected to avoid long work journeys: part-time workers would not find it worth making a long journey; only 5.3 per cent, compared with 8.4 per cent of full time workers, travelled more than an hour to work. Similarly married women might be expected to value their time at home highly; only 5.6 per cent travelled more than an hour compared with 11.0 per cent of unmarried females.

The time taken to get to work varies with the size of a city, partly because more people live further from where they work in the large cities, but also because a higher proportion of work journeys in the larger cities are by public transport. For the whole of Australia 60 per cent of journeys of over one hour were by public transport. In 1974 the proportions taking more than an hour to get to work were as follows:

	Per cent
Sydney	15.3
Melbourne	10.0
Brisbane	7.0
Adelaide	3.4
Perth	4.0
Hobart	2.3
Canberra	1.7

Despite the change to private vehicles between 1970 and 1974, the proportion taking over an hour in all the state capitals combined had remained at 10.3 per cent, about 370 000 workers (over half of whom were in Sydney), suggesting some increase in the average journey length, or a decrease in average travel speeds.

One important determinant of both the method of travel and the time taken is where people work. In particular journeys to work in the central business district are more likely to be by public transport, and more likely to take a long time, than journeys to other workplaces. In Sydney in 1971, 77.8 per cent of journeys to work in the CBD were by public transport. The main reasons are the congestion on roads leading to the CBD, the cost of parking private vehicles in the CBD and the availability of public transport serving the CBD. The longer times taken (measured door to door) result partly from the higher proportion of journeys that are by slower public transport. In addition the CBD, which contains the largest single concentration of jobs, draws workers from throughout the urban area, whereas suburban employment centres draw more from suburbs in the vicinity. The kinds of workers employed in the CBD, especially in clerical and some professional occupations, more often live in middle and outer suburbs than close to the city centre.

Journeys to school (which include journeys to tertiary educational institutions) have some features in common with journeys to work. Students have little option about whether to travel, and only a limited choice about where to attend. Journeys to school are even more strongly peaked in the morning and afternoon than journeys to work. The morning peak of journeys to school coincides with the later part of the peak in journeys to work (Figure 5.11), but in the afternoon most students have reached home before the main peak of journeys home from work begins.

In other respects journeys to school are very different. Table 5.8 shows the distribution between modes for all the state capital cities combined, in 1970 and 1974. As with the journey to work, travel by car is increasing and by public transport decreasing. The most marked change is the fall in the proportion walking. The differences between cities do not relate closely to size: public transport is most important in Sydney, Hobart, Brisbane, Perth and Canberra in that order, while the proportion walking is highest in Canberra, where suburban planning has had close regard for access to schools, followed by Melbourne and Sydney.

TABLE 5.8   *Method of Travel to School in State Capitals: 1970 and 1974*
(percentage of total)

	May 1970	August 1974
Train	5.0	4.2
Bus	21.8	21.5
Tram/Ferry	1.5	1.4
Total public transport	28.3	27.1
Car driver	*	2.7
Car passenger	14.4	19.4
Bicycle	7.5	6.6
Walk	47.8	43.6
Other	*	0.6
	100.0	100.0

Source: CBCS, 1972, and ABS, 1976, Ref. 17.5
* Too few observations for statistical significance.

The journey to school puts much less of a load on the transport system because most of the journeys are short and so many walk or cycle. In the state capitals in 1974, 55 per cent took less than 15 minutes and only 6 per cent more than 45 minutes, compared with 20 per cent of journeys to work. Nearly all of the journeys that took over 45 minutes were by public transport.

Shopping trips, trips to conduct personal business, recreational and social trips are much less concentrated in peak hours than journeys to either school or work. Few of them involve a trip to the CBD—only 6 per cent in Sydney in 1971 compared with 18 per cent of the journeys to work. As a result they are less likely to use public transport. Table 5.9 shows that the journeys to the Sydney CBD for social, recreational and personal business also relied heavily on public transport, though less so than work

TABLE 5.9   *Proportion Using Public Transport for Personal Trips:*
Sydney 1971* (percentage)

Journey purpose	Trips to or from CBD	All trips
Home-based		
Journey to work	77.8	34.9
Journey to school	68.9	90.1
Shopping	83.0	24.2
Social/recreational	44.4	9.5
Personal business	57.9	12.2
Non-home-based	41.8	14.1
All purposes	68.8 m	28.3

Source: SATS, Vol.1, VI-13.
* Percentage of total who travel by public and private vehicles.

and school trips since they are more often made outside business hours, when roads and parking are less crowded.

Non-home-based trips can be for a wide variety of purposes, including shopping, social or business trips during or after work, or trips from work for educational purposes.

Transport Facilities

The volume of transport and travel within cities is influenced by the capacity of the transport system as well as by the demand for movement of people and goods. There are three main kinds of transport facilities and methods of transport in urban areas. The first and most important is the privately owned vehicle which uses a public right-of-way to transport goods and people. Privately owned cars and trucks perform most of the passenger transport within cities, and nearly all of the freight movements that begin and end within urban areas.

The second is vehicles that provide public transport (buses and trams) on the normal public roads. They charge fares and operate to a schedule. Compared with private vehicles they occupy less road space for the number of people carried and usually cost less to operate per person kilometre. But they suffer from inflexibility over both space and time. They need to operate on fixed routes and some other method of transport has to be used by those who do not live and work within walking distance of a bus or tram route. There may be a wait for the bus or tram, and it may be necessary to change from one service to complete a trip. Over one-quarter of those who used a bus in their journey to work in 1974 had to use some other mode as well, compared with only 4 per cent of those who travelled by car. Because buses use the public streets they can collect passengers by travelling within residential areas, and can distribute them in employment and business areas.

The third main type moves on its own right-of-way, and therefore is not subject to congestion as a result of competition for space from other vehicles. Trains are the main example in Australian cities, though Adelaide's sole tram route and parts of Melbourne's tramway network have their own right-of-way. These kinds of transport are even less flexible spatially than buses. They can move large numbers of people cheaply and quickly along an established route. They use large units of capacity—the train—and therefore tend to run less frequently than buses. The problems of connecting to a train service and the likelihood of having to wait are also greater. Nearly half of those travelling to work by train in 1974 had to use another mode as well.

Both kinds of public transport are labour intensive. Not only is labour required to drive the vehicles and collect fares, but it is also required for maintenance of both vehicles and rights-of-way. For most car journeys the only labour cost is the time of the traveller. As labour costs tend to rise more rapidly than other costs with increasing real incomes, public transport is less able to compete with private cars.

There are some other intermediate kinds of urban transport. Taxis and hire cars accounted for 3 per cent of personal journeys in Sydney in 1971. They have the flexibility of cars but, like public transport, experience high labour costs. Ferries operate

TABLE 5.10 *Number of Vehicles at Houses and Flats in Major Urban Areas: 1971 (per cent of dwellings)*

No. of Vehicles	Sydney	Melbourne	Brisbane	Adelaide	Perth	Newcastle	Wollongong	Canberra	Hobart	Geelong	Total
0	25.5	22.9	21.5	18.9	17.2	21.7	19.9	7.5	20.1	17.4	22.1
1	50.5	49.7	52.8	53.4	50.8	54.7	56.6	57.6	52.0	53.8	51.3
2	19.7	22.4	20.8	22.4	25.4	19.6	19.7	28.1	22.4	23.9	21.7
3+	4.3	5.0	4.9	5.3	6.6	4.0	4.2	6.8	5.6	5.0	5.0
Total	100.0	100.0	100.0	100.0	100.0	100.0	100.0	100.0	100.0	100.0	100.0

Source: Census

on a public right-of-way which costs little to maintain, but use their own terminals. They are generally less flexible even than railways.

The total length of roads in the 17 largest urban areas in Australia in 1972–73 was 63 000 km, of which 80 per cent was sealed but only 2 per cent had dual carriageways (CBR, 1973). There is some separation of through traffic on large arterials from local traffic on small roads. Some 21 per cent of the road length classified as arterial carried 75 per cent of the vehicle kilometres (CBR, 1975). Nearly half of the arterial roads in Sydney had pavements less than 12 metres wide and another third between 12 and 20 metres. Everyone living in a city has access to roads, most of which are sealed.

Access to private cars is more restricted, though a relatively high proportion (80 per cent) of all houses and flats in Australia at the 1971 Census had at least one vehicle. Table 5.10 shows that in nine of the major urban areas, between one-sixth (Geelong and Perth) and one-quarter (Sydney) of all dwellings had no vehicles. Canberra stood out from the rest—only one dwelling in thirteen had no vehicle. It is much more difficult to judge the availability of private vehicles to individuals. All of those without licenses—the young, the old, the poor and the handicapped—were at least dependent on others to drive them. In 1973 the number of licences in Australia, excluding Queensland (where no data are available), to drive or ride motor vehicles was 5.4 million, compared with a population of 11.3 million. The number of cars and station sedans registered totalled only 3.9 million, to which might be added 0.2 million motorcycles. Clearly not all of those who are licensed to drive have a vehicle available at all times. The number of cars and station sedans per 1000 of the population has been rising in every state, however. For Australia as a whole it increased from 292 in 1969 to 341 in 1973.

The performance of the urban road system is usually assessed by the average speeds during periods of peak traffic flow on arterial roads. The Australian Roads Survey estimated the proportion of length of arterial roads in each state capital with peak period speeds of less than 25 km per hour, and the proportion of peak period travel on those roads (Table 5.11). More details for Sydney are provided by the Sydney transportation study (SATS, 1974, Vol. 1, pp. III–30 to III–33). On most arterial roads in the inner suburbs the average *daily* travel speed was less than 32

TABLE 5.11   *Capital City Arterials with Speeds Less than 25 kph*

	Per cent of length	Per cent of peak period travel
Sydney	24	31
Melbourne	25	35
Brisbane	13	23
Adelaide	4	6
Perth	11	15
Hobart	7	7

Source: CBR, 1975, 108.

kilometres per hour. It takes about 40 minutes to get 16 km out from the city centre in most directions (average speed 24 km per hour), though to the north, along some routes it can be reached in 35 minutes (average speed 27.4 km per hour).

In the Sydney area in 1970 there were 978 143 motor vehicles registered of which 70.5 per cent were cars or station sedans, 2.5 per cent motorcycles and 26 per cent goods vehicles. Taxis comprised only 0.3 per cent. Table 5.12 shows the number of vehicle kilometres travelled by public transport vehicles in 1960–61 and 1973–74.

TABLE 5.12   *Vehicle Kilometres Travelled by Public Transport Vehicles:*
1960–61 and 1973–74 (1000)

		Trains[a]	Trams	Trolley buses	Govt buses	Private buses
Sydney	1960-1	17 982	b	—	63 737	25 852
	1973-4	15 952	—	—	58 808	48 965
Melbourne	1960-1	12 714	31 047	—	9 535	28 433
	1973-4	13 584	23 873	—	11 918	36 927
Brisbane	1960-1	3 232	14 611		7 770	7 147
	1973-4	4 355	—	—	20 137	9 985
Adelaide	1960-1	3 263	874	1 138	16 597	5 622
	1973-4	3 393	673	—	21 799	7 746
Perth	1960-1	2 183	—	1 873	24 598	4 586
	1973-4	2 245	—	—	35 690	n.a.
Hobart	1960-1	325	—	1 728	4 463	n.a.
	1973-4	184	—	—	6 413	n.a.

Source: Bureau of Transport Economics (BTE), 1972. 1973-74 figures were supplied by the Bureau.
a   Train kilometres
b   Included with government buses. They were phased out during the year.
c   Suburban train services in Hobart ceased in 1975.

While car ownership and kilometres travelled has increased rapidly, the public transport fleets of the state capitals have been relatively stable and the distance travelled by some of them has declined. In Sydney the fleet of private vehicles is estimated to have increased by 38 per cent in the five years from 1965 to 1970, from 286 to 357 per thousand population. In Australia as a whole between 1962 and 1971, the number of vehicles per head increased by 42 per cent, and the distances travelled per vehicle increased 32 per cent. The total increase in vehicle kilometres travelled was 121 per cent (ABS *Survey of Motor Vehicle Usage*, 1962 and 1971, Ref. No. 14.4).

In Sydney the fleets of trains and government buses remained about the same size while the distance travelled fell, presumably because of reductions in off-peak services. The private bus fleet and the services it provides have expanded with outer suburban development. In Melbourne train services have remained about the same since 1962 while tram services have declined. Some of this decline has been taken up by expansion of government bus services, but private bus services have experienced even stronger growth.

Brisbane's tram and trolley bus services ended in 1968–69 and were replaced by City Council buses. The total vehicle kilometrage has fallen slightly and train services have just been maintained. Even private bus services have grown very modestly. In Adelaide trolley buses went out of service in 1963 and the main growth was in private bus services until most were taken over by the government Tramways Trust in 1973–74. The main growth in services in Perth was on government buses, replacing trolley buses in 1969 and expanding into some private routes. In Hobart the situation is similar, though there are no data on private buses. Hobart lost its tram services in 1961, its trolley bus services eight years later and its suburban trains in 1975. Meanwhile Melbourne is building an underground rail loop in the central business district, Sydney is linking its eastern suburbs with the CBD through a new suburban rail route and suburban routes are being electrified to improve their services in Perth, Adelaide and Brisbane.

Choice of Mode

Much of the discussion so far has distinguished between private and public transport. In this section changes in the relative importance of different modes of transport are examined in more detail, along with some of the reasons for the increasing role of private transport relative to public transport. It deals with passenger transport since nearly all goods transport between places within urban areas is by road, though of course railways move large volumes of goods within urban areas as a part of a longer inter-city movement.

The choice between public and private transport is not a simple matter of comparing prices. Access to a car is necessary to be able to travel by car, and for most people that means purchase. A car may be bought mainly for social and recreational reasons but, once it has been purchased, the money cost of using it for a particular trip is not high. Using the car for, say, travel to work deprives other family members of its use. By contrast, public transport offers its level of service to all who pay the fares on a particular day. Many people value it as a standby facility they can use on the occasions when they cannot travel by car.

Journey times by public transport are almost always significantly longer than by private transport. This is partly because of slower speeds on the main journey and because buses and trains make more frequent stops and cannot accelerate as quickly as private vehicles. The main reason is that public transport services follow fixed routes, which seldom coincide exactly with the best route for any particular journey. Therefore at both ends of a public transport trip, passengers have to walk or transfer to another vehicle. Consequently public transport is often slower when the journey time is calculated from door to door, even if the main-line part of the trip is faster (by train for example). In addition many studies have shown that travellers making a choice of mode take more account of time spent waiting for a bus or train than of the time spent travelling. Public transport also suffers from the fact that the time taken for a trip is not readily predictable. Buses and trains do not run at very frequent intervals on most routes in Australian cities and are not always able to operate on schedule. As a result the time taken for a journey by public transport tends to vary more than the time taken by car. The average time taken in journeys by private and public transport from the Sydney G.P.O. in 1971 is shown in Figure 5.12. Even for radial travel public transport is significantly slower than travel by private vehicle. It takes about 90 minutes by public transport to get as far as one can get in an hour by car in most directions. Public transport would compare even less favourably for cross-town travel.

It has already been pointed out that, even in the short period between 1970 and 1974, the proportions of journeys to work and to school by public transport fell significantly. In fact the fall in the proportion travelling to work was sufficiently great that the actual numbers travelling by public transport also fell significantly. Table 5.9 gives evidence about two of the factors affecting the choice of mode of transport. Public transport is used more frequently on the journey to work than on other trips by adults, and it is used more frequently on journeys to the city centre than on journeys to other destinations.

The number of journeys to work increases in fairly direct proportion with the workforce. Trips for other purposes are likely to increase with income (and consequently car ownership), with participation in educational programmes, and with social and recreational activity. Estimates of the increase in non-work journeys and the slight decrease in work journeys in Melbourne between 1964 and 1972 were reported earlier.

It has been shown in the previous chapter that the proportion of jobs found in city centres has fallen in recent years. This has been one of the reasons for the fall in the proportion using public transport in the journey to work. It also affects other journeys. If the proportion of retail jobs—and sales—in the city centre declines, the proportion of shopping trips to the city centres also falls. For similar reasons a smaller proportion of trips for recreational and cultural purposes will be to the city centre.

One of the main reasons that people do not use their cars on journeys to the CBD is that parking is difficult to find and expensive, but in recent years, at least in some CBDs, there has been a significant increase in the number of available parking spaces. For example, between 1964 and 1973 the number of parking spaces in the Melbourne CBD increased from 30 905 to 42 585—a large increase in public, and especially private, off-street parking outweighing a small fall in kerbside parking (BTE, 1975).

The growing suburban centres of employment, shopping and services tend to be dispersed and relatively small. They can provide more parking at lower cost close to drivers' destinations. Furthermore they cannot be well served by public transport because of the small volume of trips to them along any one route. Much of the suburban employment is in industrial areas which are built at a low density, and many factories have on-site parking for employees.

Car ownership increases with income, and car owners make more of their trips by car, and make more trips in total, than other families. Indeed it seems that households with more cars make as many trips by public transport as those with fewer cars, though this may be partly because families with more than one car are, on average, larger families.

Attempts to estimate the effect of income on choice of mode using data from

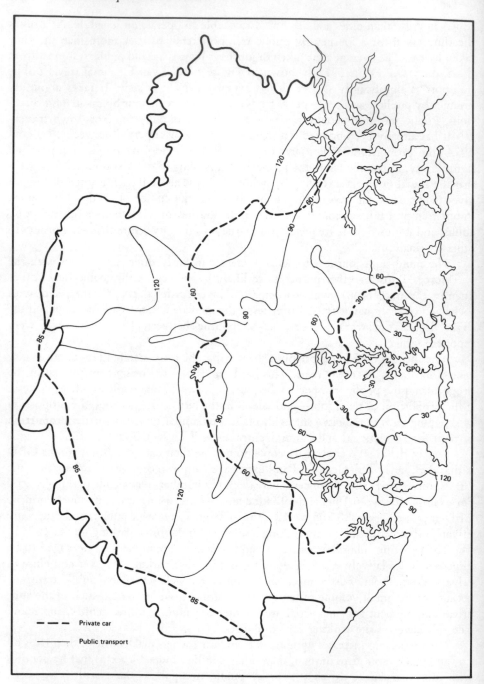

Figure 5.12 Travel time from Sydney G.P.O. by private and public transport: 1971, in minutes.

Source: SATS (1974), Vol. 1, pp. III–33, IV–18.

household surveys conducted for transportation studies have suggested that the effects are relatively small. An example of the results is reproduced in Table 5.13. There is little difference in choice of mode within the range of family incomes from $4000 to $12 000 per year. One reason is that family income is strongly affected by the number of family members in the workforce, and working family members other than the head are less likely to travel to work by car. For example, the ABS May 1970 Survey showed that 65 per cent of married women travelled to work by car compared with 71 per cent of the other members of the workforce.

TABLE 5.13   *Family Income and Main Mode of Travel: Sydney 1971*
(*percentages*)

Family income $ per annum	Car driver or passenger		Bus		Train	
	Work trips	All trips	Work trips	All trips	Work trips	All trips
4 000 or less	59	65	19	20	17	9
4 001 — 5 000	67	71	12	14	16	9
5 001 — 6 000	68	74	14	13	13	7
6 001 — 7 000	67	76	14	11	16	7
7 001 — 8 000	66	75	15	13	14	7
8 001 — 9 000	66	77	14	11	16	7
9 001 — 10 000	66	77	15	11	16	8
10 001 — 11 000	65	76	15	11	15	8
11 001 — 12 000	61	78	13	10	18	9
Greater than 12 000	72	81	12	9	12	6

Source: CBR (1975), 131.

A study of the demand for motor vehicles by the Industries Assistance Commission (Talbot and Filmer, 1973) concluded that 90 per cent of the growth in demand for ownership of motor vehicles (per head) has been due to growth in real income per head. The other 10 per cent was due to a fall in the real cost of motoring. It was estimated that a 1 per cent increase in real income per head produces a 2.1 per cent increase in vehicle ownership per head, while a 1 per cent fall in the real cost increases ownership by 0.9 per cent. A further possible influence is the practice of companies providing motor cars to their employees as a fringe benefit.

While the cost of motoring has been falling relative to the general price level as measured by the Consumer Price Index (CPI), the relative cost of using public transport has been rising (Figure 5.13). The main reasons for these different trends are that most of the products used in motoring are produced by capital intensive industries where there are opportunities for technical advance. Public transport, by contrast, is a labour intensive service. Labour costs account for nearly two-thirds of the total costs, and there are few opportunities for increases in productivity. The opportunities that are available, such as one-man bus operation, have already been taken. Public transport is also called on to finance at least part of the costs of its unprofitable weekend and late night services, which are really run for welfare reasons, from its revenue from other services. Its costs are also increased by the increasing proportion of its customers who want to travel at peak hours as off-peak travellers transfer to private cars as far as they can.

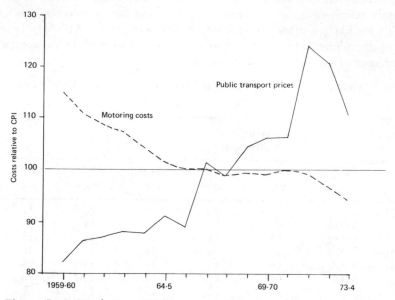

Figure 5.13 Trends in costs of transport relative to the Consumer Price Index: 1959–60 to 1973–74, with 1966 = 100.
Source: BTE (1975), 4–5.

There is some further evidence that changes in fares have a quite direct effect on choice of mode of travel. Fares often change at irregular intervals and by relatively large amounts. If changes in patronage of public transport result from changes in fares they should occur mainly in the years when fares change. In Figure 5.14 patronage is measured as expenditure on public transport. Both expenditure and fares are corrected for changes in the general price level. These data suggest that a 10 per cent increase in fares leads to a fall in patronage of about 5 per cent.

The overall effects of changes in incomes, relative prices, workplaces and other factors has been an increase in car ownership and use and a fall in the use of public transport. The fall in the number of public transport journeys in the mainland state capital cities is shown in Table 5.14. It has been greatest in Melbourne and Brisbane and smallest in Perth.

Distribution of Trips

A distinction has been made in the above discussion between journeys to the CBD and other journeys. Journeys to the CBD are more frequently made by public transport and a higher proportion of them are work journeys. The CBD, despite its relatively

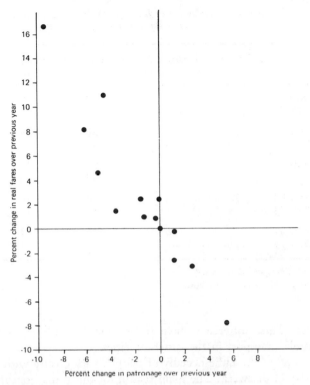

Figure 5.14 Annual variations in public transport patronage and fares: 1960–61 to 1973–74.

Note: The change in real fares is a change relative to the general price level as measured by the CPI.

Source: BTE (1975), 10, derived from Australian National Accounts.

declining role, is still the focus of most of the public transport system. It is the single area within the city which has the best access, at least by public transport, to the whole urban area. It has the greatest single concentration of jobs, the greatest variety of shopping, and the widest range of services, cultural and recreational activities.

Despite the fact that only 10 per cent of journeys in Sydney in 1971 were to or from the CBD, transport flows are much heavier on facilities near the city centre. No other single centre attracts so many trips; the areas surrounding the CBD also have high concentrations of population, jobs and activities. Land values are highest in these areas, and the cost of increasing the capacity of transport routes is correspondingly high. As a result road transport in the inner city is especially expensive, partly because in these older parts of most cities the roads were not constructed to carry high volumes of traffic, and partly because road transport needs more high-value land than rail. The main cities vary greatly in the adequacy of their inner city road systems. Melbourne and Adelaide central areas were originally laid out with wide streets, though some of the main arterials are narrower in the inner suburbs. Sydney and Brisbane streets are

TABLE 5.14   *Number of Journeys by Public Transport*
1960-61 and 1973-74 (millions)

		Trains	Trams and trolley buses	Government buses	Private buses	Ferries	Total
Sydney	1960-61	222	*	249	60	13	544
	1973-74	192	—	184	114	12	503
Melbourne	1960-61	146	172	30	74	—	422
	1973-74	110	109	22	70	—	312
Brisbane	1960-61	25	83	24	13	6	150
	1973-74	32	—	56	15	e 2	e 105
Adelaide	1960-61	15	3	50	10	—	81
	1973-74	13	1	46	11	—	72
Perth	1960-61	12	6	46	7	0	72
	1973-74	11	—	59	e 1	0	e 71

Source: Bureau of Transport Economics
Notes: *   Included with government buses
           e   estimates

much narrower. These differences help to account for differences in the roles of private and public transport in the different cities.

Movements of goods, and especially of people, vary greatly with the time of day and with the day of the week. The main reason for this is that journeys to and from work are heavily concentrated into about a $2\frac{1}{2}$ hour period in the morning and a similar period in the evening (Figure 5.15), so that transport facilities have to be designed to cope with these journey peaks. Some relief is possible through staggering of working hours, though in most cities with a range of economic activities the different working hours of factories, shops and offices probably provides about as much staggering as is socially acceptable.

The effect of peaking on the need for capacity is accentuated by the fact that the proportion of traffic in each direction often changes significantly between the morning and the evening peaks. In the morning the dominant flow is inwards towards the city centre and in the evening outwards. This is illustrated in Figure 5.16, which shows flows on the Sydney Harbour Bridge. The imbalance is greatest in arterial routes which link primarily residential areas with primarily employment centres. On the Bridge the number of lanes available for north and south bound travel can be changed, but that cannot be done on most routes, so that each carriageway must be wide enough to cope with peak flows in the direction it serves.

Peaks in traffic flows on roads are generally less pronounced than the peaks in trips by public transport, as shown in Figure 5.15. The main reason for the sharper peaks in use of public transport is that it caters for a higher proportion in journeys to work and to school. The extreme case of highly peaked flows occurs in journeys by public transport to and from the CBD. This is illustrated in Figure 5.17, which shows the number of passengers using the city railway stations in Sydney. Over 40 per cent

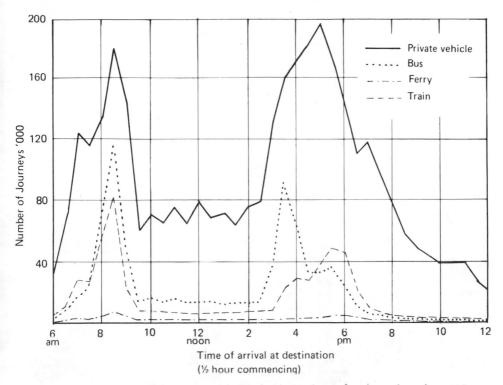

Figure 5.15 Distribution of trips through the day by main mode of travel: Sydney 1971.
Source: SATS (1974), Vol 1, p. VI-5.

of arrivals occur in one hour, from 8 a.m. to 9 a.m., and the two-hour period from 4 p.m. to 6 p.m. accounts for two-thirds of the departures.

Peaks in public transport pose some of the same problems of right-of-way capacity as peaks in private car journeys, and buses suffer the same peak period congestion as cars. There are some additional problems—because of peaks in demand the capital invested in trains and buses is used for only a fraction of its possible usable time; on some of the longer routes a train or bus can only complete a single trip in the peak period in the direction of peak flow, and labour utilisation is also difficult. Since the peaks are too far apart to be served by a single shift some workers work part of the off-peak as well as one peak. Others work split shifts and are paid penalty rates.

It seems likely that, as private cars provide for an increasing proportion of non-work and non-school trips, and an increasing proportion of all trips are wholly outside the central area, the use of public transport will become increasingly concentrated in peak hours. The strains that this puts on the financial viability of public transport affect its ability not only to meet peak needs but also to perform the social service-type function of providing off-peak transport for those without access to a car.

Although peaks of traffic in most urban transport facilities provide for the journey to and from work there are some facilities which experience their peak demand for recreational trips. This is illustrated by traffic flows on the Hawkesbury River Bridge

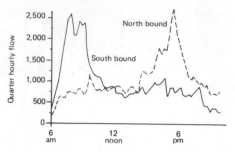

Figure 5.16 Traffic flow on Sydney Harbour Bridge, 1971.

Source: SATS (1974), Vol. 1, p. III–25.

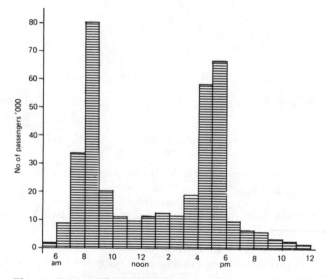

Figure 5.17 Rail passengers using city stations: Sydney 1971.

Source: SATS (1974), Vol. 1, p. IV–27.

between Sydney and Gosford. The peak hour flows are much higher on Saturdays and Sundays than on week days (SATS, Vol.1, p. III–24). Similar conditions occur on roads leading to beaches and, on occasions, on roads and public transport facilities giving access to sporting arenas.

Summary

Despite a reduction in the amount of scattered fringe development since the Second World War, there remains a lot of vacant land in the outer suburbs of Australian cities. Nearly half of the land that is used for urban purposes is used for residential purposes, and over one-third for open space, institutions, education, transport terminals and the like. The proportion used for manufacturing, retailing, offices and commercial activities is only about one-tenth. Apart from a concentration of these major employment-providing activities in the city centre, the main impression from an examination of land use is that land use composition varies little between different parts of urban areas.

The effects of the increasingly dispersed pattern of activities within cities can be seen in the transport system. It can best be served by private cars which provide a highly flexible transport system that does not need large traffic volumes. The decreasing role played by public transport is also partly a result of its high labour costs. Because it has lost a particularly high proportion of non-peak traffic the public transport systems find themselves in difficult financial positions where they need to call on general government funds to meet their deficits.

Although Australian cities have invested a great deal in road improvements in recent years, they have not established a freeway system that could provide fast, efficient travel by private car within urban areas. At the same time public transport services have barely been maintained, in the face of falling patronage. Relatively poor transport services are one of the reasons why industry, retailing and other kinds of employment are moving to the suburbs where they are less dependent on a metropolitan transport system.

6 Housing

In this chapter a number of the characteristics of housing in Australia are described. Changes in the housing stock since the Second World War will be examined in more detail than in Chapter 2. This chapter describes the kinds of dwellings that have been constructed, and the physical features and tenure of the dwellings counted at each census. It attempts to assess how far the growth in the dwelling stock since the Second World War has kept up with demands in terms of quality and adequacy. It then goes on to examine trends in housing costs and relates these to changes in tenure.

At the end of the Second World War Australia was suffering from a housing shortage, after some fifteen years when there had been very little new construction and even maintenance had been neglected. There was overcrowding, especially in the poorer inner areas of the major cities, and many people were living in temporary accommodation. Many houses were shared by two or more households and others lived in dwellings without their own kitchens or bathrooms. Because of shortages of building materials it took some years for the building industry to pick up, but once the recovery got under way it began a period of sustained construction which, during the fifties and sixties, not only made up for the backlog of construction and maintenance during the thirties and forties but also raised housing standards to higher levels than ever before. With higher incomes most Australians could afford to be well housed. There was a decline in the number of shared houses, temporary and non-self-contained dwellings. The number of occupants per house or flat, and per room declined so that overcrowding became less prevalent. Brick houses became more common relative to timber and asbestos cement.

Among the reasons for the increase in housing standards were the activities of government housing authorities, which built large numbers of houses and flats for lower income families. They sold about half of the dwellings they built to tenants and in that way contributed to the increase in the proportion of households that owned their own dwelling. Between the Second World War and the late 1950s, nearly all of the dwellings built in Australia were single family houses and, except for government houses, nearly all were for owner-occupation. At the same time, partly as a reaction to rent control and partly to satisfy the demands of migrants from southern Europe, many of the older rented houses were sold for owner-occupation. Two developments curtailed the spread of owner-occupation. One was an upsurge in flat building in the late fifties and early sixties, in large part to meet the housing demands of the increasing numbers of young families and young single people. Although Strata Titles legislation was passed in each state to make it easier for people to own their own flat or home unit the majority were rented (Department of Housing, 1968). The other development was a rapid increase in the cost of land, contributing to house price inflation, and increases in the interest rates at which buyers could borrow to purchase a house. By the late sixties and early seventies this began to make it more difficult for the average family to become an owner-occupant (AIUS, 1975b; Bromilow, 1975).

These large cost increases threaten not only the ability of households to become owner occupants but also their ability to purchase housing services in any way. Increasing costs of land and increasing interest rates affect the cost of providing rental housing as well as the cost of buying for owner occupation. Land costs have risen, partly because private developers have been required to provide services which were previously the responsibility of public authorities, and partly because land use controls limit the supply of land available for development. Mainly because of land prices and interest costs, Australia in the mid-seventies faced the possibility that housing standards could stop rising and might even fall.

Immediately after the war government housing policies were focused on overcoming the housing shortage, paying particular attention to the needs of families who could not afford to pay market rents and of returned servicemen. Home ownership became an important policy goal. Home finance on favourable terms was provided to help more people to become home owners. Today, with the increasing cost of housing, many of these measures are no longer having the desired effects. New policy measures will be needed to assist those who find the higher costs a burden.

The Stock of Housing

Although the major trends are clear, it is difficult to get a precise picture of changes in the stock of housing in Australia in the post-war period, mainly because of changes in the definitions of dwellings used at successive censuses. One difficulty is that shared houses were treated differently in 1947 and in 1954–1966. In 1971 they were included with 'other private dwellings'. An estimate can be made of the number of shared dwellings at each census from 1947 to 1966, however. Table 6.1 shows the number of structured dwellings—houses and flats, whether shared or not—and the additional households either sharing a structured dwelling or living in a non-structured dwelling such as a room, tent, shed or hut.

The table shows that the number of structured dwellings more than doubled over the 24-year period covered, while the total population increased by only 68 per cent. One of the reasons for the more rapid increase in structured dwellings was that a decreasing number of households either shared dwellings or lived in non-self-contained or temporary dwellings, the proportion falling dramatically from about 14 per cent in 1947 to 3 per cent in 1971. The proportion of individuals living in such dwellings fell from 6 per cent in 1954, the first year they can be identified, to 1.6 per cent in 1971. Among the structured dwellings the number of houses increased less rapidly than the number of flats. Most of the growth in the number of flats occurred after 1954, and during the 1960s alone the number doubled.

TABLE 6.1   *Dwelling Stock in Australia: 1947–1971*
('000)

	1947	1954	1961	1966	1971
Occupied structured dwellings					
Private house	1 538*	2 008	2 393	2 683	3 119†
Flat	111	127	218	346	453
Shared house or flat	83	51	38	13	—
Total	1 733	2 187	2 649	3 042	3 572
Occupied structured dwellings					
per 1000 population	229	243	250	262	280
Other households					
Sharing a house or flat	92	56	42	14	—
Rooms, tenements, etc.	38	53	50	67	56
Tent, shed, hut, etc.	49*	49	42	33	41
Total	179	158	133	113	98
Total households	1 912	2 345	2 782	3 155	3 671
Total number of rooms in					
private dwellings	9 143	11 811	14 355	16 427	18 353

Source: Censuses.
Notes: * Tents, sheds and huts were included with houses in 1947. It has been assumed that there were
as many in 1947 as in 1954. Very likely there were more so that the number of private houses
in 1947 is over-stated.

    † Includes 39 000 villa units, which may have been counted as houses or flats in previous years.

The main way in which the housing stock increased was through the construction of new dwellings. This is the only source of change for which anything like adequate data are available—even data on new dwelling completions is imperfect because of the inclusion, until 1972–73, of major alterations and additions as new dwellings. Between the 1947 and the 1971 Censuses 2.176 million dwellings were completed while, according to Table 6.1, the number of structured dwellings rose by something over 1.8 million. This suggests that some 0.3 to 0.4 million dwellings were lost as a result of demolition or conversion to non-residential use. It is not possible to be more precise than this because of differences in dwelling classifications at the censuses and the inclusion of alterations and additions with completions. Apart from conversion to non-residential uses, conversions of houses into flats or rooms and of flats or rooms back to houses, affect the numbers of dwellings. Only since 1971 have some estimates of the number of demolitions (net of conversions) become available. They suggest a loss of about 0.4 per cent of the dwelling stock each year. If the same rate had continued throughout the 1947–71 period it would account for 0.2 to 0.3 million of the dwellings apparently lost.

Figure 6.1 shows the numbers of dwellings completed in each year since the 1947 Census. After a rapid growth in house construction as post-war material shortages were relieved the industry stabilised in the early 1950s, completing around 75 000–85 000 houses a year, which added some 3.4 per cent a year to the dwelling stock. The actual number of houses built increased very little until the late 1960s, but in the late fifties and throughout the sixties there was a rapid increase in the number of flats built. It was accompanied, in the late sixties, by a further increase in house construction. By this time about half as many flats as houses were being built.

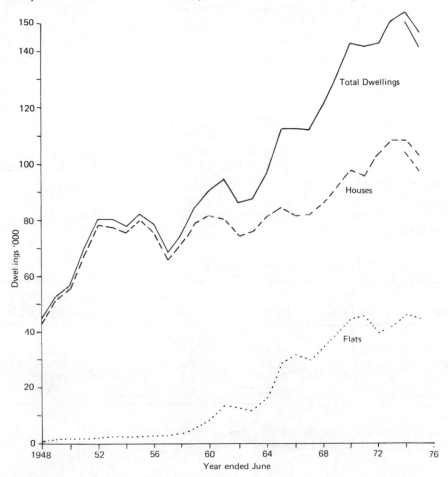

Figure 6.1 Completions of dwellings: 1947–1975.
Note: Lower lines for 1974 to 1975 exclude alterations and additions.
Source: ABS, *Building and Construction*.

The flat building boom seems to have been mainly a result of a rapid increase in the number of people in the late teens and early twenties who prefer to live in flats. The large number of war-time and post-war babies began to form separate households at about the time of the boom. There were other factors as well: rent control was relaxed during the 1950s, especially in respect of new dwellings; young single people and married couples increasingly formed separate households, many of them preferring to live in flats, and some older couples whose children had left home preferred to sell their houses and buy flats. Finally, as the fringes of the cities became more remote there was a market for flats among those who prefer to live closer to the city centre.

Partly because its site is more confined, Sydney has experienced more flat building than any other city in Australia. Nearly all of Australia's flats have been built in the major cities and a few holiday resorts (Department of Housing, 1968).

The data in Table 6.1 refer only to occupied dwellings. There has also been a rapid increase in the number and proportion of unoccupied dwellings. Table 6.2 shows the number and the percentage of structured dwellings vacant at each census. The high proportion of dwellings vacant in rural areas is partly because of the number of rural holiday homes. Nearly half of the vacant holiday homes in 1971 were in rural areas, and most of the others were in smaller centres. The increasing proportion of vacant dwellings is in part a reflection of increasing housing standards as more people have second homes and move more frequently. In 1971, 5 per cent of home owners owned at least two dwellings. These 20 000 second homes accounted for over half of the vacant dwellings (half were holiday homes and half temporarily vacant, presumably because their owners were on holiday). One-fifth were either for sale or for rent. There were more flats (11.3 per cent) than houses (8 per cent) vacant, and one-third of the vacant flats were 'to let', reflecting the greater frequency of movement among tenants of flats.

TABLE 6.2   *Percentage of Dwellings Unoccupied 1947–1971**

Year	Urban	Rural	Total	Number of Unoccupied Dwellings ('000)
1947	—	—	2.6	47.0†
1954	3.7	9.5	4.9	112.6†
1961	4.8	14.1	6.5	183.4
1966	5.9	14.7	7.4	241.4
1971	6.9	17.4	8.5	330.1

Source: Censuses.

Notes: * Percentage of unoccupied to total stock of structural dwellings.

  † Includes private and non-private dwellings as defined in Census.

Dwelling Quality

The number of dwellings is an inadequate measure of the housing available in Australia. Dwellings vary greatly in size and in the quality of the accommodation they provide. The total number of rooms, a more adequate measure, slightly more than doubled over the 24-year period, keeping well ahead of the population increase.

Even the number of rooms in a dwelling is an imperfect indication of its size. The number of bedrooms per head is an indicator of privacy but the number of living rooms mainly reflects changing fashions and tastes. In the post-war period the combined living-dining room has often replaced two separate rooms with much the same total area. Kitchens combined with family or dining rooms have also become common. Multi-function living rooms have been built into new houses and flats, and in renovating old dwellings the number of rooms has often been reduced by removing separating walls. As a result the increase in the number of rooms almost certainly understates the increase in the floor area. This should be kept in mind when interpreting Table 6.3, which shows the average numbers of rooms in different types of dwellings from 1947 to 1971. There have been only minor increases in the average number of rooms per dwelling in total, and in any dwelling class. In the case of flats the average number of rooms has fallen significantly, because of the large number of small flats (at least in terms of rooms) built during the 1960s. The fall in the average number of rooms in private dwellings between 1966 and 1971 may reflect some reduction in size as well as the continuing decline in the proportion of separate living and dining rooms. We return to this question in discussing room and dwelling occupancy.

TABLE 6.3   *Average Numbers of Rooms per Dwelling: 1947–1971*

	1947	1954	1961	1966	1971
Private house	5.1*	5.3	5.4	5.5	5.3
Flat	4.1	4.1	4.0	3.7	3.5
Share of private house	3.2	3.4	3.3	3.5	
Rooms, tenement, etc.	2.1	2.2	2.2	2.4	2.2
Tent, shed, hut, etc.	—*	1.9	2.0	1.7	
Total occupied private dwellings	4.9	5.0	5.2	5.2	5.0

Source: Censuses.
Notes: * 'Tent, shed, hut' were included with private houses in 1947.

Since 1970–71 the average floor area of private contract-built houses commenced in the capital city statistical divisions has been recorded. For all capitals combined the average floor area increased nearly 11 per cent from 1970–71 to 1973–74, to 148 square metres, but fell slightly in 1974–75 to 143 square metres. Although the series is short it does suggest that standards continued to increase until the slump in the industry in 1974–75.

Another indicator of the quality of the dwelling stock, already described, is the proportion which are self-contained. The proportion of the population living in self-contained dwellings increased from 87 per cent in 1954 to 94 per cent in 1971. Apart from the fall in the number in non-self-contained private dwellings there was also a fall in the number and proportion of the population living in non-private dwellings (boarding houses, hotels, institutions) from 6.9 per cent to 4.5 per cent.

Most dwellings in Australia, especially those in urban areas, are provided with those services that are generally regarded as necessary. The major shortcoming in many areas is the lack of mains sewerage. Table 6.4 shows that even in 1971 one-third of all private dwellings were not connected to mains sewerage. About two-thirds of those relied on septic systems and the remainder still had pan services or other means of waste disposal. Even in the major urban areas one-fifth did not have mains sewerage. Nearly all, even in the rural areas, have electricity.

Partly because of the way self-contained houses and flats are defined they nearly all have cooking facilities in some kind of kitchen. Even when non-self-contained

TABLE 6.4   *Percentage of Private Dwellings Lacking Facilities* 1947, 1971*

	1947			1971			
	Urban	Rural	Total	Major Urban	Other Urban	Rural	Total
Lacking electricity							
(houses and flats)	2.8	46.1	17.2	0.1	0.2	2.2	0.4
(private dwellings)	2.6	45.4	16.0	0.1	0.3	3.6	0.6
Without bathroom							
(houses and flats)	3.7	22.1	9.8	0.2	0.3	1.5	0.4
(private dwellings)	10.1	22.9	14.1	0.6	1.1	3.4	1.1
Without kitchen							
(houses and flats)	0.1	0.9	0.5	0.2	0.2	0.5	0.2
(private dwellings)	3.3	1.7	2.8	0.6	0.8	2.0	0.9
Without flush toilet							
(houses and flats)	23.3	78.5	41.2	4.7	9.5	31.1	9.1
(private dwellings)	28.1	78.6	43.3	4.7	9.9	32.5	14.5
Without main sewer							
(houses and flats)	—	—	—	19.6	33.5	94.8	32.2
(private dwellings)	—	—	—	19.4	33.8	94.3	32.2

Source: Censuses.
* Without cooking facilities.

dwellings are included very few are without a kitchen. Bathrooms are also provided in nearly all private dwellings. Only about one-third of those without a kitchen (or a bathroom) lack both facilities. In every respect where it is possible to make a comparison, the proportions, and indeed the actual numbers, of dwellings lacking these facilities have fallen between 1947 and 1971.

TABLE 6.5   *Material Used for Outer Wall Construction: Houses and Flats 1947, 1971 (percentage of total)*

	1947			1971			
	Urban	Rural	Total	Major Urban	Other Urban	Rural	Total
Houses:							
Brick, stone & concrete	48.1	14.8	36.3	57.6	29.1	23.7	46.4
Wood	44.6	52.3	50.9	29.2	45.7	51.2	36.0
Fibro-cement	4.6	10.6	6.8	12.6	22.8	21.1	16.1
Other	2.7	22.3	6.0	0.7	2.4	4.0	1.5
Flats:							
Brick, stone & concrete	83.3	36.4	81.7	89.4	56.4	36.4	84.3
Wood	11.1	46.2	12.3	7.2	26.1	33.3	10.0
Fibro-cement	3.4	12.7	3.7	3.2	18.2	25.2	5.4
Other	2.2	4.7	2.3	0.2	1.2	5.2	0.4

Source: Censuses.

Another measure of dwelling quality, though one which is more ambiguous, is the building material (Table 6.5). Generally solid external wall materials such as brick, stone and concrete are more durable and give better temperature and sound insulation. As was shown in Chapter 2, building materials vary considerably between states. Figure 6.2 shows that in the early post-war building boom many of the cheaper houses were built of timber and asbestos cement. As a result, between 1947 and 1961 the proportion of houses and flats with solid external walls remained constant. During the sixties there was a return to predominantly brick construction of houses so that the proportion with solid external walls increased from 36 per cent to 46 per cent.

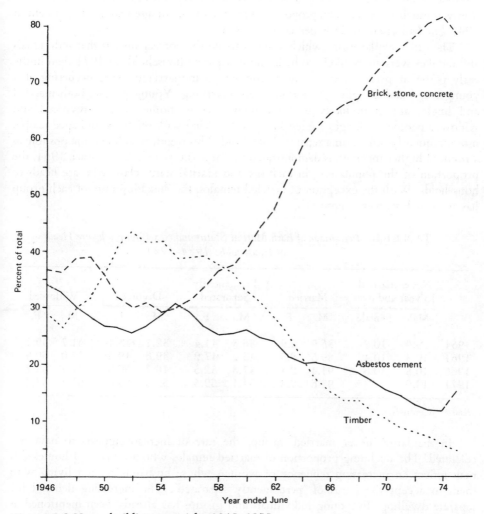

Figure 6.2 House building materials: 1945–1975.
Note: 1945–46 to 1973–74 data refer to completions; 1974–75 data to commencements.
Source: ABS, *Building and Construction*.

Dwelling Occupancy

Since the number of dwellings increased more rapidly than the population there was a fall in the number of occupants per dwelling between 1954 and 1971, the number of persons per private dwelling falling from 3.8 to 3.3. The fall occurred in both houses (3.7 to 3.5) and flats (2.6 to 2.3). There are two possible explanations for the decline. The first is that the average size of families declined. In fact it almost certainly increased. In 1947 the average nuclear family must have been quite small as a result of low birth rates during the Depression of the 1930s. Only the 0–5 age group showed the first effects of the war and post-war baby boom. By contrast, in 1971 the population was much younger. The proportion under 15 years of age was 25.05 per cent in 1947 but had risen to 28.8 per cent in 1971.

The other explanation, which appears to be the correct one, is that individuals and families were more likely to be living in separate households in 1971 than in the early post-war period. Part of the reason was that marriages were occurring at a younger age and a higher proportion were marrying. Young people, both married and single, are more likely to leave their parents' home. Single, divorced and widowed people of all ages are less likely to be living with relatives, and aged people more frequently remain in a separate household. This trend, which became possible as a result of higher incomes, is demonstrated in Table 6.6 which shows, since 1954, the proportion of the population, in each sex and marital status class, who are heads of households. With the exception of married females, the 'headship rate' of each group has increased at every census.

TABLE 6.6   *Percentage of Each Marital Status and Sex Group who are Heads of Households: 1954-1971*

	Never married 15 year and over		Married		Permanently Separated		Divorced		Widowed	
	Male	Female	M.	F.	M.	F.	M.	F.	M.	F.
1954	9.9	10.2	85.9	2.9	36.8	44.4	32.1	43.4	51.7	59.1
1961	10.3	10.4	89.5	2.5	43.2	47.2	39.6	49.3	55.0	60.9
1966	10.8	10.6	91.4	2.4	47.8	52.5	46.7	56.6	57.4	63.2
1971	13.0	12.3	92.6	2.3	54.1	59.5	52.3	63.0	61.8	67.2

Source: Censuses.

In the large 'never married' group, the rate of increase appears to have accelerated. The declining proportion of married females who are heads of households may reflect an increasing tendency of women whose husbands are not living with them to accept the status of 'permanently separated'. The increasing demand for separate dwellings by young individuals and groups has already been mentioned as one of the reasons for the increase in flat building during the 1960s.

Table 6.3 showed that the average number of rooms per dwelling had changed very little in the post-war period, rising slightly from 1947 to 1966 and then declining again in 1971. Although these data may understate the increase in the space available in dwellings, because of increasing openness of floor plans, trends in room occupancy rates give some indication of changes in the standard at which people are housed. The average room occupancy for each dwelling type is shown in Table 6.7.

TABLE 6.7   *Average Room Occupancy (Persons per Room) 1947–1971*

	1947	1954	1961	1966	1971
Private house	0.76*	0.70	0.68	0.66	0.66
Flat	0.70	0.62	0.64	0.64	0.65
Shared house/flat	0.94	0.80	0.86	0.81	
Other private dwelling	1.05	0.95	0.88	0.76	0.96
Tent, shed, hut	—*	1.41	1.38	1.36	
Total private dwellings	0.77	0.76	0.69	0.65	0.66

Source: Censuses.
* In 1947 tents, sheds and huts were included with private houses.

The post-war decline in average room occupancy was halted in 1966, at the same time as the average number of rooms per dwelling began to fall for reasons already discussed. This is further evidence of increasing pressures in the housing market. To examine this further we turn to some aspects of the distribution of room occupancy, to see how many dwellings were over-crowded and how many under-used at each census. Table 6.8 adopts a relatively low level of room occupancy to define when a dwelling is over-crowded so that over crowding may be exaggerated. It also adopts a high level of room occupancy before a dwelling is regarded as under-used, which decreases the proportion so classified (King, 1973).

TABLE 6.8   *Percentage of Dwellings Over-Crowded and Under-Used: 1954–1971*

	1954	1961	1966	1971
Over-crowded				
Private houses	8.92	7.05	6.20	5.79
Flats	6.74	10.36	8.19	13.88
Other	24.57	18.99	25.04	30.09
Total	9.87	7.86	7.16	6.77
Under-utilised				
Private houses	14.69	16.54	18.82	17.29
Flats	8.18	7.54	6.07	8.02
Other	5.34	3.01	4.16	5.57
Total	13.70	15.21	16.84	15.19

Source: 1954, 1961 Censuses.
1966, 1971 King (1973).
Notes: *Over-crowding standard:* Households with up to and including 4 persons need 1 room per person and thereafter 1 bedroom for each 2 persons with 2 additional living rooms.
Under-utilised standard: 1 person occupying 5 rooms or, 2 persons occupying 6 rooms are over-supplied and thereafter an over-supply is more than 1 extra room per extra person.

The table shows that the proportion of dwellings that are over-crowded has fallen at each census since 1954. The main reason has been a consistent fall in the number of *houses* that are over-crowded. In the case of flats there has been an increase, possibly reflecting the large proportion built since the mid-1950s with open living areas. An increasing proportion of the declining number of 'other private dwellings' are also over-crowded. These are very likely housing some people who find it difficult to afford adequate housing, including Aborigines and old people.

Until 1966 there was a corresponding increase in the proportion of dwellings that were under-used, but that proportion fell in 1971. This might reflect an increasing tendency for people whose children have left home to sell their house and buy a home unit. The slight increase in average room occupancy between 1966 and 1971 is a result of a fall in the number of under-used dwellings rather than an increase in the number that are over-crowded.

Tenure and Housing Costs

Changes in tenure of housing since 1911 were described in Chapter 2. After remaining almost static between the wars, the proportion of dwellings that are owner-occupied increased markedly in the post-war period, from less than one-half to around 70 per cent. Table 6.9 shows that nearly all of the increase occurred between 1947 and 1961. Although there was a slight increase in the first half of the 1960s it was followed by a decrease in the later years of the decade. Up to 1966 it appeared that a new level of saturation was being approached. Some part of the decline since then is probably due to the new households being formed—reflected in the increasing headship rates—most of which would be renters. Even if all of these additional households were renters, the proportion of owner occupants among the others would still have declined by two percentage points. During the post-war period, following the 1945 and subsequent Commonwealth State Housing Agreements, rental housing provided by government housing authorities has also become significant. Privately rented housing declined in relative significance up to 1966, but has since increased marginally. As with previous tables the comparability of 1947 data with the data for later years is limited because of the inclusion of tents, sheds and huts with private houses, and because of some 27 000 private houses, shared by two or more families, which were counted as single dwellings. The effects would probably be to slightly over-state owner occupancy of private houses in 1947.

The table also shows that a much smaller proportion of flats than of houses are owner-occupied, and few of either are rented from government authorities. Up to 1961, when purchasers were distinguished from owners, over 60 per cent of owner-occupants were outright owners, apparently without mortgage debt. The increase in owner-occupancy in the first twenty years after the Second World War can be explained by the taxation, privacy and security advantages of owning rather than renting a home, in a period when incomes and wealth in the community were increasing, and relatively cheap finance facilitated house purchase. The tax advantages of home ownership result from the fact that an owner-occupant receives the rental value of his home—in effect part of his income since it is a return on his investment in the

TABLE 6.9   *Nature of Occupancy of Private Dwellings 1947–1971*

	Owner	Purchaser by instalments	Outright Owner	Govt tenant	Other tenant	Other	Total
Private House							
1947	50.0	8.9	58.9	36.7		4.4	100.0
1954	52.3	16.7	69.0	4.5	23.4	3.1	100.0
1961	51.8	24.9	76.7	4.2	16.5	2.7	100.0
1966	—	—	79.2	5.0	13.5	2.4	100.0
1971	—	—	75.8	5.3	13.9	5.0	100.0
Self-Contained Flat							
1947	9.6	0.5	10.1	88.6		1.4	100.0
1954	12.5	1.4	13.9	3.9	81.0	1.2	100.0
1961	16.5	3.5	20.0	6.4	71.3	2.3	100.0
1966	—	—	21.0	7.9	68.7	2.3	100.0
1971	—	—	20.2	7.5	67.2	5.1	100.0
All Private Dwellings*							
1947	44.7	7.9	52.6	43.4		4.0	100.0
1954	47.9	15.1	63.0	4.2	29.9	2.9	100.0
1961	47.5	22.4	69.9	4.2	23.2	2.6	100.0
1966	—	—	71.4	5.2	21.5	1.9	100.0
1971	—	—	68.6	5.8	22.1	3.4	100.0

Source: Censuses.
* Includes other private dwellings, shared houses, tents, sheds, huts.

house—free of tax. By contrast a landlord must pay income tax on the rental income received, and a tenant's rent payments have to be correspondingly higher than the rental value of an owner-occupant's housing. Someone who decides to rent and invest in shares is taxed on the return on the investment. An owner-occupant is not. The privacy and security of owner-occupation are major attractions. The owner-occupant has an incentive to maintain his own property, and can often carry out maintenance much more cheaply than a landlord who usually has to employ tradesmen. Furthermore an owner-occupant can frequently adapt or add to his house in ways which suit his purposes but which are very difficult if not impossible for a landlord and tenant to negotiate.

In some respects the decision to buy or rent housing is similar to the decision to drive or travel by public transport although it is more difficult to compare changes in costs in the two ways of buying housing than in the two ways of buying travel. Housing usually absorbs more of a family's income and the capital cost of a house is much higher than the cost of a car. As a result interest costs are usually a higher proportion of the total cost of housing.

Changes in rents are indicated in the Consumer Price Index. The costs of home ownership in the index are compiled from data on construction costs, repairs and maintenance, and local government rates and charges. They exclude two of the important costs of home ownership: the cost of house sites and interest on mortgage borrowing (Neutze, 1972b). A more adequate measure would be the price of houses, including sites, and the interest rate on mortgages. The latter is very important in explaining changes in owner-occupation because families usually progress from renting to ownership when their savings and ability to make mortgage payments permit. Interest rates have a direct and almost proportionate effect on mortgage payments. Over a whole family life cycle mortgage payments may not be a high proportion of the total costs of housing, but they loom large when the decision is being made to buy for the first time. They affect the ability of families to get over the initial hurdle to become owners.

Figure 6.3 shows the two main components of the housing section of the CPI, and average weekly earnings. Construction costs increased less rapidly than average earnings, except for a short period in 1974, and rents rose less rapidly throughout the period. During the 1960s construction costs rose less rapidly than rents. About 1972 the position changed. Construction costs accelerated, reflecting the rapid increase in labour costs, and began to increase faster than private rents. On top of this, increased interest rates on working capital were reflected in construction costs. On the other side, private rents were not keeping up with the replacement cost of building new housing. This could be because rents, some of which are subject to rental agreements between landlords and tenants, adjust slowly and because landlords recognise that their tenants could not afford rents high enough to cover replacement costs. Furthermore, landlords may be willing to accept relatively low rents in return for capital gains as their properties appreciate. This change in the relative rate of increase in rents and construction costs, occurring about 1972, cannot explain the fall in home ownership between 1966 and 1971, though it suggests that the fall might have accelerated since 1971. The two costs of home buying which are not included in the CPI house price series might have increased more rapidly than construction costs in the late sixties. Since these two costs—land prices and interest costs—enter into housing costs in different ways they need to be discussed separately.

Interest costs directly affect the ability of prospective buyers to purchase a dwelling. The amount borrowed to purchase a house is multiplied by the interest rate (plus a small repayment factor) to determine regular repayments. Figure 6.4 shows changes in interest rates charged by banks and permanent building societies along with the long-term bond rate. It also shows the constant 3.75 per cent at which loans were made under the War Service Homes Act until 1975, when loans over $12 000 began to attract a higher rate. Interest rates charged by other significant lenders have been closely related to the rates shown. Thus life offices lend at around the overdraft rate or somewhat higher. Terminating building societies get most of their funds from the Federal Government through the Commonwealth States Housing Agreement and from government banks. For most of the period their Agreement funds cost them one per cent less than the long-term bond rate. They lend at rates a little above their borrowing rates. Government housing authorities (the main 'other government' lenders) also borrowed at one per cent less than the bond rate during most of the period, and lent at the same rate plus a small administration charge. Finally finance companies lend at higher rates than any of those shown.

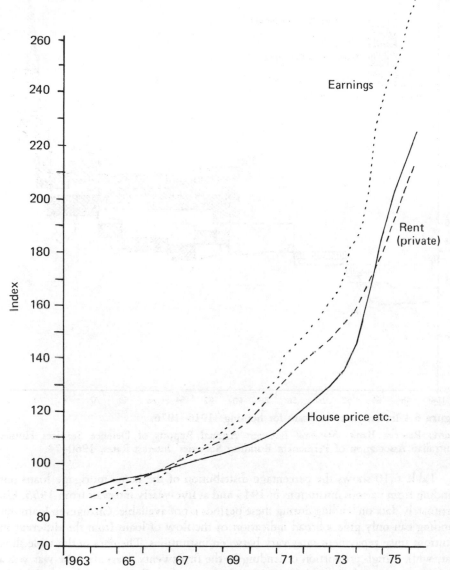

Figure 6.3 Consumer Price Index housing groups and average weekly earnings: 1963–1976 with 1966–67 = 100.

Source: *Labour Reports*.

The figure shows that until the mid-1950s interest rates were low, and trading and savings banks lent at quite similar rates. The move to higher rates in 1956 was accompanied by an increased margin between savings and trading bank lending. During the 1960s rates, especially for overdrafts, edged upwards. The main increase occurred in late 1973 when the low interest rate policy was abandoned.

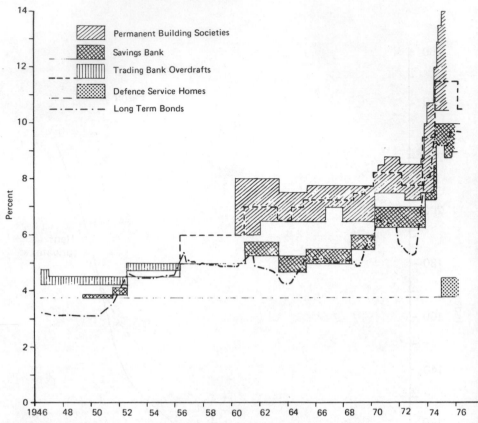

Figure 6.4 Interest rates on loans for housing: 1946–1976.

Source: Reserve Bank, *Statistical Bulletins*: Annual Reports of Defence Services Homes; Australian Association of Permanent Building Societies' Interest Rates, 1960–74.

Table 6.10 shows the percentage distribution of the home mortgage loans outstanding from various institutions in 1945 and at five-yearly intervals from 1955. Unfortunately data on lending during these periods is not available. Changes in loans outstanding can only give a broad indication of the flow of loans from the different institutions since repayment rates vary between institutions. The data in the table show that, while a high proportion of lending in the first twenty years after the war was at low interest rates, during the late 1960s there was a small shift from low to high interest sources. Thus average borrowing rates increased during the 1960s to a greater extent than the changes in any particular interest rate suggest.

The first decade after the war saw an expansion of lending by trading banks, terminating societies and especially the War Service Homes Scheme. During this period trading bank overdraft rates were only marginally above savings bank rates. With the establishment of private savings banks they began to become more important lenders at the expense of trading banks and the other (state) banks. Permanent building societies and life offices were relatively unimportant.

TABLE 6.10   *Housing Advances Outstanding to Individuals: 1945–1974*
(*percentage of total*)

	1945	1955	1960	1965	1970	1974
Savings banks	17	14	16	24	27	27
Major trading banks	13	18	11	9	7	8
Other banks	10	3	8	3	3	3
Permanent building societies	10	6	6	7	14	23
Terminating building societies	13	18	14	13	10	6
Life offices	17	12	11	9	6	4
Finance companies*	—	—	—	6	8	14
War Service Homes	11	24	24	20	13	8
Other Government	9	5	10	9	11	8

Sources: Hill (1974) and Australian Housing Corporation (1976, 63-4).
     Some of the data has been estimated.
*   No data is available before 1965.

During the 1960s terminating societies continued to decline in relative importance, along with life offices, while two of the high-interest lenders—permanent societies and finance companies—grew rapidly. Savings banks also increased their lending but overall there was a shift from low to high interest sources. The main institutional source to decline in importance, the War Service Homes Scheme, lends at the lowest rates. Its decline as a lender was even more pronounced than the decline in advances outstanding suggests, since most of its loans are for long periods. In 1965 high interest lenders (trading and other banks, permanents and life offices) accounted for 34 per cent of loans outstanding. In 1970 the same lenders, together with finance companies, held 38 per cent and by 1974, 52 per cent. The increase in new lending from high-interest sources would be much greater because of the short period for which loans from trading banks and finance companies are usually given. The government policy of requiring savings banks to both borrow and lend at low interest rates forced them to ration their loans to some maximum sum. As a result many buyers were forced to borrow from sources charging higher interest rates.

Since 1970 all interest rates have increased substantially with inflation. As Bromilow (1975) has pointed out, this has reduced the percentage of families who can afford to meet the repayments on a loan large enough to finance the purchase of an average house. As a result families wishing to become home owners in the 1970s face high costs and this could have caused a further fall in the proportion of owner-occupants.

The other component of the cost of buying a house that is not included in the CPI is the cost of a site. Unfortunately the data available on land prices before the mid-1960s is very sparse. The price of sites on which houses financed by War Service Homes loans have been built has been used (Neutze, 1972b), despite the disadvantage that many of the sites are purchased some years before the building takes place. Auc-

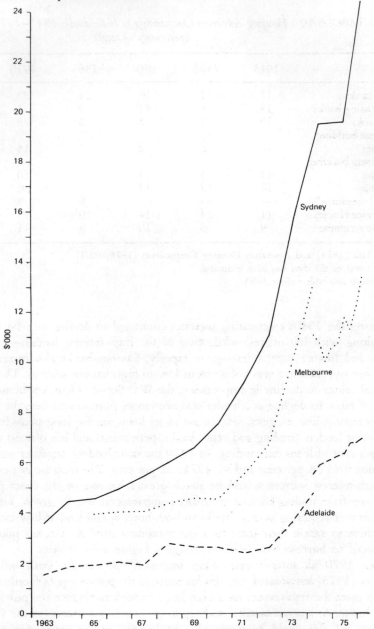

Figure 6.5 House site prices, Sydney, Melbourne, Adelaide: 1963–1976.

Note: March 1976 data for Melbourne and Adelaide are provisional.

Sources: Sydney: Philip Shrapnel & Co. Pty Ltd. Melbourne: 1963 to March 1974, Philip Shrapnel & Co. Pty Ltd; March 1974 to March 1976, Valuer General, land sales in 'developing areas' which account for 75 per cent of sales. Adelaide: 1963 to March 1974, Philip Shrapnel & Co. Pty Ltd; March 1974 to March 1976, Valuation Department, land sales in five outer developing areas.

tion price data for Sydney, Melbourne and Adelaide collected by Philip Shrapnel, consultants, seems likely to reflect price movements more adequately (DURD, 1974b). A 12-month moving average of median house-site prices is plotted for June of each year in Figure 6.5. More complete data for a number of outer suburban areas in Melbourne and Adelaide for each quarter since March 1974 is also included on the graph.

Land prices in Sydney increased somewhat faster than construction costs in the 1960s, but in Melbourne and Adelaide there was no significant difference. A boom in Adelaide in 1967 and 1968 was followed by a period of stability. Although precise data is not available for Perth, prices collected by John Worthington at the West Australian Institute of Technology (unpublished) show a pronounced boom in the mid-1960s, peaking in 1968–69, followed by a period of stable prices. It was not until 1971 in Melbourne and 1973 in Adelaide that prices began to rise very quickly. There was a period of stability in 1974–75 while restrictions on credit were in force but by early 1976 prices were rising rapidly again in Sydney and Melbourne, despite the low level of activity in the building industry.

The combined effect of construction costs and land costs can be seen in the prices of houses in the same three cities. Like the land prices they are derived from Philip Shrapnel's 12-month moving averages of monthly median auction prices of houses up to 1974, and more comprehensive sources since then (Figure 6.6). As with land prices, housing prices in Melbourne and Adelaide prior to 1973 increased only a little faster than construction costs. In Sydney, however, they started to take off as early as 1968.

Another interesting comparison is between prices and average earnings. Earnings increased somewhat faster than either construction costs or rents, less rapidly than Sydney land and house prices, but at about the same rate as house and land prices in Melbourne and Adelaide up to 1973. One way in which this comparison can be made more precise is by estimating the number of years of average earnings required to buy a house. This is shown for four areas of Sydney in Figure 6.7 and four similar areas in Melbourne in Figure 6.8. Data on prices in particular suburbs reflect changes in those suburbs as well as changes in the general level of house prices. Suburbs like Bankstown in the 1950s and Liverpool in the 1960s changed from being on the fringe of development to becoming fully developed. For this reason prices in such suburbs would be expected to rise faster than the general price level. Similarly the demand for housing in North Melbourne, St Kilda and Redfern received a major boost from the influx of southern European migrants during the 1950s. This local effect is even more marked in the case of house sites. Worthington has recorded increases of 15 to 23 per cent per year compound for particular developing fringe suburbs in Perth.

These figures confirm the difference between Sydney and Melbourne. House prices in all four areas in Melbourne declined relative to earnings during the 1960s whereas in Sydney increases occurred in two of the four suburbs in the early years and in the other two areas the levels remained stable. It is of interest to compare changes in owner-occupancy between 1966 and 1971 in the three urban areas for which we have house price data. In all three the proportion of houses and flats that were owner-occupied fell by between 5.2 and 5.7 per cent. This suggests that owner-occupancy is not very sensitive to differences in the rate of change of prices.

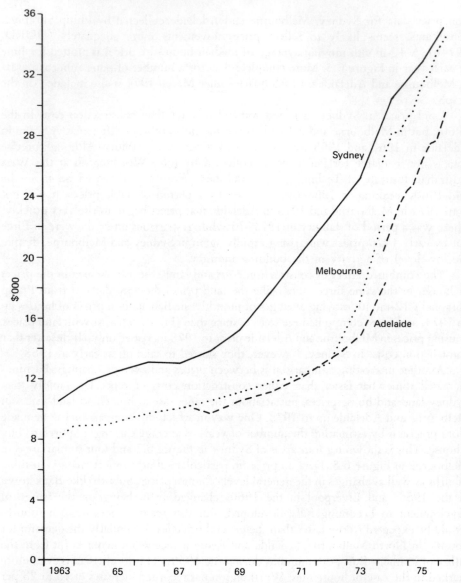

Figure 6.6 House prices, Sydney, Melbourne, Adelaide: 1963–1976.

Note: March 1976 data for Melbourne and Adelaide are provisional.

Sources: Sydney: Philip Shrapnel & Co. Pty Ltd. Melbourne: 1963 to March 1974, Philip Shrapnel & Co. Pty Ltd; March 1974 to March 1976, Valuer General, house sales in Melbourne Statistical Division. Adelaide: 1967 to March 1974, Philip Shrapnel & Co. Pty Ltd; March 1974 to March 1976, Valuer General house sales for Adelaide Statistical Division.

A further factor which reduced the ability of households to save for house purchase and to meet repayments was the increasing percentage of income taken in income tax. An adult male on average earnings in 1954–55, with a dependent wife and two dependent children, paid 5 per cent of his earnings in tax. By 1960–61 this had risen to 7.3 per cent, to 13.9 per cent in 1970–71 and 17.3 per cent in 1974–75. Despite this, his after-tax earnings increased more rapidly than either private rents or construction costs. The relatively small effect of tax changes can be seen in Figure 6.9.

In summary, although the costs of buying a house increased more rapidly than construction costs, they probably did not increase as rapidly as average earnings in the 1960s, except in Sydney and during short parts of the decade in Adelaide and Perth. Since 1971 costs have increased more rapidly than average earnings, mainly becuase of inflation in land prices and higher interest rates.

The comparison between Sydney and other cities shows that high house prices do not directly have a large effect on owner-occupancy. Many of the costs of buying a house are also found in rents. Investors in rental property have to pay similar costs for sites and construction and have to pay higher interest on borrowed funds than owner-occupants. Their interest rates have also increased. Because the historic costs faced by many landlords are lower than current replacement costs, there is often a lag in the adjustment of rents to increased costs, but in the long run rents would be expected to move in much the same way as the costs of owning. There may be some divergences because of the cost of collecting rents and the higher cost landlords usually have to pay for maintenance. However, if rents fall below the cost of providing new rental accommodation, new building for renting will slow down and some landlords will sell to owner-occupants. A shortage of rental accommodation will result, and rents will rise to a level where investors can again get an acceptable return on thier investment.

The fall in rents relative to house prices in 1973 and 1974 is largely responsible for the dramatic fall in flat building in 1975.[1] This may result in a shortage of rental accommodation. As a result, despite rapid increases in the cost of home ownership since 1972, there may not have been a large increase in the proportion of families renting. Capital gains from investment could attract more funds into rental housing in the following way, however.

When inflation produces high interest rates the effect is to force borrowers to repay the real value of their loans more quickly. In return it offers a larger capital gain to the borrower on his investment. Most borrowers cannot afford to meet the high interest rates but investors with their own funds to invest may well be attracted to an investment that yields more of its return as a capital gain and less as a regular periodic return, especially if they operate on a sufficiently small scale to avoid tax on their capital gains. Despite the recent high interest rates investors have found it difficult to maintain the real value of their assets. One of the best ways to do so is to buy real property such as rental housing. Such investors would be interested in the capital gains which allow them to protect the value of their assets and may accept quite a low current rate of return. As inflation accelerated in the late 1960s and the early 1970s more equity capital of this kind might have been invested in rental housing. If there is

---

[1] This fall was not fully reflected in completions in 1974–75, shown in Figure 6.1. Between 1973–74 and 1974–75 commencements of flats fell by 38 per cent while commencements of houses fell by 24 per cent.

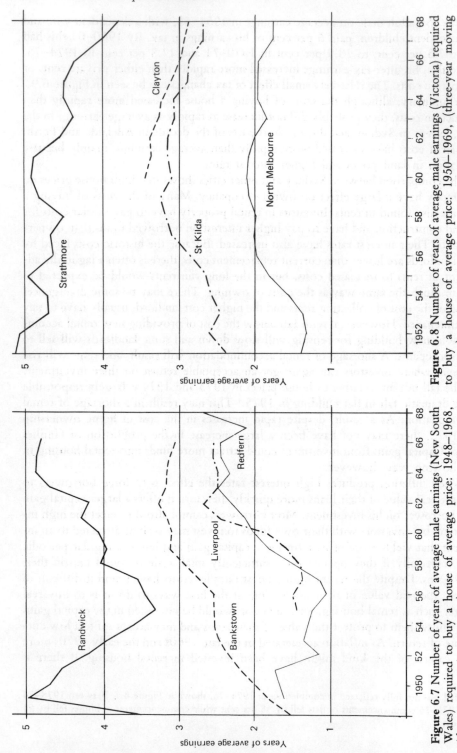

Figure 6.7 Number of years of average male earnings (New South Wales) required to buy a house of average price: 1948–1968, (three-year moving averages).

Source: Sales price data collected from New South Wales Valuer-General's valuation rolls.

Figure 6.8 Number of years of average male earnings (Victoria) required to buy a house of average price: 1950–1969, (three-year moving averages).

Source: Sales price data collected from council valuation records.

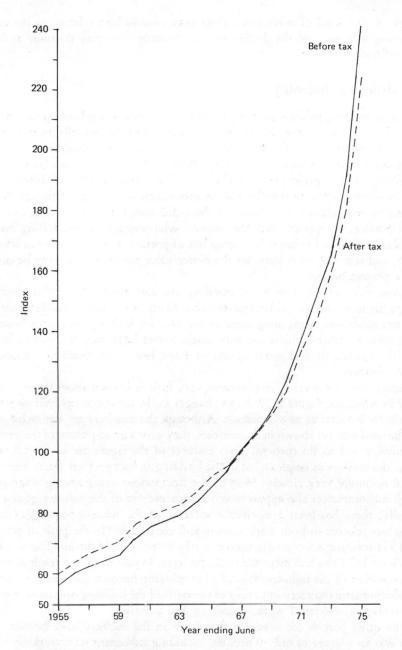

Figure 6.9 Average male earnings before and after tax: 1955–1975, with 1966–67 = 100.

Note: Calculated for a man with dependent wife and two dependent children.

Source: *Labour Reports* and *Year Books*.

enough of that kind of investment, rents may remain low relative to the costs of purchasing a home, and the decline in owner-occupation may continue as long as rapid inflation continues.

The Building Industry

The house building industry includes a number of different kinds of operations (Hutton, 1970). The speculative builder builds houses and flats and sells them after completion. An alternative is for the owner of a site to engage a builder to construct a custom-built house on his land, or for an owner to build on his own land, engaging subcontractors. The project home builder builds a limited number of different house plans for clients, either on their land or on sites which he provides. Although there are no data on the relative importance of these different kinds of builders, except the owner-builder, it appears that the owner who engages a builder to build an individually-designed house is becoming less important. Only the rich can afford the luxury, and many of them settle for the better value-for-money that can be obtained from a project builder.

Some firms engaged in home building are also involved in related activities. Perhaps the most common is land subdivision. Many of the largest builders buy broad acres and subdivide them, using some of the sites for building their own houses and selling some to other builders and individuals. Other large builders produce building materials, operate as real estate agents or have links with building societies that provide finance.

Apart from the level of employment very little is known about the building industry in Australia. Figure 6.10 shows changes in the number employed on jobs carried out by builders of new buildings. Although the numbers are somewhat smaller than the total number shown in the censuses, they give a good picture of the growth of the industry and its fluctuations. Two features of the figure are of special interest. Firstly, fluctuations in employment in the building industry follow fluctuations in the general economy very closely. Most of the fluctuations occur among wage earners, though subcontractors also appear to move into and out of the industry quite readily. Secondly, there has been a significant increase in the relative importance of subcontractors relative to both wage earners and contractors. In the peak of activity in June 1951 subcontractors accounted for nearly 11 per cent of the building workforce, but in June 1974 this had increased to 23 per cent. In part this was a result of a change in organisation of the industry. Instead of employing his own tradesmen a contractor gets subcontractors to carry out many of the parts of the building operation, for example bricklaying, electrical work, plumbing and painting.

The other part of the reason is that firms in the industry have become larger. There was an average of only 9 persons, including subcontractors, working for each contractor in June 1951 compared with 12 in 1974. However, the size of building operations remains small—in 1968–69 only 25 of the 3792 house builders operating in Sydney took out permits for more than 100 houses (Housing Industry Association, 1970), though they accounted for 40.5 per cent of all permits issued. This percentage increased between 1967–68 and 1970–71 (Vandermark and Harrison, 1972). Flat

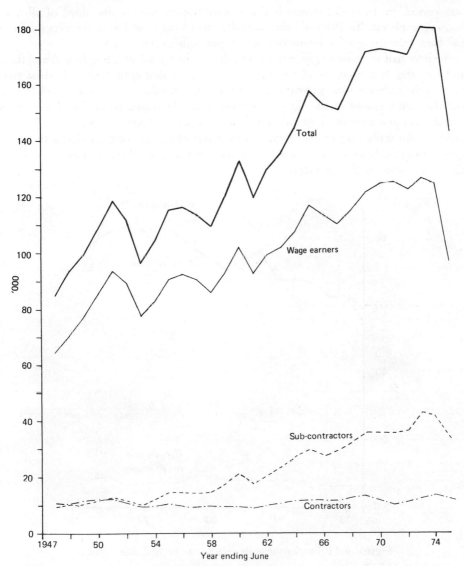

Figure 6.10 The building workforce: 1947–1975.
Source: ABS, *Building and Construction*.

building was also in the hands of small firms. Only 19 builders took out permits for more than 100 dwellings and they accounted for only 21 per cent of all permits. This may understate the importance of the large operator, since firms often form separate companies for particular developments, especially for home units.

Of the 3792 house builders in Sydney in 1968–69, 2263 were owner-builders who were building their own houses, and accounted in that year for 15 per cent of all permits issued. The owner-builder has become much less important during the post-war period. In 1951–52 owner-builders were responsible for one-third of all new houses completed. By 1964–65 this had fallen to 13 per cent, but more recently there has been something of a recovery—to 18 per cent in 1974–75.

About half of those engaged in the building industry are building houses and flats, and the other half other buildings. Figure 6.11 shows that employment in these two parts of the industry have grown at about the same rate during the 1960s and 1970s, but that employment in dwelling construction has fluctuated more sharply, perhaps because construction of most non-residential buildings takes a long time. Because many of the skills required to build factories and offices are different from those required to build houses it may not be possible for many workers to transfer between these two parts of the industry.

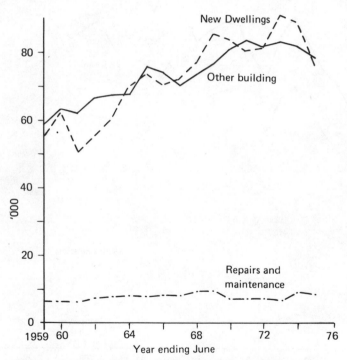

Figure 6.11 Employment in sectors of the building industry: 1959–1975.

Note: Includes only those working for builders of new buildings.

Source: ABS, *Building and Construction*.

There has been a considerable increase in the use of manufactured materials, parts and components in the industry. Ready-mixed concrete, pre-cut frames, factory-made joinery and plumbing components are all produced in factories. On the other hand industrialisation of a more radical kind to produce houses, or even rooms or panels for on-site assembly, has not made a great deal of progress, partly because of the high transport cost and partly because of the high overhead costs (Burkitt, 1974).

Government and Housing

Probably the main objective of governments' housing policy is to ensure that all families can get housing of an acceptable standard. Families that cannot afford to buy housing in the market should be assisted in some way. Other objectives have also been pursued, including home ownership, regional development, and slum clearance (Jones, 1972). Sometimes these objectives have come into conflict, especially when scarce capital resources have to be allocated between different kinds of housing for different groups and in different locations. The measures adopted by governments include building of housing, provision of finance for housing on favourable terms and favouring home owners in tax legislation.

Public housing began in Australia with the passing of an Act in Queensland in 1909 for provision of subsidised housing for workers. Within the next ten years the other states followed. For the most part these schemes provided new housing for those who could afford to buy. During the 1930s and early 1940s a strong housing reform movement resulted in the establishment of housing authorities in all states to improve the housing conditions of the poor. A Commonwealth Housing Commission was established in 1943 and its report (1944) led to the first Commonwealth State Housing Agreement in 1945, which significantly increased the funds available to the state housing authorities by providing loans from the Commonwealth at 1 per cent less than the long-term bond rate.

The funds provided under the Agreement were to be used for rental housing for families who met a means test. There was also provision for rebates for those who could not afford the 'economic' rent for the dwellings built under the agreement. From 1956, by which time the immediate post-war housing shortage had mostly been overcome, changes were introduced into new Agreements. Perhaps the most important was that home ownership was to be encouraged, both by the sale of houses built by the authorities to eligible families or to tenants, on attractive terms, and by the diversion of 30 per cent of the funds allocated to housing under the Agreement through the Home Builders Account to co-operative (terminating) building societies for lending to home buyers.

There has been considerable diversity in how the states used Agreement funds, and even more in how they used their own state funds. For example, Victoria has put more of its funds into redevelopment, often at high density, whereas South Australia used state funds to provide housing for middle-income families. From 1956 to 1973 considerable differences appeared in the means tests applied by the various states, but the 1973 Agreement specified the maximum income for a family to be eligible. Once a family is admitted to public housing it can stay there: no further means test is applied.

From their inception just before or during the Second World War until June 1973, the housing authorities in the six states built 379 000 houses and flats. On 30 June 1973 they had 191 000 rent-paying tenants. Almost exactly half of the dwellings completed had been sold. One in ten of the houses and flats in the six states in 1971 had been built by a housing authority. Up to June 1973 the proportions of dwellings completed by the authorities in each state that had been sold were as follows:

	Per cent
New South Wales	38.3
Victoria	45.8
Queensland	59.3
South Australia	52.6
Western Australia	59.1
Tasmania	67.1

Comparable data is not available for the Territories, where government authorities have built a higher proportion of the housing (see Figure 6.12), although sales have been much more common in the A.C.T. than in the Northern Territory. Between June 1960 and June 1973 the number of government dwellings completed in the Northern Territory was 6949, but the increase in the number of tenants was only 3731 (53.7 per cent). The comparable figures for the A.C.T. were 12 273 completions and 1928 more tenants (15.7 per cent). These percentages are not direct measures of retention since some of the dwellings that were rented in 1960 would have been sold between 1960 and 1973.

In the ten years from July 1963 to June 1973, 45 656 dwellings were built with Housing Agreement funds paid through the Home Builders Account and co-operative housing societies, compared with 156 308 by all government housing authorities, of which 105 234 were built by State Housing Authorities under the Housing Agreements.

Figure 6.12 shows the proportions of houses and flats completed by governments in each state and territory in the 20-year period from 1955–56. Nearly all have been built by the state housing authorities: in the period 1969–70 to 1972–73 over 95 per cent. Over the period covered by the diagram there has been a large and almost continuous decline in the relative importance of the public sector in housing. Data calculated by Jones (1972, 16), covering only the state housing authorities, show that the peak in the public contribution to construction occurred in the mid-1950s. In the late 1940s and early 1950s the public component had been about 16 to 18 per cent.

States vary greatly in the relative importance of the public sector in housing. Apart from the Territories, South Australia, until its policy changed in 1968, was the state with the largest public share in housing construction. Since 1968 it has ceased to build outside the low income housing range and consequently has fallen behind Western Australia and Tasmania in terms of market penetration. The differences between states derive mainly from the different policy objectives of state governments (Jones, 1972).

The Defence Services Homes Scheme began in 1918, to 'make provision for Homes for Australian Soldiers and female dependents of Australian Soldiers' (Defence Services Homes Act, 1918–1975). The scheme aims primarily to provide finance to servicemen (or their widows, or widowed mothers) who served Australia overseas in two world wars and in Korea, Malaysia and Vietnam. In 1973 eligibility was extended to those who served in the armed services during peace time.

The main feature of the scheme is the provision of long-term low interest loans for the purchase of a house. The interest rate charged has usually been lower than the rate at which funds could be obtained from any other source, but often the maximum

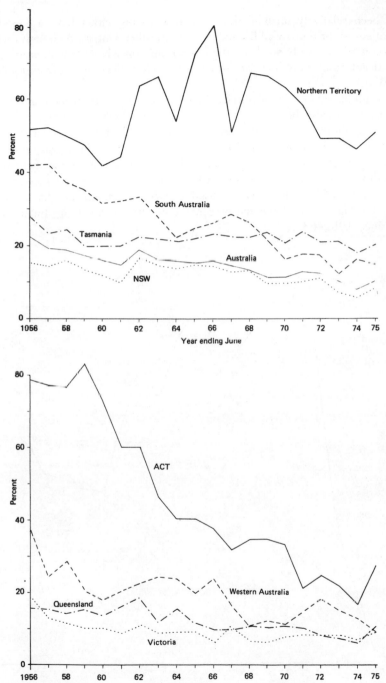

Figure 6.12 Percentage of houses and flats completed by government: 1955–56 to 1974–75.

Source: ABS, *Building and Construction*.

loan has been relatively small so that a borrower must either have a considerable amount of equity or borrow additional sums from other sources. Although each eligible person is allowed only one loan, there is no limit on when the loan must be taken up. Significant numbers of loans are still being made to servicemen from the Second World War.

Although lending for home purchase has been the most significant contribution of the scheme it has also been used to purchase land which was subsequently made available to applicants. In the 1920s the Commissioner built houses in large numbers. Up to 1930, 40 930 homes were financed under the Act. There was little activity during the depression and the war, but after the war there was a rapid increase in activity, as shown in Figure 6.13. Many of the loans were for the purchase of existing dwellings. Up to December 1975 a total of 359 068 home purchases had been financed. The figure also shows the percentage of all new dwellings financed under the Act since 1962–63.

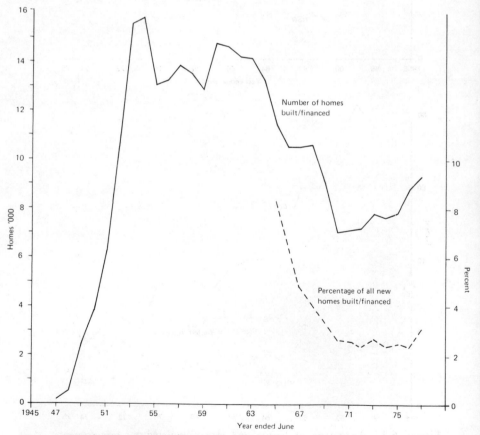

Figure 6.13 Defence Services homes built/financed: 1945–1975.
Source: Australian Housing Corporation (1976, 62).

Under the Aged Persons Homes Act, 1954, funds have been made available to non-profit bodies and local governments for housing for aged persons. Even before 1969, most state authorities made housing available to pensioners at heavily rebated rents, but in that year further housing assistance for this purpose was made available to the states by the Commonwealth Government.

A home savings grant scheme, which came into operation in 1964, offered young couples a grant of $1 for each $3 saved with a financial institution which allocated at least 20 per cent of its annual lending to housing. Other ways in which the government has acted to encourage home ownership include a limited tax deductability of mortgage interest introduced in 1974–75, establishment of home loans insurance, and controls over interest rates at which savings banks lend for housing. This latter has been an important advantage for those who can get loans from savings banks, but it has resulted in savings banks having to ration their loans, and in the emergence of building societies as competitive saving and lending institutions. It has also required the savings banks to pay low interest rates, which has probably limited the ability of many families on low incomes to accumulate the savings necessary to buy a home.

From a strong emphasis on helping poorer families to get adequate rental housing, government housing policy has moved to an increasing emphasis on helping people to become home owners. At a time when housing costs and interest rates made it possible for many lower-income families to buy a house this policy was not particularly regressive in its effects, especially if it was accompanied by a strong welfare housing policy. However, when the cost movements described earlier in the chapter began to limit the ability of many families to buy, policies to encourage home ownership relative to renting increasingly helped only those who were wealthy enough to take advantage of them. While these other policies have been expanded, the welfare role of the housing authorities has tended to contract.

Summary

There was a rapid improvement in housing standards in Australia in the first twenty years after the Second World War. This was a time of vigorous home building— mainly houses in the early part of the period but increasing numbers of flats after about 1958. The proportion of homes that were owner-occupied increased, larger homes were built and occupancy rates fell. A significant contribution to the improvement in housing standards was made by government housing authorities, which built from 15 to 20 per cent of the new dwellings and rented them to low income families. After 1956 the authorities also contributed to the increase in owner-occupation by selling houses to their tenants on generous terms. Other government policies on interest rates, taxation and the provision of loan funds to co-operative housing societies also boosted owner-occupation.

In the decade since 1966 progress in housing has been slowed and there are some signs of a fall in standards. Government housing authorities have played a decreasing role in construction, owner-occupation has become slightly less common and the number of occupants per room has increased slightly. On the other hand increasing numbers of families and individuals are establishing separate households. The main reason for the change since the period before 1966 is that housing costs are rising more rapidly relative to income. Land prices and mortgage interest rates have been the main contributor to increased costs. By the mid-1970s the house-building industry was in a very depressed state with costs in excess of returns from investment in housing. It seems likely that these economic conditions will cause a further fall in the proportion of Australian families who own their own home.

7 Investment in Urban Development

The previous chapters have been mainly concerned with the results of urban development. They have described the development of Australian cities over a long time period, concentrating on those changes in conditions which influenced the shape of cities and changed the living conditions of residents. The suburbanisation, first of residential development, and then of retailing, manufacturing, wholesaling and some service jobs were at the centre of attention. From one point of view, however, urban development is building houses, shops and factories, providing them with transport, 'wire and pipe' services, and providing residents with health, recreation and education services. This chapter looks at urban development as investment carried out by private firms, government authorities and non-profit organisations. It shows the relative importance of the main parts, where it is occurring and how it is financed. The next chapter takes up in more detail the role of government in urban development, both as a provider of services and as the instrument through which communities decide how they will develop.

One of the important policy issues in urban development is how to pay for it. The previous chapter showed how the difficulty of financing housing is placing strains on what appeared to be a satisfactory system until a few years ago. One reason is that authorities responsible for servicing have found it difficult to finance and pay for the services demanded by growing city populations, and have charged some of the costs to land developers. This chapter assesses the magnitude of the problem by estimating the level of investment in urban development, and describing how it is financed at present. Investment in urban development also has to compete with other demands on funds for investment and sometimes is restricted when the general level of investment is curtailed. The estimates that follow begin to provide a framework for assessing the effects of such policy measures.

Measuring the Level of Investment

If urban development is looked at as investment, it should be possible to measure it in dollars. Apart from growth in the population of a city and the jobs it provides, and (with more difficulty) growth in the area it covers, quantitative measures of urban development are scarce. Table 7.1 contains an estimate of the investment in urban development in Australia during the four-year period from July 1970 to June 1974. This section of the chapter describes how these estimates were derived and some of the difficulties in making them. There are two major problems in measuring the dollar value of investment in urban development. The first is a difficulty in principle. Does urban development comprise only investment that occurs within urban areas, or does it also include investment outside the urban boundaries that is necessary to serve the urban population? Using the former definition gives the unusual result that a city which generates its electric power within its boundaries has more investment in development than one whose generators are located on a nearby coalfield. The latter definition makes it difficult to decide just what to include. For example, how much

TABLE 7.1   *Composition of Investment in Urban Development:*
1970–71 to 1973–74

	$ m	Percentage of total
1. Land development	2 180	10.4¹
2. Government services		
Sewerage, drainage, sanitation	1 023	4.9
Water supply	658	3.1
Electricity* and gas	400	1.9
Roads	1 384	6.6
Rail	20	0.1
Airports	123	0.6
Ports and harbours	251	1.2
Education	958	4.6
Hospitals and health services	406	1.9
Communications	1 367	6.5
Open space	127	0.6
	6 717	31.9
3. Housing and other buildings		
Houses	5 843	27.8
Other dwellings	1 681	8.0
Hotels and hostels	352	1.7
Shops	533	2.5
Factories	1 007	4.8
Offices and other business	1 889	9.0
Religion	54	0.3
Entertainment and recreation	305	1.5
Miscellaneous buildings	471	2.2
	12 131	57.7
Total Urban	21 028	100.0
Total Gross Fixed Capital Formation	40 236	
Urban as a percentage of total	52	

Source: See text.
* Distribution only.

urban-rural, or indeed inter-city, transport services are needed to serve the urban populations. This chapter is confined to investment within urban areas.

The second is a practical difficulty. Apart from new houses and other buildings, and the capital expenditures of local governments, very little data is available on *where* investment takes place. The rural-urban distribution of capital expenditure by state governments is rarely recorded. Although some efforts have been made to produce a set of regional accounts for government expenditure they have so far been only experimental (DURD, 1975, 85–6).

A useful criterion for deciding what kind of investment constitutes urban development is the type of asset created. Since urban development is site works and buildings rather than plant and equipment, a financial criterion might be appropriate in the private sector. Investment in urban development creates assets which can be used as security for mortgage borrowing—put another way, urban development creates real property assets rather than moveable assets. In the public sector this criterion is less helpful. Electricity substations and sewer mains cannot be mortgaged, and investment in moveable assets such as buses and suburban railway rolling stock might be regarded as part of urban development. As far as possible we confine ourselves to buildings, construction and site works in both the private and the public sector.

We are interested in gross investment rather than net investment because both redevelopment, and development of vacant or agricultural land, are important ways of changing cities. Cities can grow by using the areas they occupy more intensively and by spreading into new areas at their fringes: colloquially, they can grow both up and out. Depreciation, which accounts for the difference between gross and net investment, is difficult to estimate for many buildings and for site works. A building is usually replaced when its site becomes more valuable for some other kind of building. The depreciated value of a building depends more on the value of the site for other purposes than on the age or physical condition of the building. Depreciation due to age and obsolescence is more important for some public service capital investments such as water and sewer pipes and pumps, and electricity and telephone installations which do not occupy much land. But even those service installations, which are usually fixed in location and serve localised consumers, are as likely to be replaced because of a change in land use in the areas they serve as because they are worn out or obsolete.

In the following discussion, investment in urban development is described in two parts which often occur in sequence. The first is development and servicing of land, including the provision of those services which are provided to properties rather than individuals. The second is construction of buildings for housing, employment and services. Information about investment in land development and servicing is sketchy, but investment in buildings, especially dwellings, is recorded much more fully.

Development and Servicing of Land

There is only fragmentary evidence available about the volume of investment in land development and servicing. Data for Canberra give some indication of the order of magnitude of the total private and public costs involved. The data are from *Annual Reports* of the National Capital Development Commission and *1975–76 Budget Paper No. 9* (p.23). From July 1970 to June 1974 sites were created for 19 200 dwellings in

Canberra—mostly single family housing—as well as for shops, offices and local industries. During that period $73.9 millions was spent on land development, which includes reticulation of water and sewerage, local access roads and drainage, but excludes headworks costs; an average of $3850 per dwelling site. The figure is probably somewhat high because the rate of land development was increasing during the period (3530 dwelling sites in 1970–71 to 6561 in 1973–74) and some of the investment in 1973–74 related to sites which were completed in later years. Cost levels were also increasing due to inflation during the period. On the other hand, costs in Canberra are widely believed to be lower than in other cities due to the large contracts that are let for complete land development. An average figure of $3500 per dwelling would probably be conservative. In February 1975 the costs of servicing a site for a new house was estimated by the National Capital Development Commission, as a basis for setting site prices, at $5000.

During 1970–71 to 1973–74, 623 000 dwellings were commenced in Australia. This would suggest that the total national investment in land development would have been of the order of $550 million per year, or about 5.5 per cent of gross fixed capital formation. This estimate assumes that enough sites were developed during this four-year period to replace those used up when dwellings were commenced. We know in fact that stocks of developed housing sites were being run down in several cities (Paterson, 1974; DURD, 1974b). Nevertheless, this estimate shows the replacement cost of sites used for building, although some of the dwelling commencements were outside urban areas. During this period some 84 per cent of the dwellings completed in Australia were located in the seven capital city statistical divisions alone.

The estimate may be too high because the cost of developing land for flats is lower than for houses, and flats (more precisely 'dwellings other than houses') comprised 29 per cent of dwelling commencements in Australia compared with only 11 per cent in the A.C.T. On the other hand no separate estimate is made of the cost of developing industrial or commercial land, which would be more important outside the A.C.T. In the period 1967–72 in Sydney 157 hectares were used for industrial development each year (AIUS, 1975). This compares with about 1500 ha per year needed for house sites.

Other Government Services

The dividing line between land development and the provision of public services in urban areas is unclear and has varied over time and between different areas. In an assessment of the level of investment in urban services there will be some duplication of investments that have already been counted since their cost is *recovered from* land developers. The measures of public sector capital formation do not include, as a general rule, the value of public assets created *by* private developers, and the extent of overlap is difficult to determine.

Although the costs of land development are quite closely related to the number of dwelling sites produced, other capital costs are incurred by service authorities to cater for population growth and to meet the demand for increased levels of services for the existing population. Table 7.2 shows for Canberra the costs of basic community services. In a rapidly growing city like Canberra most of the investment is required to service population growth. Therefore the data are also expressed in dollars per additional person. The table excludes postal and telephone services, which require large capital investments.

TABLE 7.2   *Public Capital Expenditure on Basic Services in the A.C.T.:*
1970–71 to 1973–74

	Total expenditure over 4 years ($m)	Expenditure per additional person ($)
Land development	73.9	1496
Utilities: Water supply	8.2	166
Sewerage	12.2	247
Electricity*	7.4	150
Town services†	4.4	89
Local transport: Roads	30.8	623
Public transport	6.8	138
Recreational and cultural facilities	5.0	101
Social services: Schools, colleges	43.8	887
Hospitals, health services	26.9	545
Other	0.7	14
General services	6.6	134
Professional fees, etc. (part)	12.5	253
Total	$239.2m	$4842

Source: Calculated from Table 6 in *1975-76 Budget Paper No.9*, and NCDC *Annual Reports*.
* Reticulation only.
† Includes garbage and sanitation, storm water drainage, emergency services, control of animals, public rest rooms, cemeteries, etc.

A similar estimate of costs of government services for urban development was made for Melbourne between 1953–54 and 1965–66 (Paterson, 1970; 1975). As a study of government costs it excludes land development costs borne by private developers. Councils in Melbourne were empowered to require developers to pay for water reticulation from 1962, and to lend 80 per cent of the capital cost of sewerage to the Board of Works until the catchment area was close to fully developed. Dr Paterson's figures do not distinguish services that are a part of land development from other services. His gross cost of urban public services per additional person from 1960–61 to 1965–66, when electricity generation is omitted, was $2769, of which 13 per cent was due to telephones. He used a crude method to allocate the capital expenditure between the part required to cater for growth in use of the services by existing users (25 per cent) and the part needed to cater for population increase (75 per cent). In Canberra population growth would have been an even more important element of the cost because it was more rapid. The resulting figure for Melbourne for 1960–61 to 1965–66 was $2061 per additional person, compared with an unadjusted gross $3855 in Canberra (excluding land development, but adjusted upward to allow for telephones). Prices increased by nearly 40 per cent between the two periods so that it seems likely that investment costs in Melbourne would have been $2900 per additional person by the early 1970s.

Capital investment per additional person appears to have been lower in Melbourne, especially since some elements of land development are included. In part this may have been because investment in Melbourne's capital plant, at least in water, sewerage and major roads, probably lagged behind increased demands during this period, but the figures are not sufficiently accurate to permit a detailed comparison.

Some idea of the level of investment in urban services can be gained by assuming an expenditure of $3500 per person added to the Australian population, and (following Paterson) adding 33 per cent for additional demands by the existing population. Since substantially all of the population increase in Australia occurred in urban areas this would suggest a total gross capital formation of $975 millions per year, or about 9.75 per cent of gross fixed capital formation. If, relying mainly on Canberra data, we regard this as additional to land development, it would follow that 15 per cent of gross capital formation takes the form of land development and the provision of public services.

National accounting estimates of public capital formation by function can also be used to derive some estimates of investment in urban development. Again there will be some double counting of costs included as land development. We use data for the same four years where possible and apply it to the financial division found in *1975–76 Budget Paper No. 9*. These estimates are summarised in the second and third parts of Table 7.1.

1. Sewerage, drainage and sanitation Capital expenditure amounted to:

1970-71	$190.9m
1971-72	$231.0m
1972-73	$277.9m
1973-74	$322.5m
	$1022.3m

There is no way of separating urban from non-urban expenditure included in this total but the large majority seems likely to be urban.

2. Water supply. Since the early 1960s water supply has absorbed a decreasing proportion of public capital expenditure. A rather larger proportion of this expenditure will be for farm water supply. The national totals were:

1970-71	$127.1m
1971-72	$152.0m
1972-73	$180.5m
1973-74	$198.5m
	$658.1m

During this period the capital expenditure of the Sydney Metropolitan Water, Sewerage and Drainage Board (which serves Sydney and Wollongong) on water, sewerage and drainage ranged from $100m to $130m, which suggests that most of the capital expenditure on both water and sewerage and drainage occurred in urban areas.

3. **Electricity and gas** The national total public capital expenditure has been very large. Private expenditure in this area, mainly in gas supply, has also been significant.

	Government	Private
1970-71	$422.3m	$10
1971-72	$409.3m	$11
1972-73	$419.5m	n.a.
1973-74	$436.9m	n.a.
	$1688.0m	n.a.

Much of the expenditure is on generation and transmission outside urban areas, though it is difficult to judge how much. Paterson's estimates for Melbourne were that about three-quarters of the capital expenditure is for generating capacity. This is consistent with data from the Victorian State Electricity Commission's annual reports showing that about a quarter of fixed capital expenditure is on distribution. Allocating the investment in proportion to population would imply that an average of about $90m per year was invested in the distribution network for electricity in urban areas. To this should be added $10m per year of capital expenditure on gas supply, which is all assumed to be in urban areas. Both estimates are, of course, based on a geographic definition of investment in urban development, and assume that none of the new generating capacity was provided in urban areas.

4. **Roads** The Commonwealth Bureau of Roads (1973, 127) has made an estimate of expenditure on urban roads for three of the four years in our period. Applying the urban-rural division of the third year to the fourth year as well gives the following:

1970-71	$291.7m
1971-72	$320.3m
1972-73	$364.4m
1973-74	$407.5m
	$1383.9m

5. **Rail Services** There is no objective way to divide the total capital expenditure on rail services between urban and rural areas. Most of the construction investment has been replacement rather than expansion during this period, though construction of the Melbourne Underground Loop commenced and work proceeded on the Eastern Suburbs Railway in Sydney. A considerable amount of new rolling stock was purchased for suburban services, but this should be omitted on the criterion that has been adopted. On the other hand signalling improvements, track duplication and the like in urban areas should be included. Total capital expenditure on rail services was between $137m and $155m per year, but only a small proportion was clearly investment in urban development.[1] Only a token $5m per year has been included in the summary table for investment in rail services in urban areas.

6. **Urban Public Transport** Apart from rail services, urban public transport accounted for capital expenditure of $10–13m per year. Since nearly all would have

[1] The Annual Report of the Commissioner for Railways in N.S.W. reported that $12m was spent on the Eastern Suburbs Railway in 1971–72.

been for the acquisition of new buses and perhaps trams, it has not been included in Table 7.1.

7. Air Services The two main kinds of capital expenditure are on airports and aircraft. Capital expenditure on aricraft is made by public corporations (mainly airlines) while that on airports is made by general government (mainly the Department of Transport). Using this method of identification capital expenditure on airports is:

1970-71	$49.9m
1971-72	$37.6m
1972-73	$18.8m
1973-74	$17.1m
	$123.4m

Capital expenditure on airports is necessarily lumpy. During the first two years of this period Melbourne's new international airport at Tullamarine was completed.

8. Shipping, Ports and Harbours The major capital expenditures are on ships and on port and harbour installations. Capital expenditure on ports can be identified as it is made by state and local government in the states and by the Federal Government in Darwin. Some investment in ships by the Western Australian Coastal Shipping Commission will also be included in the following estimates:

1970-71	$54.0m
1971-72	$74.3m
1972-73	$61.9m
1973-74	$60.4m
	$250.6m

9. Schools, Colleges and Universities Nearly all of the investment in education facilities occurs in urban areas. In New South Wales in 1973–74 nearly three-quarters of the total volume of building for educational purposes occurred in the Sydney and Outer Sydney Statistical Divisions, plus the Statistical Districts of Newcastle and Wollongong. Less than 10 per cent was in rural shires, and much of that would have been in unincorporated urban areas within those shires, including areas of population spill-over from municipalities. Although this section is concerned with government services it is appropriate to include here private capital expenditure on educational facilities.

There are two sources of data on capital expenditure on educational facilities. The National Accounts data identify only public expenditure on educational facilities, but include expenditure on equipment as well as buildings. They may also include some

	Government		Private	Total
	Total	Buildings	Buildings	Buildings
1970-71	250.9	174.1	37.5	211.6
1971-72	291.3	197.1	34.0	231.1
1972-73	332.5	212.2	31.2	243.4
1973-74	384.2	236.3	35.4	271.7
	1258.9	819.7	138.1	957.8

expenditure on land. The value of work done on new buildings from the building statistics includes both government and private buildings separately, and will be used in subsequent estimates.

10. Hospitals and Other Health Services The sources of data and the involvement of the government and private sectors is similar to education:

	Government		Private	Total
	Total	Buildings	Buildings	Buildings
1970-71	102.8	70.1	28.0	98.1
1971-72	115.9	69.4	28.5	97.8
1972-73	118.8	75.9	29.5	105.4
1973-74	149.2	81.3	23.5	104.8
	486.7	296.7	109.5	406.1

11. Communication Capital expenditure over this period was made by the Australian Post Office and the Overseas Telecommunications Commission. As in the case of electricity there is no ready way of identifying the urban portion of the total, either on the basis of the cost responsibility of urban residents or the physical location of the assets. Nor is there any ready way to distinguish the parts of the investment, in buildings, fixed cables and equipment, which might be regarded as urban development. Exchange equipment could well be regarded as a part of capital expenditure on urban development. Perhaps a reasonable estimate might be that three-quarters occurs in urban areas. Capital expenditure on communications would then be as follows:

1970-71	$280.8m
1971-72	$320.0m
1972-73	$345.2m
1973-74	$421.0m
	$1367.0m

12. Other Services Although a number of other services provided in urban areas require development expenditure by some level of government, they are difficult to identify from national accounts. It is more appropriate to deal with them in the next section on housing and other buildings, since the main part of capital expenditure that can be classed as urban development comprises buildings. One part that does not is the development of open space for recreational use. An estimate of at least a part of this expenditure is:

1970-71	$27.3m
1971-72	$26.8m
1972-73	$33.9m
1973-74	$39.3m
	$127.3m

Housing and Other Building

Most of the investment in land development and government services involves site works, the laying of wires and pipes and the provision of transport and communications networks. In this section we deal with investment in housing and in private and public buildings that have not been included in the previous section. A good deal of data is available showing how much building work is carried out in local government areas and statistical divisions, but none which shows how much occurs within urban areas. For most practical purposes, however, all housing and other building can be counted as occurring in urban settlements, and has been in Table 7.3. The error involved is quite small, given the location of population and jobs, and of growth in both. The value of work done on buildings during the four-year period is shown in Table 7.3. As far as possible buildings which have been included in the expenditure on government services have been omitted. Education and health buildings have been omitted and an adjustment was made for the 11 to 12 per cent of Post Office capital expenditure which was on buildings. No similar adjustment was possible for the other service authorities, so there is a small amount of double counting in the value of work done on government factories (which include power-houses and workshops) and other business premises (which include bus depots, television stations and studios and warehouses), some of which is also included in investment in services.

TABLE 7.3   *Value of Work Done on Buildings ($m)*
1970–71 to 1973–74

	Private	Government	Total
Houses	5376.5	466.3	5842.9
Other dwellings	1560.9	119.1	1680.0
Total dwellings	6937.3	585.4	7522.7
Hotels–hostels	332.7	17.9	350.7
Shops	526.9	5.5	532.5
Factories	912.5	94.1	1006.7
Offices*	1141.0	337.9	1888.6
Other business premises*	409.7		
Religion	54.0	—	54.0
Entertainment and recreation	203.9	100.8	304.6
Miscellaneous	225.4	245.3	470.7
Total other buildings	3806.2	801.5	4607.8
Total	10743.6	1387.1	12130.6

Source: *Building Statistics*, Australian Bureau of Statistics
Notes: Value of work done on buildings used for education and health purposes have been omitted.
      * The value of buildings built for the Post Office have been excluded from this data. Since the distribution between the two classes is unknown they have been combined.

Perhaps the most notable feature of the table is that when health services and education buildings are excluded, capital expenditure on buildings by governments has been small, amounting to only 9 to 14 per cent of the total expenditure on buildings.

Total Investments

The results of all of the above estimates are summarised in Table 7.1. The table must be interpreted with caution, partly because of the very broad approximations that had to be made in deriving the estimates. It does give an indication of the importance of investment in urban development—it absorbs about half of the national gross fixed capital expenditure—and the relative size of its major components. Table 7.1 also shows, for the four-year period, the percentage composition. Apart from the building of houses no single element accounts for much more than 10 per cent of the total. The data in the table show a considerably higher volume of investment in government services than estimates derived from Canberra expenditure ($6717m compared with $4300m). Despite their shortcomings the data in the table are likely to be more accurate.

Location of Metropolitan Investment

Chapter 3 showed that population growth in Sydney has been concentrated in the fringe municipalities and that growth has occurred in some inner municipalities when flats have been built. Although most houses and flats are built where population is growing, other kinds of investments often occur elsewhere. Shops and schools may be mainly built in growth areas but offices and factories are built in employment centres. This section describes the distribution of investment in building between local government areas in Sydney from June 1970 to June 1974. Unfortunately data about the location of other investments in urban development are not available for parts of the urban area.[2]

The distributions of the value of building completions for each of the main kinds of buildings are shown in Figure 7.1, parts (i) to (viii). Each dot represents approximately 3 per cent of the total and any LGA with less than 1.5 per cent has been left blank. Although the data refer to LGAs, only the urban areas are shown in the figure since nearly all of the building would be within the urban area. The distributions are summarised geographically in Table 7.4, which includes all classes of building for which data are available, but groups LGAs into broad rings similar to those used in earlier chapters.[3] The concentration of house completions in the outer ring of suburbs is to be expected. Because the map shows value of completions the North Shore outer suburban areas stand out more strongly than if the number were shown. This applies particularly to Ku-ring-gai where the number of completions was nearly 20 per cent less than in Liverpool, though the value of completions was nearly 80 per cent greater. The average value per house was more than twice as high. The lower value of completions in the south-west sector was only partly a result of the relatively cheap houses being built there. After rapid growth in Liverpool in the 1960s growth swung further

[2] Expenditure by local governments is, of course, recorded by local government areas. Most data for expenditure by individual local governments does not distinguish between current and capital expenditure.
[3] The difference is that the City of Sydney in Table 7.4 is the area within its post-1968 boundaries.

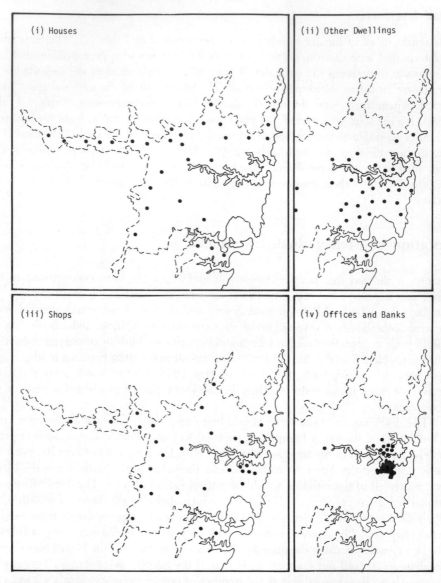

Figure 7.1 Distribution of value of building completions: Sydney 1970–1974. Each dot represents 3 per cent of the total for the Statistical Division.

Source: ABS (NSW), *Value of Building Jobs Completed in Statistical Divisions and Local Government Areas.*

north to Blacktown and Penrith. By the end of the period rapid growth had resumed in the south-west, spreading along the main lines of transport into Campbelltown.

The building of other dwellings, mainly flats, has been distributed widely throughout Sydney. Except in Warringah and Sutherland, where flat dwellers are at-

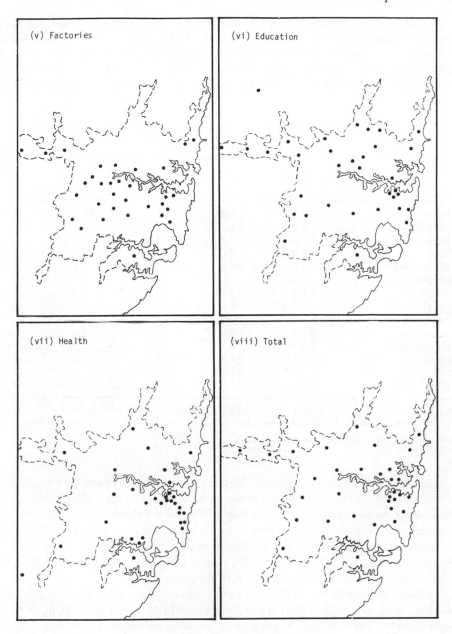

Figure 7.1 (contd.)

tracted by the coastal amenities, relatively few have been built in outer suburbs,
though suburban rail stations in Hornsby, Fairfield and Liverpool have also attracted
some. The volume of building is influenced by the willingness of councils to permit

flat building in predominantly single-family housing areas. Randwick and Canterbury have stood out in this regard. In North Sydney many of the flats are built at a high density near the harbour foreshores and the commercial centre. There are few suburban areas, either inner or outer, that have not experienced some flat building. Usually flats are located near public transport routes and close to shopping centres.

TABLE 7.4   *Distribution of Value of Building Completions Between Rings of LGAs in Sydney: 1970–71 to 1973–74*

	City of Sydney	Inner Ring	Middle Ring	Outer Ring	Total
Houses	0.1	4.4	15.3	80.2	100.0
Other dwellings	2.3	31.2	41.9	24.7	100.0
Hotels, hostels, etc.	51.8	20.8	13.5	13.9	100.0
Shops	13.0	12.0	18.2	56.7	100.0
Offices, banks	50.9	29.3	14.1	5.6	100.0
Other business premises	11.1	33.6	30.9	24.4	100.0
Factories	4.5	16.4	41.2	37.9	100.0
Entertainment, recreation	55.3	10.9	15.3	18.8	100.0
Educational	10.9	14.7	20.3	54.2	100.0
Health	20.8	28.4	30.7	20.2	100.0
Religious	3.4	14.0	27.9	54.8	100.0
Other	10.8	21.8	26.8	40.6	100.0
Total	14.1	19.2	25.2	41.5	100.0

Source: ABS, N.S.W. Office, *Building Statistics.*

Over the half the value of 'hotel, hostel, etc.' completions have been in the City of Sydney, and the remainder scattered throughout the urban area. Shop building was much more widely spread with over half in the outer suburbs. More was spent on retail space in the City of Sydney than in any other local government area. Alterations and additions are also likely to be an important part of total investment, especially in the inner suburbs. Baulkham Hills and Ku-ring-gai stand out as LGAs where there was a lot of house building but relatively few shops.

Offices and banks have been more concentrated than any other major kind of building, with over half in the City of Sydney, and less than 6 per cent in all of the outer suburbs. The City and North Sydney together accounted for three-quarters of the total. The office buildings in suburban areas are less obvious than the high-rise buildings in the CBD, but as the census data shows, there are a significant number of office jobs in suburban areas—though few are in office buildings.

Nearly four-fifths of all factory buildings was in the middle and outer suburbs. In this case the sectoral location is even more striking than the distribution between the suburban rings. There was very little factory building north of the harbour.

Altogether these LGAs, from Baulkham Hills to Warringah, accounted for only 15 per cent of the total. Some factories were built in the old industrial suburbs such as Botany and South Sydney, but the largest volume was in the Parramatta-Auburn-Bankstown area in the middle western suburbs, spilling over into outer western suburbs such as Blacktown, Holroyd and Liverpool.

Completions of entertainment and recreation buildings were unusually concentrated because of the completion of the Sydney Opera House. Other business premises include transport terminals, warehouses and service stations. They have been more concentrated in inner areas than factories or shops. Botany ranks high because of the completion of the international terminal at Kingsford Smith Airport.

Two classes of buildings used for government services are distinguished. Educational and health buildings are both remarkably centralised, considering the concentration of population growth in the outer suburbs. Major tertiary educational institutions are located in Ku-ring-gai, Ryde, the City of Sydney and Randwick. These last two LGAs are even more prominent in the case of health buildings, and together accounted for 39 per cent of the value of completions. This reflects the extent to which hospital facilities are being expanded in traditional locations close to the medical schools, locations which were most convenient when access to hospitals was mainly by public transport, and before the post-war expansion of the western suburbs, but not in the 1970s. The only other large expenditure on health buildings was on the St George district hospital in Kogarah.

When the different kinds of buildings are combined in part (viii) of Figure 7.1, the City of Sydney had over twice the value of completions of any other LGA. Over half of those were offices and banks. The same class was even more dominant in North Sydney where they comprised two-thirds of the value of completions. At the other extreme, in the outer suburbs, houses account for about half of the total, followed by 'other dwellings', factories, shops and schools. 'Other dwellings' (flats) are the most important kinds of buildings in both inner and middle suburbs, comprising about one-third of the total. Altogether building activity is widely dispersed throughout the urban area. The proportions in each ring are not very different from the proportions in the population in 1971 (see Chapter 2), except for the over-concentration already noted in the City and the lower level of building in the middle ring.

Investment in Adaptation

All of the data about investment in urban development in Australia is gross in the sense that it makes no allowance either for the depreciation of the assets created or for those that must be demolished when a new building replaces an old one or an area is resubdivided so that the old streets, water and drainage mains have to be replaced. No estimates have been made of the depreciation of the urban fabric due to age and obsolescence. Although this kind of depreciation undoubtedly occurs, its effects are often masked by the increased value of sites as cities expand and available sites become relatively more scarce. Even if the prices are corrected for inflation it is uncommon for developed properties in a growing city to fall in real value. Furthermore the concept of an economic lifetime is not very helpful in estimating depreciation because demolition usually occurs when a site is needed for another purpose, rather than when the building becomes too old. The only information that is available about depreciation of the urban fabric is some data about the demolition of dwellings. It is not possible to get any useful data on depreciation from the accounts of utility or other service authorities. In 1974–75, when the fixed assets of the Sydney Metropolitan Water, Sewerage and Drainage Board were worth some $1464m, the 'provision for renewals and other purposes' totalled only $11m.

Apart from demolitions, conversions also affect the dwelling stock. Conversions can be to a non-residential use, or can involve subdivision of dwellings (houses to flats) or amalgamations (flats or rooms to houses). In the mid-1960s there were up to 500 flats produced each year by conversion, but by 1973–74 the number had fallen to less than 100 (*N.S.W. Statistical Register*, 1973–4). There is some evidence from a few case studies (Neutze, 1971a, 46; 1972a, 63) of amalgamations of rooms and non-self-contained dwellings increasing the stock of self-contained dwellings. The number of non-private dwellings also fell between 1966 and 1971, from 5934 to 3627, either through conversion or demolition.

Unpublished estimates by the ABS Sydney office of the number of demolitions of houses and flats in the Sydney statistical division from June 1970 show an annual total of 3500 to 3800 demolitions from 1970–71 to 1973–74. In 1974–75 the number fell by about half. These numbers can be compared with annual completions around 30 000 per year. In the five years from June 1970 to June 1975 nearly 12 dwellings were demolished for every 100 newly constructed. The distribution of demolitions within Sydney is of interest, particularly since other authors have made estimates of the extent of redevelopment by assuming that all building in inner urban LGAs is redevelopment. The LGAs of Sydney which Vandermark (1974) used for this purpose only account for 21 per cent of the demolitions in this five-year period. A large number occur in the outer suburban LGAs and presumably were mainly holiday houses (especially in Warringah, which had the greatest number of demolitions—1106) or semi-rural houses. Many also occurred in middle suburbs where there was rapid flat development. There are two ways in which the distribution of demolitions can be shown. If demolitions occur mainly with the building of new dwellings the loss-to-construction percentage is valuable. If it is a more general phenomenon occurring because of obsolescence and conversion of areas to non-residential use, the percentage of the 1971 stock lost by demolition is the best indicator. Chapter 6 recorded that some 0.4 per cent of the dwelling stock is demolished each year. The rate of loss in Sydney was slightly lower—1.5 per cent were lost in four years. Figures 7.2 and 7.3, show the distribution of these two measures of demolitions within Sydney in the four years June 1971 to June 1975. Figure 7.2 shows that the greatest rates of loss dwellings occur in some inner and fringe LGAs. Apart from the City of Sydney, demolition was most rapid in several middle suburbs which were experiencing rapid flat construction, and in a series of outer suburbs where redevelopment was from ex-urban and rural dwellings to urban. Demolitions can occur in a cyclical pattern as an area experiences successive waves of redevelopment. Demolitions occur at the beginning of a wave and are often followed by a large number of new completions. The three St George suburbs (Rockdale, Kogarah and

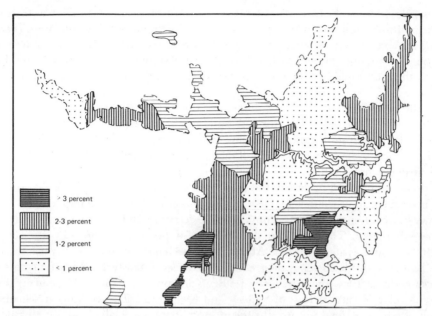

Figure 7.2 Percentage of 1971 stock of dwellings demolished: 1971–1975.
Source: ABS, NSW, unpublished data, and Census.

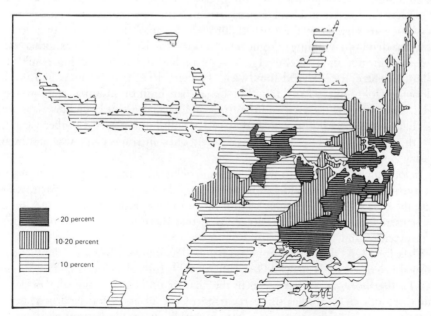

Figure 7.3 Demolitions as a percentage of completions: 1971–1975.
Source: ABS (NSW), unpublished data, and *Value of Building Jobs Completed in Statistical Divisions and Local Government Areas.*

Hurstville) were at the early part of a wave in 1971 to 1975. Not only was their rate of demolitions high but there was a high ratio of demolitions to completions (Figure 7.3). By comparison, in some other suburbs where flat redevelopment had been occurring for a longer period, such as Canterbury, Randwick, North Sydney and Lane Cove, the most rapid demolition phase was over even though redevelopment was still active.

The ratio of demolitions to completions is generally highest in the inner suburbs where there is little or no space for new buildings of any kind without demolition, but there is by no means a uniform decline with distance from the centre. Parramatta, which is mostly developed, has a high ratio, and Warringah and Fairfield, which are still growing quite rapidly, have moderately high ratios.

Redevelopment is of interest not only because of the distinction between gross and net investment in urban development but also because of its spatial importance. A city grows by spreading out and occupying more territory and by using its existing area more intensively. The trends in the location of population and jobs described in Chapters 3 and 4 suggested that Australian cities have not only been spreading out, but have actually been using their existing areas *less* intensively. According to some measures this is true—there are fewer residents and not many more jobs in many of the fully developed parts at least of Sydney and Melbourne. This is, however, mainly a result of a secular trend towards the use of more space, especially land, for all kinds of human activities—production, living, recreation, transport and storage. It has not resulted in the abandonment of property in inner suburban areas, as has occurred in the United States, or in large areas becoming vacant and unused. Rather, as Vandermark (1974) has shown, a considerable proportion of the new building occurs in parts of cities which are already used for urban purposes. Some of this new building occurs on sites cleared of old buildings. Some of it occurs on land which was either unused previously or not used intensively. For example, studies in the inner suburbs of Redfern (Neutze, 1972a) and Randwick (Neutze, 1971a) in Sydney, and in North Melbourne (Johnson, 1973b), found blocks of flats built on sites that were previously stables, a derelict factory yard and the front and back yards of large houses, as well as those built on cleared house sites. A new office building replaced a timber yard. In all cases the site was used more intensively but only in some cases was a substantial building demolished.

In looking at the extent to which urban development of various kinds is spreading the city, and the extent to which it is intensifying the use of established parts, we need to use the data from the previous section on its *location*, rather than whether or not it represents redevelopment. That data showed that there is a great deal of building in the city centre and some inner suburbs.

Data for LGAs does not distinguish fringe development from development in established urban areas, as many LGAs contain both fully developed and undeveloped areas. Furthermore, as we have seen in the chapter on land use, the edge of development is seldom clear. Rather the percentage of vacant and rural land increases continuously away from the centre of a city. For its purposes the Bureau of Statistics has adopted a criterion for distinguishing urban areas based on 200 persons per square km. If this can be taken as the edge of the city, Table 7.4 shows broadly the proportions of

TABLE 7.5   *Importance of Additions and Conversions: Sydney-Wollongong: 1961-2 to 1975-76*

	All additions as a % of total cost of buildings	Flats resulting from conversions as % of all new flats	Ratio of no. of house additions to no. of new houses
1961-2	17.3	6.8	0.27
1962-3	24.3	8.5	0.33
1963-4	20.3	9.1	0.40
1964-5	19.1	5.1	0.36
1965-6	18.2	5.2	0.40
1966-7	19.7	5.2	0.45
1967-8	19.9	4.7	0.51
1968-9	18.4	5.3	0.54
1969-70	23.5	5.5	0.55
1970-1	20.6	5.5	0.60
1971-2	18.1	5.3	0.68
1972-3	21.5	2.9	0.85
1973-4	22.5	3.4	1.32
1974-5	20.4	0.7	1.35
1975-6	25.9	2.2	1.18

Source: Metropolitan Water Sewerage and Drainage Board *Building Operations Annual*, Sydney.

various kinds of buildings built at or beyond the fringe. The outer ring comprises LGAs through which the 1971 urban boundary passed.[4]

Even without redevelopment there can be a good deal of investment in existing areas in the form of alterations and additions to existing buildings. Bureau of Statistics data on building operations until June 1973 include all alterations and additions costing $10 000 and above as new buildings, whereas those costing less were ignored. Since June 1973 some data on alterations and additions to dwellings have been published separately. In capital city statistical divisions there were 1493 alterations and additions to dwellings in 1973–74 and 4441 in 1974–75. This compared with 97 000 and 87 000 new dwellings in the two years. For all of Australia alterations and additions costing $10 000 and over accounted for 2.6 per cent in 1973–74 and 4.0 per cent in 1974–75 of the value of work done on dwellings. The Sydney Metropolitan Water Sewerage and Drainage Board publishes annual statistics on building operations—non-residential as well as residential—which include a much wider range of additions, and distinguish flats produced by conversion from newly-built flats. Table 7.5 is derived from those statistics and shows that about one-fifth of the investment in building comprises alterations and additions to existing buildings. This proportion remained relatively stable through the 1960s and early 1970s. Conversion of buildings for use as flats was quite significant in the early 1960s, at least in terms of numbers of flats, but became much less important by the mid-1970s.

[4] The boundary actually passed along parts of the outer municipal boundaries of both Holroyd (outer ring) and Bankstown (middle ring). The Bankstown boundary in that area comprises an unbridged part of Georges River, whereas the Holroyd boundary coincides with no natural barrier to expansion.

In contrast, the number of additions to houses has increased dramatically relative to the number of new houses. Unfortunately it is not possible to compare the values of the two kinds of investment, but unless additions became much smaller on average it appears that this form of investment in houses became much more important in the early 1970s. The main reason is that, in an inflationary situation, established home owners' equity in their housing increases rapidly and allows them to upgrade their housing either by buying a larger house or adding to their existing house. In a period of inflation investment in housing also protects the real value of the funds invested.

Redevelopment usually occurs in a piecemeal fashion. Only one or a few properties may be involved. Partly because of the difficulty of acquiring adjacent properties, and partly because it is rarely necessary to supply utility services that are common to a number of properties, redevelopment usually occurs in a more fragmented fashion than conversion of rural land to urban use. Except in government-sponsored schemes it is relatively rare for the street layout to be changed, though many planners and others have pointed out the opportunities that comprehensive redevelopment affords to change to a more appropriate pattern of subdivision as well as overall land use.[5]

The difficulties of attempts at comprehensive redevelopment are now well known. In the private sector the most that can usually be achieved is to buy a few old low density buildings in a city centre for an office building such as Australia Square. Over a number of years a manufacturer may be able to buy up a number of houses near his factory to allow him to expand. One of the most ambitious private redevelopments involved the acquisition of about 100 houses to provide a site for a regional shopping centre at Bankstown. The difficulties experienced, because of property owners who did not want to sell, and in negotiations wtih councils in the Sydney area, are described by Vandermark and Harrison (1972).

It has usually been recognised that government authorities have an advantage in urban redevelopment because they can use powers of compulsory acquisition to ensure that they only have to pay market price. Jones (1972, 72) estimated that the two main public authorities involved in redevelopment, the New South Wales and Victorian Housing Commissions, had cleared 30 hectares and 111 hectares respectively by 1970. This had involved demolishing 1430 and 3788 houses. Up to 1970 the number of dwelling units built on cleared sites was 3472 and 8635. Although they have the legal powers necessary for redevelopment the Commissions have increasingly been subject to political pressures opposed to redevelopment, some of which emanate from owners and occupants of housing that might be subject to demolition.

Part of the investment in urban areas is required to cater for increases in population. Another part is needed to cater for the increased demands for housing space, working space and services from the established residents. Conceptually the two elements, sometimes called widening and deepening investment, are quite distinct. In practice the distinction is difficult to make, especially when the amount of capital, in services, housing and employment, varies significantly between different groups of

---

[5] The advantages of comprehensive redevelopment were described by a number of authors who presented papers at a seminar on urban redevelopment at the Australian National University in 1966. The papers have been published; 'P.N. Troy (ed); 1967'. See especially papers by Grahame Shaw and L.M. Perrott.

residents. It may be useful to separate deepening investment into two parts. One part could be called 'catching up' and is the investment needed to provide an acceptable level of housing and services for all residents, and the other more conventional deepening investment. Although this distinction is particularly important for government services, it is almost impossible to make empirically without a clear definition of what is an acceptable level. Paterson (1975) used a very simple procedure based on the physical utilisation rate to separate deepening from widening investment in urban services. The additional demand is shared between existing and new users on the assumption that utilisation rates are the same for each, and responsibility for investment is allocated in proportion to responsibility for addition to demand. On that basis he estimated that one-third of the total capital spending on public services could be attributed to increased utilisation—deepening investment. Paterson points out that his estimates make simplifying assumptions about the determinants of costs and utilisation which are not likely to be strictly valid (Mushkin, 1972). It does serve to remind us that not all new investment in urban development is needed to accommodate population growth.

Financing Urban Development

It is unusual for firms or individuals investing in urban development to rely entirely on their own resources to finance the investment. Usually a large part of the cost is borrowed, either through an institution or privately, and much of the borrowed finance is secured by a mortgage over the property. Nor is it only the investment in site development and buildings that needs to be financed. Since long-term site leases are uncommon in Australia, a developer usually has to buy the site to secure the funds he invests in development. Purchase of a site for development is a 'transfer payment' and does not involve investment in a national accounting sense, but it is a necessary outlay for development, and needs to be financed along with investment in servicing sites and building structures on those sites.

The first part of this section, describing the demand for finance, is limited to the private sector's need for different kinds of finance at different stages of development. The public sector also needs finance but does not borrow for particular developments over particular periods. Rather each authority borrows for its general purposes. Partly because of the interactions between the two sectors, they are considered together in the following section which describes sources of funds. The amount of finance needed for urban development can be estimated under three headings which correspond to different stages of development and to categories which are recognised by financial institutions.

Firstly, land finance is required for the purchase, subdivision, servicing and holding of land until the completed project is financed by a long-term loan, either by the developer-investor or by a purchaser. In the case of redevelopment or development of a purchased site the whole outlay occurs at the time of purchase. It is only necessary for the developer to own the land outright during the period of land development and building construction, but he usually needs to at least hold an option during the period prior to development while he is negotiating for planning and building permits and designing the subdivision or building. He may even purchase it earlier so that he can be sure of sites being available to keep his development plant fully occupied. Purchase of an option is only possible if land owners wish to extend this kind of credit, and they may charge a high price for it.

The amount of funds required each year can be estimated by applying the ratio of site value to building value to the total value of private buildings completed in Australia. Using data from a number of sources[6] it was estimated that the proportion of the total cost of completed developments attributable to the site was 20 per cent for flats and 25 per cent for houses, factories, office buildings and other private buildings. If they are in error these estimates are probably on the low side. They give values of sites for new private buildings as follows:

1970-71	$664m
1971-72	$766m
1972-73	$843m
1973-74	$998m
1974-75	$1090m

These estimates are higher than the estimates of the costs of servicing land because they include the cost of purchasing land and the interest cost of holding land and developed sites.[7]

There is very little information available about how far in advance of development developers usually purchase land. In any case ownership prior to development could be regarded as investment or speculation rather than a necessary part of urban development. To estimate how much land finance is required we need to make some judgement about the period land needs to be held, and the amount of the total cost which is outstanding for various parts of that period. One set of estimates was made in the *Report of the Committee of Inquiry into Residential Land Development* (1975, 105) which suggested that it was necessary for a developer to own zoned land for 18 months in order to develop it in 1970 and that this period had increased to 36 months by 1975. In 1970 the last six months of this would have been required for actual development and selling; this had expanded to 9 months by 1975. The report gives no source for its estimates except that they are 'broadly consistent with what private developers believe to have been the case'. Other estimates for Sydney (Vandermark and Harrison, 1972) and for flat building for the whole of Australia (Department of Housing, 1968) suggest rather shorter time periods.

The time periods assumed for the calculation of the amount outstanding are an average period for which the whole site cost is outstanding. Therefore the period should start sometime between when the raw land is purchased and when all of the services are installed. In the case of developments which usually occur in serviced areas, or on redevelopment sites, the corresponding time period is shorter. The times used for estimation are shown in Table 7.6. It should be noted that the time period over which finance for land ownership is required includes the period during which

[6] Housing Industry Association (1971); Vandermark and Harrison (1972).
[7] Because of the different methods used in estimation, the difference between the two sets of figures does not give an estimate of raw land and interest costs. Recent direct estimates of these dimensions for Melbourne are given in the *Report of the Committed of Inquiry into Residential Land Development*, (1975).

TABLE 7.6   *Time Taken for Development (months)*

	From development application (or purchase of site) to end financing	From commencement of construction to end financing
Houses	18	5
Flats	12	8
Factories	12	8
Offices	24	12
Other private buildings	12	8

Source: See text.

the building is being constructed as well as when a site is being held, and possibly developed, prior to commencement of the building. The second column of the table represents the construction period.

The amounts outstanding at any time are the same as the annual flow, if the average period that the full cost is outstanding is 12 months. It is 50 per cent greater in the case of housing and twice as great for office buildings. The estimate of the total outstanding each year is as follows.

1970-71	$706m
1971-72	$820m
1972-73	$904m
1973-74	$1045m
1974-75	$1153m

On this basis single family housing sites account for just under one-half of the total finance required at any one time for holding land for, and during, development.

The second requirement is for bridging finance during the construction period, either to cover construction costs directly or to make progress payments to the contractor. Although building contractors and suppliers of building materials extend short-term credit from when work is done to when payment is made, there is still a very considerable amount of finance needed by the developer before the building is completed and sold or before a long-term mortgage is negotiated. An estimate of the amounts required can be made using the average time from commencement to end financing or sale for the major types of buildings. The estimates are shown in the second column of Table 7.6 and are derived from the same sources as the estimates of the period for which land finance is required. If we assume that construction occurs at the same rate over the period, the total amount of bridging finance increases at a constant rate from zero at the beginning to the value of the building at the end.

As in the case of land finance, requirements can be expressed in two different ways. The flow required during any one year is approximately equal to the total value of private buildings completed during the year. The total amount of bridging finance outstanding· at any one time can be estimated by multiplying the value of buildings completed in a year by half of the time required for construction (in years). This may seem to over-estimate the requirements since provision of finance lags behind the value of work done. On the other hand it makes little allowance for delays between completion and end financing or sale. The amounts outstanding are shown for each major class of building in Table 7.7. The amount required at any one time is about one-third of the value of completions each year. Bridging finance for single family houses is only about one-third of the total.

TABLE 7.7   *Bridging Finance Required: Amount Outstanding ($m)*

	1970–1	1971–2	1972–3	1973–4	1974–5
Houses	204	239	282	328	355
Flats	114	103	121	149	182
Factories	64	74	61	87	95
Offices	84	115	121	146	146
Other private buildings	139	156	159	160	192
Total	605	687	744	870	970

Source: Derived from Tables 7.3 and 7.6.

The third requirement is for end finance, arranged on completion of the building and usually secured by a mortgage over the developed property. It varies greatly in the time period over which it is lent. In the case of owner-occupied housing the period is usually long (20 years and over), repayment is required during the period of the loan (the loan is amortised) and refinancing is uncommon. Mortgages for commercial buildings or investment flats are usually for much shorter periods and refinancing is common. Interest rates are usually lower than for land or bridging finance—especially for end finance for owner-occupied housing—for these are relatively long-term loans with good security and low administrative costs.

The gross flow of end finance required each year is equal to the value of the completed property, including the site, as shown in Table 7.8. It does not seem to be useful to try to calculate the amount outstanding at any one time, since end finance for newly developed property cannot be distinguished, even in principle, from finance for the purchase of existing property and refinancing of mortgage loans on existing property. The amount of end finance outstanding at any one time on developed property can be more usefully compared with the total value of that property, rather than with new developments over any given period of time. Such a comparison, which would be valuable for studies of the ownership of wealth, would take us outside the scope of this chapter.

All of the funds used to finance the servicing, development and subsequent holding of urban property come from personal or corporate savings or taxation. Figure 7.4 sets out the various ways in which finance flows from the original source of the savings, either directly or through financial intermediaries, into urban development. Savings in the corporate and the personal sectors of the economy amounted to $8460m in 1972–73. Most of the corporate savings take the form of depreciation allowance ($3348m), undistributed (company) profits ($970m), and increase in income tax provision ($423m). Household savings amounted to $3719m. A number of public authorities run surpluses on their current accounts ($2318m in 1972–73) and use

TABLE 7.8   *Value of Newly Completed Private Buildings — Including Sites ($m)*

	1970–1	1971–2	1972–3	1973–4	1974–5
Houses	1300	1529	1805	2097	2274
Flats	426	387	453	557	683
Factories	255	295	245	346	380
Offices	222	306	321	389	390
Other private buildings	556	625	636	640	769
Total	2759	3142	3460	4029	4502

Source: Derived from Table 7.3.

these for investment in capital assets for their own use, including real property. Of the gross accumulation of $10 778m, all except the $937m lent overseas was available for use in Australia. That part of taxation which is used to finance capital investment can be regarded as forced savings. Perhaps one should also include here government borrowing from the Reserve Bank.

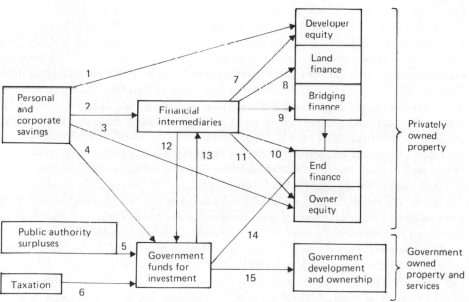

Figure 7.4 Flows of funds into urban development.

The solid arrows in Figure 7.4 show flows of funds. In each case where lending occurs some debt instrument passes in the opposite direction. The broken vertical arrow on the right side of the diagram shows that property passes from the development phase, represented by the top box, to the developed phase, represented by the lower box. Only limited information is available about the magnitudes of most of the flows represented by the numbered solid arrows. Some of the flows of finance for urban development can be distinguished from other financial flows because a particular debt instrument, often a mortgage, is involved and the flows, or stock of financial loans, are identified by the security offered. Others can be identified because a lending or a borrowing organisation is almost exclusively involved in financing the development or holding of urban property or services. Building societies among lenders, and property developers among borrowers, are obvious examples. The numbers 1–15 which follow refer to the numbered arrows in Figure 7.4

1. The equity of developers in the properties they are developing or holding prior to development comes either from their own savings, in the form of un-distributed profits or other reserves (in 1972–73 the gross operating surpluses of enterprises in the building and construction sector amounted to $740m, of which $560m occurred in unincorporated enterprises), or from borrowings from the public or other corporate savers. Savings are channelled into development enterprises through the purchase of shares and debentures. Since the term 'developer' includes any person or organisation that takes the initiative and the risk involved in development, it includes the individual who has saved to purchase a house site and then employs a contractor to build the house, and the commercial firm that builds its own factory or office building on land which it owns.

2. Much personal and corporate saving is channelled through financial intermediaries such as banks, finance companies, life offices, pension funds and building societies. The money may be lent to these intermediaries in the form of deposits, by purchasing shares or debentures, or by paying superannuation or insurance premiums. The personal or corporate lender does not know what his money will be used for, unless he lends to a specialised intermediary like a building society. The security for his loan is the assets and profitability of the intermediary rather than security over the property or other collateral on which the intermediary may lend. While most of these intermediaries are large institutions, often fairly closely regulated by government, others such as small merchant banks, building societies, mortgage brokers, unit trusts and solicitors investing clients' funds, are small.

Table 7.9 shows the lending in 1972–73 for urban development by some of the most important financial intermediaries involved in this field. Table 7.10 shows, from October 1975 when the data first became available, lending to individuals for owner-occupied housing. Part of the difference between the two sets of data is because they were for different time periods and part because of difference in coverage. The second table is limited to housing, but includes government as well as private lending. Much of the data, even in the first table, relates to lending for housing because this has become a specialised and identifiable function of financial intermediaries and is of particular interest in policy.[8] There are four major lenders of funds for urban development: savings banks, trading banks, building societies and finance companies.

Of these, savings banks borrow from the public at low rates of interest and primarily make low interest, long-term loans to owner-occupants. Because they lend at lower interest rates than the other major private lenders, they are often unable to

---

[8] Hill (1974) describes sources of finance for housing in some detail.

TABLE 7.9   *Institutions Financing Private Urban Development; 1972–1973 ($m)*

	Lending: 1972–73 Net	Gross	Assets 30 June 1973
Savings bank loans to individuals for housing	433.2	1076.6	2825.3
Trading banks:			
loans to individuals for housing	134.7	702.4	475.4
loans to builders	125.8	n.a.	293.1
Building societies (mortgages)	773.8	1111.2	3258.9
Life offices:			
loans for housing	−5.5	71.6	448.0
other non-rural mortgages	−21.7	63.6	666.0
Public pension funds			
housing mortgages	4.4		48.6
other mortgages	96.6		383.3
Private pension funds (mortgages)	26.7		226.2
Non-life insurance	−13.1		403.5
Finance companies			
housing purchase and construction purchase of house site	416.6	(901.1 (183.4	1622.4
construction other than housing other common purposes*	806.0	(363.2 (1241.5	1549.0
Development Finance Companies	64.8		380.4

Source: Reserve Bank *Flow of Funds,* and Australian Bureau of Statistics.
* Includes loans for development and servicing of raw land.

TABLE 7.10   *Loans Approved to Individuals for Construction or Purchase of Dwellings for Owner Occupation: October 1975—June 1976*

	$m	Per cent of Total*
Savings banks	1616.3	41.1
Trading banks	531.2	13.5
Building Societies		
Permanent	1135.0	28.9
Terminating	116.2	3.0
Finance companies	240.6	6.1
Government housing authorities	189.8	4.8
Other government	22.6	0.6
Credit unions	12.2	0.3
Insurance companies	66.0	1.7
Total*	3930.0	100.0

Source: Australian Bureau of Statistics, Ref. No. 5.56.
* For these institutions only.

meet all of the demand for loans, and they ration them by limiting the size of the loan to any individual and by requiring borrowers to maintain a minimum deposit with them for a specified period before qualifying for a loan. They also charge higher interest rates to higher-income borrowers.

Terminating building societies borrow mainly from institutions, their members and governments, and lend to their members at low interest rates. They receive low-interest loans from the Federal Government through the Commonwealth State Housing Agreement, which since 1956 has required that 30 per cent of the low-interest moneys available to each state should be made available to individuals for home purchase through terminating building societies or other approved institutions. These funds have become an increasing part of these societies' loanable funds and allow them to lend to low-to-middle income families at low rates. They also have low loan limits and are not very important as sources of funds.

Permanent building societies borrow funds at market interest rates, mainly from individuals, and lend at rates 1½ to 2 per cent above borrowing rates. They lend almost exclusively for housing, and mainly make long-term loans to individuals for owner-occupation. Their interest rates and loan limits are higher than the savings banks or terminating societies, and there is no means test on their borrowers. They grew rapidly in importance during the 1960s and 1970s, being able to attract funds by offering relatively high interest rates.

Trading banks lend mainly for relatively short periods, at higher rates of interest than savings banks or permanent building societies. They lend on second mortgages to owner-occupants who need to borrow more than they can get from savings banks. They also lend to investors in rental housing and non-residential property, and lend finance for land and bridging finance to builders and developers. The extent to which their loans are for short periods can be seen from the fact that they lent $702m to individuals for housing during 1972–73, but at the end of that year only $475m was outstanding.

Life insurance offices lend for both housing and investment property. In recent years their lending for both purposes has been falling and they have increasingly taken equity interests in investment property. In effect they have been financing their own investments rather than the investments of others. Pension funds, non-life insurance companies and development finance companies (which include merchant banks) lend mainly on non-residential property. In those fields they have become quite important, lending to builders, developers and investors.

Adequate data about finance company lending for urban development has only been available since mid-1972. In 1972–73 they lent almost as much for buying a site, building or purchasing a house, as savings banks or building societies. Since their loans were for shorter periods, the amount outstanding at the end of the year was only 50 per cent more than gross lending during the year. The much smaller role they assume in the lending in Table 7.10 suggests that they make many of their loans to enterprises. Finance companies lend at the highest rates of interest of the major intermediaries, they lend for the shortest periods, and are most likely to be providing second mortgage and bridging finance. Much of their lending is for land development or to finance building operations—both housing and other buildings.

A number of institutions not listed in Table 7.9 provide finance for urban development. For example, in 1972–73 Friendly Societies in Victoria lent $5m to persons building or buying houses, and a good deal of private lending occurs through solicitors and real estate agents. In Victoria in 1972–73, the distribution of 'type of mortgages' lodged on properties of under one acre, most of which would be urban properties, was as follows:[9]

	per cent
Banks	30.7
Building societies	19.5
Co-operative housing societies	2.5
Friendly societies	0.4
Insurance companies	3.6
Government institutions	4.7
Trustee institutions	2.0
Finance companies	12.7
Private individuals	13.3
Other mortgagors	10.4

Banks and building societies together have been responsible for almost exactly one-half of all mortgages of this kind.

3. The equity of the long-term owner in his property is initially financed by savings. Over time the equity will increase as the value of the property increases, as long as the property is not mortgaged to correspondingly higher levels. This is especially significant if, as is usually the case with loans to owner-occupants of houses, the mortgage agreement includes provision for repayment over a specified period. Financial intermediaries and developers themselves act as long-term owners when they invest in properties for their own use or for renting to others. Table 7.11 shows the investment in fixed capital during 1972–73 and the value of fixed assets, at 30 June 1973, of the major financial institutions. Most of the fixed assets would be real property. Some of the intermediaries, especially life offices and some finance companies, regard investment in property as an alternative to lending on the security of a mortgage over property, and land trusts are formed to invest members' funds in property. The individual house buyer's equity, initial deposit and subsequent loan repayment, come from personal savings. Results of surveys carried out by the Urban Research Unit and by Macquarie University suggest that owner-occupied houses are to a very large extent owned by their occupants with relatively little mortgage indebtedness (Neutze, 1972b).

4. A part of the finance used by governments at different levels to develop and service urban property is derived from borrowings from the public. Individuals and corporations subscribe to Commonwealth, local and semi-governmental authority loans. Government regulations require that a certain proportion of the assets of banks and life offices must be held in these forms. There is some information about the kinds of holders of government securities in total, but relatively little about who holds securities issued by those particular authorities which develop urban property and provide services in urban areas.

A large proportion of the borrowing by local and semi-governmental authorities is to finance the kinds of services in which we are interested. Electricity supply

[9] ABS, Victorian Office, *Mortgages on Real Estate Lodged for Registration*, Ref.No. 27.

TABLE 7.11   *Investment in Fixed Capital by Financial Intermediaries ($m): 1972–1973*

	Fixed Capital formation 1972–73	Value of fixed assets 30.6.73
Savings banks	13.3	121.0
Trading banks	41.6	200.0
Life offices	271.3	1315.6
Non-life insurance offices	69.6	421.3
Public pension funds	7.9	59.9
Private pension funds	11.5	54.9
Building societies	23.1	63.9
Finance companies	150.5	803.9
Development finance companies	7.5	16.2
Unit trusts, land trusts and mutual funds	40.7	107.7
Total	637.0	3164.4

Source: Reserve Bank *Statistical Bulletins, Flow of Funds Supplement*, April 1975.

(including small amounts for gas) accounts for about half of the indebtedness of semi-governmental authorities and water supply and sewerage for another fifth. Public housing is the next most important accounting for just under one-fifth. The two most important uses of local government loans which are distinguished are water supply, sewerage and drainage, and roads and bridges. However, nearly half is borrowed for 'general works'. Some 44 per cent of the semi-governmental authorities' (but only 4 per cent of local governments') debt is to the central (state) government. Nearly all of the rest took the form of local and semi-government securities.

Table 7.12 shows the principal holders of local and semi-governmental securities in 1973 and the net change in their holding during the ten years 1963 to 1973. Among the institutional holders the savings banks are by far the most important, followed by public pension funds, life offices, non-life insurance offices and private pension funds. With the data available we cannot separate the holdings of the general public from those of public authorities. Of the increase in amounts outstanding in the ten years up to June 1973, the savings banks account for nearly half and life offices and public pension funds for another third. Savings banks are probably the only group that significantly increased their proportion of total securities held during the decade.

In addition to these public loans, some of the money borrowed by the Commonwealth, on its own behalf or on behalf of the states, is used for urban development. Investment in airports, housing under the Commonwealth States Housing Agreement, and in post and telephone services, is financed to some extent from these sources. At 30 June 1975 nearly one-fifth of Commonwealth securities were held by governments, mostly the Commonwealth itself. Eighteen per cent were held by savings banks, 22 per cent by trading banks, 8 per cent by the Reserve Banks and 11 per cent by life offices.

TABLE 7.12   *Major Holders of Local and Semi-Governmental Securities: 1963–1973*

	Net change 1963–73		Value held 30.6.69	
	$m	%	$m	%
Trading banks	13.8	0.4	34.5	0.6
Savings banks	1602.0	47.4	2437.5	39.2
Life offices	380.4	11.3	666.5	10.7
Public pension funds	742.7	22.0	1315.6	21.2
Private pension funds	109.9	3.3	296.5	4.8
Non-life insurance offices	253.9	7.5	392.3	6.3
Building societies	125.4	3.7	130.6	2.1
Friendly societies	7.3	0.2	18.9	0.3
Health societies	24.9	0.7	44.6	0.7
Development finance companies	9.4	0.3	9.4	0.2
Other financial institutions	38.3	1.1		
Australian Government	−66.6	−2.0		
Rest of world	−26.0	−0.8	868.3	14.0
Persons & unincorporated entities	147.3	4.4		
Other	15.3	0.5		
Total	3378.0	100.0	6214.7	100.0

Sources: Reserve Bank, *Flow of Funds*, and ABS, *Public Finance*.

An alternative way to measure financing is the gross investment in various securities. In the case of semi-governmental securities this is useful because most of the loans are for relatively long time periods. Table 7.13 reproduces some of the results of a study by J.D. Ewart (1970) of the buyers of Victorian semi-government securities, mainly from the records of the Melbourne and Metropolitan Board of Works, the State Electricity Commission and the Gas and Fuel Corporation. Over the period of the study all classes of institutions except the pension funds increased their purchases, while purchases by the general public declined as a proportion of the total.

5. A significant number of the public authorities which operate as trading enterprises run surpluses on current account. In 1973–74 Federal Government authorities' surpluses totalled $2138m and the surpluses of state and local authorities $818m. Perhaps the most notable are the various electricity authorities which, because they are in an industry where costs tend to decrease as demand increases, and where there are cost-saving technological advances, manage to finance a significant part of their investments from current account surpluses. Telecom Australia also finances a significant amount of its capital expenditure from surpluses. On the other hand public transport authorities are seldom able to set aside sufficient funds to cover the depreciation on their plant and equipment. Although surpluses on current account can all be used to finance gross investment, they should not all be counted as surplus (in the sense of profits) until adequate reserves have been set aside for depreciation.

6. Government investment in property and services which does not earn revenue (or special purpose taxes such as water rates) is usually financed from general taxation.

TABLE 7.13   *Buyers of Victorian Semi-Government Securities: 1947–1969*
(*percentage of total*)

	1947–69	1965–69
State Savings Bank	21.8	22.9
Other Banks	15.1	17.6
Superannuation Funds	15.1	13.0
Insurance Companies	7.0	7.9
Public Authorities	4.9	6.2
Other institutions	8.3	10.5
Public	27.8	21.9
Total	$1608m	$549m

Source: Ewart (1970).

This applies in particular to roads, schools and parks and also to police and fire stations and the like. Relatively few taxes are earmarked for particular uses. Even the various taxes on motor vehicle use, including the petrol tax, are only partly earmarked since they yield more revenue than the relevant governments spend on roads. In the case of roads it is difficult to distinguish capital investment from maintenance.

7. Financial intermediaries invest in a wide range of different kinds of assets which may include the shares or debentures of development companies.

8. Although developers tend to use their own capital to finance a good deal of their holding of land, they also borrow from financial intermediaries. Large development companies raise short-term loans, sometimes on terms similar to those for bank overdrafts, from finance companies or merchant bankers on the security of the reputation of the development company itself. Smaller firms and individuals planning to develop their own properties more frequently borrow on the security of a mortgage over the land. Not many intermediaries will lend on such security and this field is left very largely to the finance companies who lend at relatively high interest rates to individuals paying off blocks of land ($184m in 1972–3) and to small firms holding land prior to and during development (a part of the $124.5m lent for 'other commercial purposes', Table 7.9). Merchant banks are included among development finance companies. The loans by finance companies for 'other commercial purposes' include lending for land holding and development as well as other lending.

9. Bridging finance can be raised by the large company in the same way as finance for land-holding. The three most important organisations involved in this field are the trading banks, finance companies and building societies. Building societies limit their lending to those who are borrowing end finance from them for the ownership of houses or flats. Apart from lending on the general security offered by a large company, banks and finance companies may use some other asset of the developer as collateral, or take a construction mortgage over the property during construction. Trading banks also lend to individuals building their own homes. Some of the trading bank lending shown in Table 7.9 is of this type. Their gross lending is large relative to the amount outstanding, showing that most of the loans are for short

periods. Merchant banks and solicitors also provide funds to developers for this kind of operation.

10. End finance is provided by a very wide range of intermediaries as described under 2 above (see Tables 7.9 and 7.10).

11. Financial intermediaries invest in companies which in turn invest in property and either occupy it themselves or rent it to tenants.

12. Financial intermediaries as well as individuals buy Commonwealth and local and semi-governmental securities. The relative importance of their holdings has been described above.

13. The main flow in the opposite direction is the loans to terminating building societies from the Home Builders Account under the Commonwealth State Housing Agreement.

14. Other ways in which governments make loans for private ownership of property are mainly for housing and are described in Chapter 6. They include loans for War Service Homes, lending for the purchase of homes built by the state housing authorities, and a number of mostly small state schemes. In 1972–73, $74.3m was lent to ex-servicemen for the construction or purchase of homes, and the amount outstanding at 30 June 1973 was $952.5m. Table 7.10 shows that government gross lending for owner occupation is quite small relative to the major private lenders. In recent years the net lending by governments for housing has been declining, partly because some housing authorities, especially the Victorian Housing Commission, have built more flats which are not for sale. On 30 June 1972 the amounts outstanding were about $750m.

15. A proportion of the funds available to the government for investment are invested in urban development, in schools, roads, housing, office buildings, hospitals, electricity supply, water and sewerage systems.

Summary

Although measurement is difficult, it is possible to estimate the level of investment in urban development and to compare the relative importance of its major components. In the first part of this chapter the components were assessed under the headings of land development, public services, and housing and other building. House building was by far the largest component, but the other 70 per cent is widely distributed among a large number of government and private investments. The relationship between government authorities and private firms and individuals who provide closely related parts of the urban infrastructure will be described in the next two chapters.

This chapter was only able to examine the distribution within one urban area (Sydney) of one major part of urban development—namely building. Only some kinds of building—especially housing, and to a lesser extent shops and schools—are concentrated in areas of population growth. Other kinds, such as flats and factories, are scattered through inner suburban areas or the western industrial areas. Office building is by far the most concentrated in the City and North Sydney.

Urban development includes both converting land from rural to urban uses, and changing, adapting, reshaping and redeveloping existing urban areas. Investment in additions and alterations to housing are quite small but increasing, and the extent of demolition of houses—about 0.4 per cent per year—gives an indication that redevelopment is not negligible.

Those who make the decision to invest usually have to borrow in order to finance the capital cost of the investment. Financial institutions exist to channel finance from savers into profitable investments. Different kinds of institutions specialise in borrowing from particular sources, and in lending for particular kinds of development. This is especially true of housing finance institutions, partly because government policies have been used to channel finance into housing on favourable terms. Except when they are used to pursue policy objectives, financial institutions have little positive influence on the way cities develop, though in seeking to avoid losses they may inhibit innovation in development. Investment in urban development accounts for about half of all national investment, and financing it makes a heavy demand on the financial resources of the nation.

8 Government Roles in Urban Development

The characteristics that distinguish urban development from most other kinds of investment are that it is fixed in location and its different components are closely interrelated. In economic terms investments by governments in the provision of services, and by private individuals and firms in houses, shops and factories are joint inputs in the production of services in urban areas. This complementarity also occurs between different elements of private investments and of public investment. It is one of the main reasons for the need for urban planning. Its importance can be illustrated simply. Houses are of little value to urban residents without access roads, shops and places for their residents to work. This also applies in the reverse direction, and it applies to almost every kind of investment in urban development. In this chapter we are mainly concerned with describing the investments made and the services supplied by the public sector and the different levels of government involved.

Attempts to develop and implement urban policy in Australia are hampered by the fact that three levels of government are involved in urban development. Attempts to influence the relative rate of growth of different cities, to promote growth centres or to encourage existing cities to grow in particular ways usually involve all three levels, and different authorities and departments within each level. This chapter describes the responsibilities of government as distinct from the private sector, and describes the allocation of the main functions between different government authorities.

The division of responsibility for investment in urban development between the private and government sectors can be defined in several ways. The most useful are firstly, according to who takes responsibility for the decision to invest, and secondly, who is responsible for paying for the investment. Usually the decision-maker provides at least the risk capital but governments sometimes finance or subsidise private investment. Some aspects of financing were described in the previous chapter. The role of government in investment in urban development in Australia has changed in a number of ways in the post-war period, but apart from its entry into welfare housing, none of the changes have been very far-reaching. For the most part the private sector initiates urban development by subdividing land and building houses, shops, factories and offices, and the public sector follows, providing transport, utility services, and social services such as education and health. While individual developers plan their own estates it is the responsibility of governments to ensure that they conform to an overall plan for a city's development and to plan for the provision of services. The division of responsibilities between levels of government is described in a later part of the chapter.

The colonial governments which came to power in Australia as the colonies were given self-government were initially responsible for all government functions. The state governments which succeeded them after Federation in 1901 have the major responsibility for servicing and planning urban development, especially in the major cities. Part of the reason is that the capital cities of most of the states contain such a high proportion of the state's population (see Chapter 2) that the state government can afford neither to ignore the needs of the capital's residents nor to establish a potentially powerful rival in the form of a metropolitan government. Another part of the reason is the relatively small role played by local governments, and how this came about can best be understood by looking briefly at their history.

Local governments were established mainly because the colonial governments wanted to avoid some of the detailed local administration, and wanted to tap local sources for tax revenue to finance local works, especially roads and bridges. Many localities, including some in urban areas, were reluctant to become incorporated, preferring the lower level of services that the central government was prepared to provide, rather than raise their own tax revenues. It was only when incorporation was made mandatory in most states late in the nineteenth and early in the twentieth century that all urban areas came under the control of local governments. Because they were formed to take account of local interests each municipality only covered a fraction of the larger urban areas. The disadvantages of having over sixty local councils responsible for local government in a single urban area (Sydney) soon became clear and brought different responses in different cities.[1]

In both Melbourne and Sydney there have been movements for metropolitan government either by amalgamation of the existing local councils or by the formation of an additional metropolitan level of government. In neither city were the movements successful. A minor success occurred in Sydney in 1949 when the number of local government areas was reduced from 66 to its present number of 41. Since that date also there have been no further subdivisions of the rural shires surrounding the urban area of Sydney as parts of them became urbanised. As a result a number of large shires round the periphery now have populations of over 100 000 with plenty of room for further expansion. Around Melbourne, on the other hand, the urban parts of the corresponding shires have often separated and formed urban municipalities. Only in Brisbane was the movement for metropolitan government successful with the formation of the City of Brisbane in 1925 by the amalgamation of twenty local government areas. Similar amalgamations of councils formed cities of Greater Newcastle (1938) and Greater Wollongong (1947), though in all three cases the urban area now extends outside the city boundary. Canberra is the only other major urban area without fragmented municipal government. Even in that case one-tenth of the population of the urban area defined for the 1971 Census lives across the territory border in the New South Wales municipality of Queanbeyan. Canberra itself is governed by the national government, though there is a commitment to give some powers to the elected legislative assembly, which at present is solely advisory.

---

[1] Descriptions of the origins, functions and scale of local governments are found in Bowman (1976), Neutze (1974) and *Joint Study into Local Government Finances* (1976).

One result of the way local governments began in Australia is that many of their powers are permissive and they are *required* to perform relatively few functions. Another is that local governments are very diverse both within and between states. Even within urban areas the populations and budgets of the largest local authorities are often ten times as large as the smallest. This has been an important reason why they have not been given wider powers and responsibilities. The larger councils with adequate resources and qualified staff could carry out functions which could not be entrusted to the smaller councils. This becomes even more important if all local authorities must be treated alike, since rural local authorities often have very few resources, and are responsible mainly for roads and bridges. Efforts to consolidate local government areas in the different states have seldom been successful. Residents fear a loss of local identity and local control and local politicians a loss of power. Even some quite modest urban areas such as Geelong and Ballarat in Victoria are divided between several local governments. In these cases it is partly because cities have been unable to expand their boundaries as the city has spread.

Another response to the disadvantages of relying on fragmented local government to provide services and to plan urban development in the larger urban areas has been the establishment of special-purpose metropolitan authorities to perform one or more of these functions. These authorities have often included members elected from among the local councillors. In most cases they have become, to a considerable extent, responsible to the state government, one reason for this being that they depend on that government for access to loan funds for capital works. A more important reason is that state governments have found that they cannot escape political responsibility for the functioning of these authorities. In recent years there has been an increasing tendency for the state governments to assume control, especially in the sensitive areas of water, sewerage and public transport.

This chapter describes the responsibility of different levels of governments for each of the major components of urban development, including land development, housing, provision of services, and planning and co-ordination of development.

Land Development

Land development is the conversion of land from broad acres into building sites complete with services. It is important because the decision to develop land is the main entrepreneurial decision that initiates urban development. The traditional division of responsibility between the public and private sectors was that private owners developed the land while government authorities provided the services. However, investment in land development today consists mainly of provision of the necessary services. Other site works are usually much less costly. A land developer or subdivider also surveys the site and arranges titles for the individual sites. The private part of land development has often been called, simply, subdivision. It was essentially an entrepreneurial, risk-taking activity and involved little investment in physical assets. Australia is unusual in having a land development industry. In most countries the subdivision function is carried out by builders.

Between the two World Wars, and in the early post-war period, all that was necessary to put building lots on to the market was to register a subdivision and provide a cleared access road. When houses or factories were built it was the local council's responsibility to improve the roads and provide storm water drainage and footpaths, though in Victoria the councils sometimes charged owners of the abutting property through private street accounts. Government authorities were also responsible for servicing the houses with water, electricity, telephones and in due course sewerage. Much the same division of responsibility applied to subdivision of land for industrial purposes. Most commercial development occurs on sites which are already serviced but the responsibility for any servicing needed still rested with public authorities.

One major disadvantage of the traditional division of responsibility was that land owners could, at little cost to themselves, subdivide large areas of land. Such a development could be profitable even if only a small proportion of the lots were sold. Most of the costs involved in making the subdivision usable were met by the government servicing authorities. Most councils welcomed subdivision and rarely attempted to restrict it even when they had the power, so that in boom times many sites were produced and only a fraction were used for building. Public authorities found themselves unable to keep up with the demand for their services, especially in areas of scattered development where the whole area had to be serviced even though only a fraction of the service capacity would be used. Some of the more remote subdivisions of the 1920s and even a few from the 1880s still remain largely undeveloped (Paterson, 1974). One reaction in the early period after the Second World War was to restrict land subdivision to areas which were close to established urban areas and which could be readily serviced. In Sydney, from 1951 to the early 1960s, development was limited to the area inside a 'green belt'. In other cities different techniques were used. The most recent explicit control mechanism is the definition of Preferred Development Areas, in the Melbourne region.

The second method of control relied on financial restraints rather than physical controls. In the 1950s local councils began to require developers, as a condition of approving an application to subdivide, to provide sealed roads, concrete kerbs, gutters and footpaths, and to contribute a percentage of their land for local open space. In the case of small developments a cash contribution might be accepted by the local council instead of land for open space. In the late 1950s and early 1960s local storm water drainage was added to the list.

In the early 1960s in Sydney some developers came to an arrangement with the Water Sewerage and Drainage Board to pay for the cost of sewering a subdivision in order to get sewerage services earlier than they would under the Board's programme. Negotiation for the provision of water and sewerage became common and was regularised in the State Planning Authority Act, 1963, which required the Authority to certify that a subdivider had complied with any conditions and had made any contributions levied by the Board. The Board can require the subdivider to meet not only the costs of reticulation within the subdivision but also the cost of connection to the Board's existing trunk mains. The Board can exercise some discretion in the extent to which off-site costs are charged. In 1965 similar requirements were introduced in Adelaide and Brisbane, and during the 1960s and early 1970s they were progressively introduced in Melbourne, Perth and many smaller centres. In some cases the supply authority may require a loan for extending an electricity transmission line or a trunk sewer to a new subdivision. The loan is repaid over a specified period, or when some percentage of the whole area served is developed. A series of studies by the Australian Institute of Urban Studies and the Urban Research Unit have described the situation in particular cities.[2] The increasing costs of holding serviced vacant lots discouraged the subdivision of land that was unlikely to be sold and used for building in the near future. These measures also helped to relieve the financial problems of water and sewerage authorities. With a given loan allocation, and with a given rate revenue to service the loans, the authorities are better able to keep up with the demand for their services if developers are required to pay for reticulation in newly developed subdivisions.

These various requirements have greatly increased the investment in land development by private developers. As long as the demand for building sites remained strong, these cost increases could be recovered from the buyers of developed sites without depressing developer profits or the price they could pay for raw land. When the demand weakened in 1974 the rate of land development slackened and the price of raw land stabilised or fell. In the long term the costs of servicing must be either passed back to the original owners in the form of lower raw land prices or forward to the eventual purchasers in higher prices for building sites (DURD, 1974a; DURD, 1975; Tyler, 1973).

Despite these requirements, local councils are still paving access roads and providing kerbs, gutters and footpaths, mostly on streets that were dedicated before the requirements were introduced. In Victoria local councils can use private street accounts for this purpose. The council borrows to pave the street and amortises the loan from levies on the owners of properties to which it gives access. Sewerage authorities are still reticulating areas that were developed before the requirements were introduced, and some more recent subdivisions where owners installed septic tanks because they could not be connected to a sewerage system at the time they were developed. In some cities, most notably Melbourne, the land developer is required to install a package treatment plant in areas that cannot be connected to the main system at the time of initial development. Developers are also required to reticulate the area to the authority's specification, and in due course it is connected to the main system.

The provision of these services can still be regarded as part of public capital formation because the roads, sewer and water mains become the property of, and are subsequently maintained by, the government authorities. Developer contributions and requirements might be thought of as a means of financing the provision of services. Even though the actual decisions to undertake the development are taken by private developers the government authorities decide on the level and quality of services. Alternatively the services can be regarded as an extension of the house, and as being jointly owned by the private property owners. In this sense developer requirements represent an extension of responsibilities of the private sector from the property boundary to the boundary of the subdivision.

[2] For Brisbane, Murphy (1973); Sydney, Vandermark and Harrison (1972); Melbourne, Urban Research Unit (1973); and Bromilow and Meaton (1974); Adelaide, Pak-Poy (1973)

Land development by government authorities in Australia has been quite limited. The Commonwealth Government purchased the site for the development of the national capital, and the National Capital Development Commission is the sole developer of land in Canberra, as well as being the planning authority. It provides sites for public and private housing, offices, shops, factories, schools and recreation areas. It is also responsible for roads and hydraulic services. Most land for urban use in Darwin is also developed by the government. The War Service Homes Commission developed land for homes for ex-servicemen in the 1920s and again after the Second World War, but in neither period was it a large developer.

Of the state authorities the South Australian Housing Trust, which began operations in 1933, has been the most significant land developer. All of the state housing authorities have developed land for their own housing and many have sold some sites to private individuals to built their own houses. Sale of sites has never been an important part of their operations (except in Tasmania) since they see their main role as providing inexpensive housing for those who meet the means test for admission to their waiting lists. The South Australian Housing Trust has been different because it has had a role in urban development that is wider than simply welfare housing. It has been a major instrument in the state's policy to promote industrial development (Stretton, 1975, Ch.6; Sandercock, 1975, Ch.6). To this end it provided inexpensive housing for middle-income families (up to 1968) and sites and sometimes buildings for industrial and commercial purposes. It has purchased large areas of land for development, especially in Adelaide. Its most notable development is at the new town of Elizabeth, 25 km north of the centre of Adelaide.

Lands Departments in some states, most notably New South Wales, develop Crown land for sale for housing or non-residential building. The City of Perth has developed its endowment land, mainly for housing. The New South Wales State Planning Authority (later the Planning and Environment Commission) purchased quite large areas for development in the South-West Corridor to implement the Sydney Region Outline Plan. It also bought land for the town centre in the mainly Housing Commission development at Mt Druitt, in Sydney's western corridor. Some local councils, especially outside the metropolitan areas, have purchased land for housing and industrial development. A few councils have developed shopping centres.

In 1973 South Australia established a Land Commission to develop land for private use. It was assisted by a Federal programme to provide loans to the states for this purpose and has now largely taken over this function from the Housing Trust. Urban Land Councils were established for the same purpose in four of the other five states (except Queensland) in 1975 (DURD, 1974a; DURD, 1975, 27–36). They were established partly to stimulate the supply of land in order to contain the inflation in land prices. Development corporations modelled on the National Capital Development Commission have been established for urban growth centres in Albury-Wodonga on the Victoria-New South Wales border, Bathurst-Orange west of Sydney, Monarto east of Adelaide and in Sydney's South-West Sector. Except in Adelaide, where the Land Commission has established a very important role, these bodies have not yet become major land developers. Some have purchased significant areas of land and may become important developers in the future.

Government Services

Investment in government services is almost wholly a government responsibility, though, as noted above, land developers have been required to contribute a part of the cost of some of them. Table 7.1 includes among the government services some—education, health services and gas supply—which are at least partly provided by the private sector. All other data in the second part of the table relate to government investment.

Water, Sewerage and Drainage

The inability of local governments which cover only a fraction of an urban area to carry out the full range of local government functions found in other countries became obvious in the 1870s and 1880s in relation to water supply and sewerage. The problems resulted partly from classic 'spillover' effects of government activities between local government areas. In the case of sewerage a system which serves an individual municipality may cause problems for the municipality further down stream in the drainage basin. In the case of water supply economies of scale in developing the river catchments for collection and storage of water, and the major balancing storages closer to where the water is consumed, point to the need for a single authority to serve a large urban area. Initially the central cities in Sydney and Melbourne supplied water to surrounding municipalities before special purpose authorities were established. In smaller centres in Queensland, New South Wales, Tasmania and Victoria (sewerage only) these functions are carried out by the local councils. But in all of the larger centres except Brisbane they have become the responsibility of special purpose authorities. Sydney and Wollongong are served by the same authority while separate authorities serve Melbourne, Perth, Newcastle and Geelong. Water and sewerage services for Canberra are planned by the National Capital Development Commission and operated by the Commonwealth Department of Construction. In Brisbane the City Council is responsible. The special purpose authorities are formed of councillors elected from councils in the areas served. Because the larger authorities are such heavy users of scarce loan funds available to the states, the state governments in both New South Wales and Victoria have increasingly taken responsibility for their operations.

In those states where sources of water are very limited the state governments have become more heavily involved in its supply. This is especially important in South Australia, which draws much of its supplies from the Murray River. Water and sewerage services throughout the state are the responsibility of the Engineering and Water Supply Department. In Western Australia also the Metropolitan Water Supply Sewerage and Drainage Board is responsible to the state government. In both of those states and in Victoria the state government departments have developed water supplies for country towns. The only major urban area in which water supply and sewerage are primarily the responsibility of the separate municipal governments is Hobart. The Metropolitan Water Board collects and stores the water and sells it, as a wholesaler, to the four municipalities in the urban area. They are responsible for reticulation and provision of water to consumers within their areas. Each municipality is responsible for sewerage, and discharges into the Derwent estuary.

As distinct from sanitary drainage through a sewerage system, surface or stormwater drainage is more frequently a local problem. Nevertheless in most cities the water and sewerage authorities have taken responsibility for main drainage. In part this is because main drains often serve parts of a number of municipalities in a catchment. It is also because of the inter-relationships between the two kinds of drainage: polluted wastes are sometimes discharged or overflow into stormwater drains, and stormwater often gets into the sanitary sewers. Local drainage is mainly a municipal responsibility. Developers are now usually responsible for reticulation within subdivisions and are sometimes required to pay for at least part of the cost of any trunk sewer and water mains, and any augmentation of main drains needed to serve the whole subdivision. The arrangements between developers and service authorities are usually determined by negotiation. For example, the connecting trunk sewer often serves land other than that owned by the developer making an application. The developer may then, as in Melbourne, be required to finance the full cost and be repaid a part of it when the other land is developed, or after a given period, or he may have to meet only his share of the cost.

Developers may also be required to make a specific contribution to the general cost of the headworks of each system. Such a contribution may be related to cost and subject to negotiation or, as in Melbourne, fixed at so much per acre. The amounts required in Melbourne have increased significantly over time. In June 1976 they stood at $2100 per hectare for water, $3954 per hectare for sewerage and $3000–$3700 per hectare for storm water drainage; a total of $9054–9754 per hectare or about $940 per house site. Even at that level they only contribute a small proportion of the total headworks cost of the average new subdivision. Most of the finance for investment in these services comes from loan funds, either normal state government loan moneys or special-purpose loans raised by the local or semi-governmental authorities. Some funds for investment come from current revenues from rates or charges.

Garbage Disposal

Spillovers of the effects of waste discharge are less of a problem in the case of solid wastes than liquid wastes, and as a result they have remained mainly municipal responsibilities. The large cities are exhausting the sites available for sanitary land fill and some seepage from garbage dumps has been polluting streams. The alternatives of composting or incineration are often best handled on a large scale and may also produce spillovers (air pollution). Because of these problems a Metropolitan Waste Disposal Authority was established in Sydney in June 1971 to dispose of solid wastes collected by the municipalities. Municipalities also have powers to control the discharge of wastes into the air, but effective controls were only introduced when state authorities or sections of departments were created specifically for this purpose.

Electricity

The generation and distribution of electricity was originally handled by private companies and by local authorities. As the electricity production industry developed, it became dependent on large coal-fired stations or, where natural conditions were favourable, hydro-electric stations based on large dams. Fragmented local government could not handle either type of generation efficiently, except in remote areas where it is cheaper to generate locally on a small scale than to transmit over long distances. Even Brisbane City Council has recently lost its generating function, though it is still a distributor.

Local government financial statistics show that the distribution of electricity is an important activity of local authorities in New South Wales and Queensland. This is somewhat misleading for, except in Brisbane and a few, mostly isolated, areas, the territorial local authorities in each state play a very small role in electricity supply. In Queensland nearly all of the generation and most of the distribution is handled by five locally-elected regional electricity boards. They are partly dependent on state sources of funds and borrow more of their own. In New South Wales the Electricity Commission, a state body, is responsible for nearly all generation and sells power to 34 special-purpose electricity county councils which are formed by groups of adjacent local authorities. Only five territorial local authorities in the state retail electricity. Although county councillors are elected from the constituent territorial local authorities the county councils, having their own sources of revenue, enjoy a high degree of independence.

Nearly all of Victoria's electricity is generated by the State Electricity Commission. It retails all of the electricity except in eleven local government areas in Melbourne where the local councils buy from the Commission and distribute to their consumers. Electricity is generated and distributed in the other three states almost solely by state authorities. The only exceptions are isolated communities in South and Western Australia which generate and distribute their own electric power.

One of the objectives in the constitution of authorities for electricity generation and retailing has been to ensure that both operations are run as business undertakings and do not come under the direct control of ministers or elected representatives. To this end nearly all of the state bodies involved are commissions, controlled by commissioners who are appointed for a specific period, rather than coming under direct ministerial control. Even the local councils which operate electricity undertakings have to keep separate accounts and often maintain a separate department.

Although electricity is solely a government responsibility in Australian cities, part of the cost of reticulation may be borne privately in two situations. In the first, if lines within a subdivision are to be installed underground the additional cost is usually paid by the developer; in the second, a developer may be required to finance any extension to the distribution system required for his development, the cost being repaid over a period as the areas served by the extension are developed and the electricity authority begins to receive revenue from sales. Most of the investment is financed from loan funds and from current revenue. Like water and sewerage authorities they often borrow in their own right as local or semi-governmental authorities.

Postal and Telephone Services

When the colonial governments became states of the Commonwealth of Australia at the time of Federation in 1901, the Commonwealth Government took responsibility for the post office. At that time it was mainly a postal organisation, but it was also responsible for the rapidly growing telephone service. In both cases the inter-connections between all parts of Australia made a national service essential. In 1975 two separate statutory corporations, Telecom Australia and the Postal Commission, took over these services from the Department of the Postmaster-General. Like the statutory authorities at the same level they have a high degree of independence. A significant proportion of the capital for expansion of telephone services comes from operating surpluses. The Federal Government takes responsibility for all loan raisings for these services. Developers are not required to meet the costs of telephone services within their subdivisions except that where a developer or the local council requires that the cables be laid underground the additional cost is frequently charged to the developer.

Gas

The supply of gas is organised in a wide variety of ways. Local authorities are responsible in areas of New South Wales outside the main centres. Statutory corporations similar to those supplying electricity also play a significant role—for example the Gas and Fuel Corporation of Victoria. Finally, regulated private companies are still heavily involved in the Sydney region and in the smaller state capitals. Oil companies provide bottled gas in many smaller centres and rural areas where there is no reticulated supply. In recent years both government and private supply authorities have invested heavily to replace gas produced from coal or petroleum feedstocks with natural gas.

Transport Services

The provision of roads and bridges is by far the most important function of local government in Australia. Outside the urban areas this has sometimes been recognised by calling them 'roads boards'. In the states where local authorities play only a very minor role in the provision of public utilities, capital expenditure on roads accounted for 60 per cent or more of their total capital expenditure in 1968–69 (Neutze, 1974). In the other states roads are less dominant because of the capital expenditure on electricity, water and sewerage. Even so roads accounted for 40 per cent of capital expenditure in Queensland, 56 per cent in New South Wales and 62 per cent in Tasmania. These percentages would probably be somewhat lower for urban local authorities, though roads are an important part of the total activities of territorial local authorities in urban areas.

Roads perform two functions—they provide access to property and cater for through movement of traffic. Although many roads in urban areas perform both functions, urban road planning attempts to separate the two kinds of traffic as far as possible. The highest level of separation occurs with freeways, which do not allow access to adjoining property, and roads within a neighbourhood, which are not designed for through traffic. The Commonwealth Bureau of Roads (1975) has attempted a classification of all roads in the 17 largest urban areas in Australia and regards 20 per cent of the total length of roads as urban arterial and the remainder as local roads. The arterial roads are, of course, larger. In 1973–74 they carried three-quarters of the total vehicle kilometrage in the urban areas. As a broad generalisation arterial roads are the responsibility of state road authorities while local roads are the responsibility of local authorities. In practice the division of responsibility is often more complex with responsibility for several different classes of roads being shared in different proportions ranging from wholly local to wholly state. The classification of any road is also a matter for negotiation rather than being determined solely by technical criteria.

Responsibility for construction is not always the same as responsibility for financing. The state authority may employ local authorities as its constructing agents or local authorities may be required to contribute to the cost of roads built by state authorities. Where costs are shared, either authority might carry out the work. A part of the cost of roads in the Sydney area comes from a rate on property raised by local councils for the Department of Main Roads. Local government expenditure on roads in urban areas is predominantly on reconstruction and maintenance, almost wholly on roads which are legacies of the period before developers were required to build paved roads.

As well as state and local governments and private developers, the Commonwealth Government is involved in the provision of urban roads. Primarily this is through financing—because there is no direct revenue from roads they are generally financed from tax revenue. Taxes on the sale of fuel, motor vehicles and parts are levied by the Commonwealth Government and a part of the proceeds paid to the states through grants for road works. Grants of various kinds have been made since 1922. Until recently the only conditions placed on the grants was that a certain proportion should be spent on minor rural roads, but since the establishment of the Commonwealth Bureau of Roads in 1964 the conditions have become increasingly specific about the kinds of roads on which the grants could be spent, and increasing emphasis has been placed on urban roads. Although the Bureau can influence allocation to particular roads even within urban areas, if they are classified as export roads, most of the detailed allocation of the funds is made by the state authorities.

Most of the public transport in the main cities is provided by state authorities. Brisbane is again the exception because the City Council provides bus services. Suburban rail services are operated as part of the railway system of each state. In New South Wales the Public Transport Commission was formed in 1972, when it assumed control over government railways, including the Sydney and Newcastle suburban services, and government bus services in both cities. Special trusts or commissions operate the government bus and tram services in Melbourne and Adelaide, and bus services in Perth, Kalgoorlie, Hobart, Launceston and Burnie. Municipal bus services are found only in Brisbane and Rockhampton. Outside the main centres, and in parts of the state capitals—mainly the outer suburbs—bus services are provided by private firms, under regulations administered by a state government authority. Melbourne still retains an extensive tram service and Adelaide a single tram line. In both cases the operation is integrated with the government bus services. In Canberra the government bus service is provided by the Department of the Capital Territory.

It was noted in Chapter 5 that public transport services in the major cities often run at a loss. The deficits are met from state revenue and the states must also provide capital for investment in extensions of the services. In the early 1970s the Federal

Government began to make some special purpose grants to allow the states to upgrade their public transport systems in the major urban areas (DURD, 1975, 46–8).

The provision of port facilities, like the railways, is very largely a state responsibility. They are an important element in urban development, not only because of the investment immediately associated with the port, but also because of the effect of the port in generating movement of goods between it and other parts of the urban area. All ports in New South Wales and South Australia are the responsibility of single state authorities, while in other states separate port authorities control individual ports, and in Queensland harbour boards have members representing the local councils in the area served by the ports. Some ports have been built by private firms to allow the export of mineral products, most notably in the north of Western Australia. One of these, Port Hedland, has recently been taken over by the Western Australian government.

The main airports serving Australian cities are provided by the Federal Government through the Department of Transport. Like ports, airports are large traffic generators and their location within an urban area has implications for its general development. The location of new airports is usually a matter for discussion between the Federal and state governments. Improved road links between the airport and the city centre are sometimes provided when a new airport is built or its capacity expanded.

Parks

Apart from roads the main claim on the capital funds of local authorities is investment in parks and other recreation facilities. As with roads, local councils do not have to bear the full responsibility for the provision of recreation facilities. Also like roads, parks do not produce revenue and are financed from taxation rather than loans, while some of the larger and more important parks in the main urban areas are owned and maintained by the states. Adding to the amount of open space available in urban areas has been a significant function of the state or metropolitan planning authorities. There are, as noted in Chapter 5, significant areas of open space provided by private sporting clubs. The cost of providing local open space for community use has been partly lifted from local councils in developing suburban areas by the requirement that developers dedicate a part of their development site—usually 5 to 12.5 per cent—for public open space. In the case of very small developments a cash contribution is made instead of dedication of land. The municipality still has to bear the full cost of developing the land for recreational use.

Education and Health Services

Public primary and secondary education in Australia is provided almost entirely by state Departments of Education, though part of the cost is provided by the Federal Government. Universities, colleges of advanced education and other tertiary institutions are financed very largely by the Federal Government. Although administration of the state education systems is decentralised to regions, there is no significant degree of local control over the schools and local government has no role in the provision of education. There are, of course, private and parish schools (but not tertiary institutions), and pre-school education outside the Australian Capital Territory is provided mainly by non-profit bodies.

Health services cover a wide range of activities, from public health measures through hospitals to the services provided by private medical practitioners. Of these, hospital services require the largest investments and have the widest implications for urban development—they are mainly provided by state authorities. In some states local groups are quite heavily involved in both initiation and control, but in other states they have only a very small role. Hospital boards such as those in Queensland include representatives of local governments. Individual local governments are usually too small, however, to be able to sponsor hospital services. The separation of the smaller urban areas and their rural hinterlands into different local government areas also makes the local authorities unsuitable vehicles for the provision of regional services such as hospitals. In some cases, like mental hospitals and isolation hospitals, the control of the state is complete. Even where there is a local hospital board it gets most of its funds from the state, and increasingly the states have used their financial power as a means of planning hospital services on a state-wide basis. The earlier development of the system of public hospitals has led to concentration of services in the state capitals, and within them, in teaching hospitals close to the university medical schools. Some private hospitals, including many run by religious orders, are subsidised. Others are run by non-profit organisations, and still others run for profit. The only significant direct role of the Federal Government is in the provision of repatriation hospitals for ex-servicemen. Private schools and private hospitals have accounted for about one-fifth of the expenditure on new buildings. The following figures show the percentage of the value of buildings for education and health purposes that were built by governments, over an eighteen-year period to 1973–74.[3]

	Education	Health
1956–57 to 1960–61	71.6	75.4
1961–62 to 1965–66	80.3	86.0
1966–67 to 1970–71	82.4	78.9
1971–72 to 1973–74	86.5	73.6

The public sector appears to be becoming increasingly important in education whereas in health services its share has fluctuated around 80 per cent of the total.

Fire and Police

Fire brigades are organised by bodies which are constituted under state legislation. They are financed by contributions from local authorities, the state government and insurance companies, with the last paying most of the cost. Police services are almost solely a state responsibility outside the two Commonwealth territories.

[3] From 1956–57 to 1960–61 the data refer to value of completions; for later years the value of work done.

Housing and Building

Apart from providing public services the main way in which governments invest directly in urban development is through the public housing authorities. Local government authorities have rarely exercised their powers to build public housing. A few councils have built housing, often for their employees, and rather more have built housing for aged persons with financial assistance from the Federal Government, but the main public housing authorities have been formed by the state governments. They have on some occasions gone beyond the building of houses for sale or renting to needy families to build shopping and service facilities for those occupying their housing. Although local councils have had very little direct involvement in the provision of housing they have sometimes been instrumental in encouraging a housing authority to build within their jurisdictions by providing sites.

Government investment in housing in the post-war period has mainly been the responsibility of state housing authorities in each of the states and of the Commonwealth Government in the Northern Territory and the A.C.T. The majority of the finance for the state authorities has been provided in the form of long-term low-interest loans through a series of Commonwealth State Housing Agreements. These Agreements, which were described in some detail in Chapter 6, provide for construction of housing for low income families. About half of the dwellings built by the state authorities have been sold and the remainder are still rented.

The Commonwealth Government has also financed the construction or purchase of housing for ex-servicemen through the Defence Services Homes Scheme (Chapter 6). Although most of the assistance has taken the form of cheap finance, funds have also been used to buy land and to build houses.

There are two alternative measures of the importance of the government role in the provision of housing. The first is its importance as a builder and decision-maker in relation to the construction of housing. This can be shown in the value of work done on new government dwellings as a proportion of the value of all work on new dwellings. As Figure 8.1 shows, the percentage has declined from between 13 and 15 per cent in the early 1960s to between 6 and 10 per cent in the early 1970s. The second measure is the importance of governments as long-term investors in housing for rental purposes, as a proportion of the total investment in housing. For this purpose the value of houses sold is deducted from the value of new construction to give the government percentage of the total gross fixed capital expenditure on housing. The lower line in Figure 8.1 shows that the government role measured in this way has been much smaller, usually 5 to 7 per cent, and has fluctuated inversely with variations in volume of sales. On this measure there was no significant decline in the government role until the 1970s. Because the housing authorities are building dwellings for families who meet a means test, and because they try to build as much housing as possible with their limited resources, on average they cost less than privately built houses and flats. For example, in 1973–74 government houses completed accounted for 8 per cent of the number, but only 6 per cent of the value of all houses completed.

During the four years 1970–71 to 1973–74 governments carried out just over 17 per cent of the total investment in other buildings compared with less than 8 per

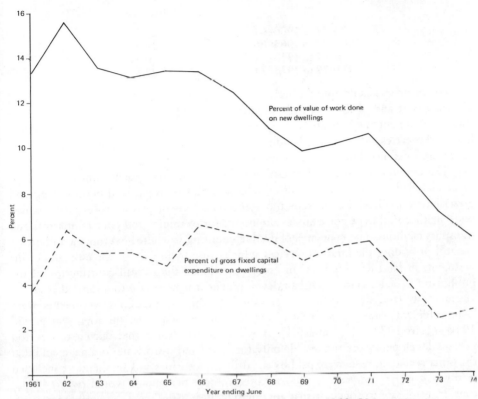

Figure 8.1 The government role in investment in housing: 1960–61 to 1973–74.
Source: ABS, *Building and Construction*.

cent of the total in housing (see Table 7.3). Government authorities built a variety of kinds of buildings, mostly used for the provision of government services. But some—most of the government-built shops for example—were owned by government authorities and leased to private businesses. The Commonwealth Government has built hostels for migrants and a number of government authorities build hostels for their workers. Government printing offices, abattoirs, railway workshops and brickworks are examples of the kinds of factories built by the government authorities.

Most factories, like the other non-residential buildings constructed by government authorities, are special-purpose structures for the use of the authorities that build them, while offices, like the shops that are sometimes built for renting, are much like those built by the private sector. Government authorities rent a considerable proportion of their office space requirements from private owners. For example, from 1956 to 1971, 12 per cent of the office space built in Melbourne CBD and its environs was built by the public sector, but government authorities rented from private investors about another 12 per cent of the total constructed. If post offices are included, the proportion of the total value of office buildings built by governments were as follows:[4]

[4] 1956–57 to 1960–61 value of completions; other years value of work done.

	Per cent
1956–57 to 1960–61	28.7
1961–62 to 1965–66	39.1
1966–67 to 1970–71	30.8
1971–72 to 1973–74	22.8

Governments build quite a high proportion of the buildings for recreation and entertainment and of those in the miscellaneous category (Table 7.2). Among those for entertainment and recreation are gymnasia, squash courts, swimming pools, public halls and theatres. Government buildings in the miscellaneous category include police, prison and defence buildings, museums and orphanages.

The attempt in Chapter 7 to estimate the level of investment in urban development included a certain amount of double counting between land development and government services. There were also some omissions of private investments which were neither buildings nor land development: for example, golf courses, marinas and transport facilities. The main area of double counting is where government authorities are still providing the kinds of services which were included, for the estimates of investment, in land development. In order to estimate the overall contribution of the public and private sectors to urban development it is necessary to assume that all investment in land development is private. On this assumption governments were responsible for some 38 per cent of the total investment over the four-year period 1970–71 to 1973–74 (Table 8.1). If we were to assume that during this period private developers were responsible only for roads and stormwater drainage, and that the other servicing costs were paid by the utility authorities and are therefore included in the cost of government services, the government percentage would rise to 41 per cent. It seems safe to conclude that government authorities were responsible for about 40 per cent of investment in urban development over this period.

TABLE 8.1   *Investment in Urban Development by Government and Private Sectors (average $'000 per year: 1970–71 to 1973–74)*

	Private	Government	Total
Land development	545	—	545
Government services	73	1672	1745
Housing	1734	146	1880
Other building	952	200	1152
	3304	2018	5322

Source: See text above, and Chapter 7.

Planning and Control of Development

As well as planning the provision of their own services, governments can exercise control over private developments. Local councils are heavily involved in regulating the quality and location of urban development within their boundaries. They are responsible for the health regulations and building regulations. In the former case they mainly act as agents for the state Departments of Health, but in the latter case they have somewhat more discretion. Controls over subdivision are also largely concerned with the quality of development, though most councils seem to identify high quality with low density, which has probably inhibited some desirable kinds of medium density development.

The location and pattern of urban development is controlled through land use planning. The first phase in planning.is deciding how the urban area is to change in the future, and formalising these decisions in a plan. The second is implementation of the plan through land use controls. The plan-making phase involves decisions at the large scale of the urban area, and even the state, as well as the small scale of the local community. Outside the major urban areas local government can deal reasonably adequately with both levels, except where development spills over into a rural shire. But in the major cities there is either a metropolitan regional (Melbourne, Geelong, Perth, Hobart) or a state (New South Wales, South Australia) planning authority. Decisions about the general pattern of growth and the desirable distribution of land uses within the urban area at a broad scale are made by the regional or state authority. Local plans are made within that broad framework by local councils.

An important role in the second, implementation, phase is played by local councils through statutory land use controls, which give them the power to approve development applications. The way in which this function is exercised is described in more detail in the next chapter. Statutory land use plans leave some discretion about what will be permitted in particular zones because of the impossibility of foreseeing all demands and eventualities at the time the plan is being devised. Furthermore, a precise definition of the locations of such high density uses as shopping centres would probably be self-defeating because of the way the property market would react. It would give an immediate and large capital gain to the owner of the favoured site and create pressures to allow the development to take place on cheaper sites nearby. It is not uncommon for all developments, except single family houses in areas zoned for housing, to require the consent of the relevant planning authority.

If the proposed development is of a kind permitted in the plan, or if it is relatively small, the local council can approve without further reference. If, however, because of its size or location, or because of the more widespread effects it may have on the way the urban area grows, it has implications outside the municipality, it is usually referred to a state or metropolitan planning authority. Most developments have implications for the provision of services, especially hydraulic services, and either the council or the planning authority refers applications to the relevant service authorities. In this way the service authorities become involved in land use planning decisions. Partly because of the increasing scale of many developments, and partly because of the increasing extent to which developers are required to reticulate services within their subdivisions, development applications are increasingly being referred to a wide range of authorities, both for information and for approval, before a decision is made by the planning authority with the statutory power.

The above description tries to show how land use planning as a function of government operates in theory. In practice there are very real constraints on the extent to which both local and metropolitan or state planning authorities can influence the way a city grows and develops. The existing pattern of land use imposes severe limitations, and pressures on planning authorities from land owners and developers restrict the ability of the community, through land use controls, to achieve the future development they desire. These problems are taken up in more detail in the next chapter.

Summary

In summarising the roles of different levels of government it is appropriate to start with the Federal and local governments, and deal last with the states, since they have the residual powers under the Australian Constitution. The direct role of the Federal Government in urban development outside the territories is limited to the provision of postal and telephone services and airports. However, it has a very large financial role and, especially during the three years of the Whitlam Labor Government (1973–75), began to use its financial powers to influence the activities of state and local authorities in urban development. This was not entirely a new initiative since special purpose grants, especially for roads and universities, had previously been given with some 'strings attached'. The states still retain most of the discretion about how to use both the tax reimbursement funds which flow through the Federal Treasury and the loan moneys which are approved by the loan council.

Local government is directly involved in two main ways. The first is in the provision of local roads and drains, parks, garbage services and some other services. The second is in planning and controlling private development within their boundaries. These two functions are combined when the councils require private developers to provide roads, local drains and open space within their subdivisions. Special-purpose local authorities, and some of the ordinary local authorities, retail electricity and provide water and sewerage services in some parts of Australia.

State departments, and authorities primarily responsible to state governments, provide the remaining urban services, and carry out planning and land use controls at the metropolitan level in the larger centres. Major roads, public transport, ports, education, housing, health services, police and fire services are all primarily state responsibilities. The special-purpose authorities which supply services in metropolitan areas are increasingly coming under state control. Some state authorities purchase land and develop it for use for housing, industrial or commercial activities.

The two major cities which are significantly different to this pattern are Brisbane and Canberra. In Brisbane a single local authority covers nearly all of the urban area and is responsible for a number of functions, such as public transport, water and sewerage, retailing of electricity, and metropolitan planning, which are carried out by state or special purpose metropolitan authorities elsewhere. In Canberra, on the other hand, Federal Government instrumentalities carry out all of the functions of both state and local governments elsewhere. The National Capital Development Commission, with the advantage of government-owned land, has been able to integrate urban planning with the land development functions which are primarily carried out by private developers in other parts of Australia.

The state capital cities are in an often unique situation. Because they house so much of the state populations, and because their local government is fragmented they rely on the state for some functions that are performed by local councils in smaller centres. In some respects there are 'city states' in Australia, and their governments often act like city governments.

Financial constraints on the level of government investment in urban development operate at several different levels. The Loan Council, which includes the Prime Minister and the State Premiers, determines the total volume of government borrowing each year in the light of the general economic situation. Loans for the Commonwealth and state governments are raised by the Commonwealth. Each state allocates these funds between competing demands within the state. Local and semi-government (mostly special-purpose) authorities raise their own loans, within the limits decided upon by the loan council. Any local or special-purpose authority, or indeed state government, which wants to invest more than it can borrow has the option of raising additional revenue for investment through taxes or charges. The level of investment is limited by their ability to borrow (because of Loan Council limits) and their ability to raise revenue, either to invest directly or to service previous borrowings. Investment in services which do not produce revenue to service loans, such as schools, parks, hospitals and roads, competes directly with other government expenditures for the tax revenue available, at all three levels of government.

9 Determinants of the Pattern of Urban Development

This concluding chapter gives an account of the main influences that have determined the shape and pattern of development of Australian cities. As in the other parts of the book the primary emphasis will be on the location of different kinds of development within the major metropolitan areas. To a considerable extent the findings which are presented derive from research carried out in the Urban Research Unit on the process of urban development in Sydney and Melbourne. Many of the results of the Melbourne study are summarised in a research report (Urban Research Unit, 1972) which also interprets the findings as they relate to that city. Although the focus of interest is intra-urban development, the same factors have helped to determine the distribution of development between cities, though their relative importance and the way they interact may differ.

The first part of the chapter is concerned with historical and physical influences. These are given for any city at a particular time, as distinct from influences described later in the chapter. The second part examines a number of possible hypotheses about how the shape of development over any particular time is affected by decisions about development. These hypotheses can be identified with different strands in the literature on urban development, including a number of formal and informal models. Each hypothesis reflects a view that a particular group of individuals or institutions has the major influence on the shape of development. The third part describes how the different kinds of influences and interests interact with one another, through market, administrative and political mechanisms. Finally, the chapter draws some conclusions about the way in which urban development in Australia occurs under these different influences.

The chapter will be concerned with some very general features of urban development: the direction of spatial spread of the city—whether Melbourne grows to the east or the west; the extent to which growth is along corridors, or spreads evenly around the fringe; the density of development and the extent to which it includes not only housing but also shops, factories and offices; the arrangement of activities within the existing urban area, the changing distribution of employment opportunities between the central area, commercial centres in the suburbs and suburban industrial areas; the income levels of residents in different parts of a city and the extent of segregation between different income groups; the extent to which cities grow by spreading at the edges, and by increasing the density of the existing urban area.

Historical and Physical Influences

There are two important influences on urban development which do not result from any current activities. The first is the influence of natural features. This is well recognised in the literature about the distribution of growth between different urban areas. The productive potential of the hinterland, its mineral and water resources, the climate and the recreational opportunities in the vicinity all influence the relative rate of growth of different cities. Chapter 2 also showed that such natural features as a safe anchorage and a reliable supply of fresh water determined the sites of the state capital cities.

Topography and other natural features of the site of a city continue to have an important influence as it develops. The early roads and stock routes from the settlements followed ridges to avoid swampy ground and river crossings. They also avoided steep grades. The railways followed similar routes for much the same reasons and linked the settlements which had sprung up along the roads. Residential development of a town usually avoided low-lying and poorly drained areas. Those who could afford it sought the higher and topographically more interesting areas with attractive views. The less well-off families concentrated in flatter areas where the costs of land and building were lower. Factories, especially since the Second World War, have mostly been located on flat land because modern industrial processes rely heavily on the horizontal movement of goods being processed, assembled or stored.

The influence of topography on the distribution of social classes is well known in many Australian cities. But probably nowhere is it more obvious than in Sydney where the broken terrain of the North Shore, the eastern harbourside suburbs and parts of the Georges River and Port Hacking foreshores contrast with the flatter topography south of the city centre and on the Cumberland Plain to the west, where land is less expensive. Even within the western suburbs richer people live along the slight ridge that extends from Ashfield through Burwood to Strathfield. In Melbourne the more interesting topography south and east of the Yarra is reinforced by the more equable climate, and the better garden soils. The flat basalt plains to the west are expensive to service because of the layer of very hard rock near the surface. One of the effects of requiring developers to meet these costs is that building in Melbourne's western suburbs has become more expensive, and therefore they are less suitable for low cost housing.

The influence of topography is sometimes indirect. Because of difficult topography, sewerage services may not be provided in an area at the time it is subdivided. Without sewerage the density and type of development is limited by the difficulties of disposal.

It can be argued that many of the features of urban development in Australia are determined by the natural characteristics of the sites and hinterlands of the cities. It is probably more useful to regard the natural features of the site as one of the conditions within which decisions about development are taken. There are still many options about the sequence and the kind of development that occurs in particular localities and individual sites. Attention in this chapter is mainly directed towards the ways in which the choices between those alternatives are made.

The chapter is concerned with the marginal changes in the use of land and the marginal additions to a city's physical infrastructure and buildings that are made during a limited period. Much of the physical plant in a city can be taken as given. The existing development also affects decisions about new development. Thus, the best use of a particular site depends on the other land uses in the vicinity, the services available and the distance of the site from different parts of the city. In many respects the previous development of a city has an influence similar to natural features of the site.

The parallel between the influence of natural and constructed features of a city is not very close. The influence of inherited structures and patterns can be explored further—made endogenous to the model—by an historical examination of decisions about development. Inherited structures can also be demolished or used in different ways. Examples of the influence of inherited developments are easy to find. Once dirty or noisy industries are established in a suburb it becomes unattractive to most residents, but may be attractive to other manufacturers and wholesalers. The income level of those who already live in a suburb is an important influence on the value of residential sites. Prices are higher in high income suburbs because it is easier to attract new high income residents to live in them. In choosing where to live people are concerned about the availability of suitable jobs within commuting distance, and employers making location decisions consider their ability to attract suitable workers. Shopping facilities, schools and recreation opportunities are all taken into account by residents when choosing where to live.

The location of some services exerts a powerful influence over a long period of time. A prime example is suburban railways. All the suburban railways in Melbourne were built before 1890, and yet the *Report of the Metropolitan Town Planning Commission* (1929) observed that 'Nothing has influenced the trend of suburban development in this metropolis to a greater degree during the last half century than the railway system' (p.129). Despite the reduced role of the suburban railways in carrying passengers since 1929, they have still exerted a major influence on development in the half century since the report was written.

The directions of growth of most of the major cities in Australia and their high and low income suburbs were established before the Second World War. Few suburbs have changed from high to low or vice versa, (Davis and Spearritt, 1974, 9–14) and most of the new suburbs that have attracted the rich are adjacent to the older high income suburbs. Industrial areas tend to be concentrated in a few sectors of the cities—south and west of Sydney, south-east and west of Melbourne. In many respects these cities have just been adding more of the same kinds of development, extending the established sectoral patterns.

Major Decision-Makers

Five major decision agents influence the shape of development of a city. Three are in the private sector—individuals and families deciding where to live, commercial and industrial firms deciding where to locate, and private developers deciding where to service land and build. The other two are in the public sector—public authorities providing utilities and services, and planning authorities exercising controls over the development of the city. These 'agents' range from a large number of individuals or firms in the private sector to a few important authorities in the public sector. Even within a group there is diversity though—developers range from large firms that develop land and build houses, factories and offices to small speculative builders. It is useful to examine the influence of these five agents under the headings of five hypotheses about the major determinants. Each hypothesis argues that a particular agent is very important.

Residential Choice

Much of the theory of welfare economics is based on the belief that consumers' tastes are given and that their choices between different goods and services, and between work and leisure, effectively determine the allocation of resources. The market transmits consumers' tastes to those making decisions about production. The price that consumers are prepared to pay for goods and services, relative to the cost of resources used for their production, determines the allocation of resources to their production. The application of this theory to urban development holds that the preferences of residents about the kind of housing they want to live in, where they want to live, the services they want in their locality and where they are prepared to travel to work, to school and to shop, largely determine the way a city grows.

When deciding where to live people take into account convenience to jobs and a range of services, but research in the Urban Research Unit (Troy, 1971; 1972) suggests that the most important factor is availability of a suitable house at a price they can afford. This suggests that developments in a range of different locations could be financially successful as long as the right kinds of housing are built. A family's choice of housing is also affected by its composition and its income, and people seem to prefer to live among others with tastes and living standards similar to their own. For these reasons developers have to pay careful attention to their particular market in any proposed location. Householders' decisions also tend to perpetuate established patterns of development. Not only do most choose to live in areas of similar socio-economic status to themselves, but when they move, they usually stay within the same sector of the city (Johnston, 1969).

The preferences of families about where to live, and in what kinds of housing, are reflected in the profitability of different kinds of residential developments, including redevelopment in inner suburbs at higher density. This first hypothesis would see these residential development decisions as determining most of the other urban developments. Once housing is established, shops and other private services will be provided to meet the demands of local residents, and the kinds of shops will be determined in large part by the incomes and tastes of the residents. Government service authorities respond to demands produced by residential development and provide schools, parks, trunk roads, water, sewerage, electricity and telephone services. Depending on the occupation of the residents, employers may find it to their advantage to locate near the new development to tap the labour available. Those employing blue collar workers have less need to locate in shopping and commercial centres and can afford to locate near their workers. Working wives also resist travelling long distances. In contrast, white collar male workers and single females are more willing to (or have to) commute long distances. As a result most of the manufacturing development is located in areas close to lower income residential areas, and most of the offices are built in locations accessible to (though not necessarily close to) high income residential areas. Thus office development outside the city centre has mainly been to the north in Sydney and to the east of Melbourne.

Groups of residents act through local councils to secure the provisions of services in residential areas and to ensure that land use controls are used to resist developments that threaten their amenity. Collective actions of this kind are not covered by the free market model from which this hypothesis derives. If, however, that model is broadened to allow for the exercise of collective choice about the environment, as well as individual choices about where and in what to live, the actions of government in both provision of services and land use planning can be seen to follow residential choices.

A number of arguments can be marshalled to support the hypothesis. The first development of a suburban area is usually for housing, and the provision of local services, both public and private, follow. In this sense residential development leads and other kinds of development follow. The boom in flat construction which began in Australia in the late 1950s was, as shown in Chapter 6, largely a response to the demand from the increasing numbers of young households without children that are more likely to live in flats. Flats were built where they wanted to live. The flat building boom has had significant influence on the distribution of population, at least in Sydney (see Chapter 3), and is an exception to the general proposition that postwar development consisted of filling in the gaps between developed areas and adding more suburbs similar to those built between the wars.

Despite these arguments, probably the best explanation of the more rapid growth of Melbourne to the south and east is that a better climate and soil provide both more attractive living conditions and lower development costs. In Sydney, the situation is different. The environmentally attractive part of the city is the most difficult and costly to develop and to build on. As a result there has not been the same imbalance in the direction of growth. The fringe of development which is furthest from the city centre is in the Cumberland Plain to the west and south-west of Sydney where low development costs are combined with a less interesting environment, a lower rainfall and wider temperature ranges.

The hypothesis can be questioned at another level. Even if consumers' tastes and preferences have a major effect on the way cities develop, it can be argued that those tastes and preferences themselves are shaped by the environment in which the consumers have been living. The same criticism applies to the use of welfare economics to argue that the market allocates resources in an optimal way. The fact that cities in different parts of the world are built in very different ways, at different residential densities, suggests that environmental preferences are influenced by experience. This view is also supported by the resistance of residents to changes in kinds of dwelling and their preference for staying within a particular sector of a city when they move.

Location of Employers

A second hypothesis puts most of the emphasis on the decisions of employers about where to locate. Once jobs are located workers choose to live where they are accessible to their jobs. Of particular importance are the decisions of employers in those private firms and government authorities that do not have to locate in each suburb to be close to their customers. Most of the formal models of urban development are based to some extent on this hypothesis. One family of models grew out of the work of Wingo (1961), Alonso (1964), Muth (1969) and Mills (1972a), all of whom assume that these kinds of jobs are concentrated in the city centre. The main objective of the models was to explain how population and housing densities, income levels, household structures, house rents and land values vary with distance from the city centre. By assuming that workers want to live close to the centre, the models are able to show how, as they locate further from the centre, families will gain from larger house sites at the expense of increases in commuting costs. They take the location of employers as given.

Another group of models, derived from the work of Lowry (1964), are mainly designed to predict future development patterns. A number of city zones are identified by their distance from every other zone. The first step in operating the model is to locate employers in 'basic' activities, that is activities which serve a metropolitan, regional, national or international market rather than the local suburban market. Those locations are determined by considerations that are exogenous to the model. The next step is to decide where people who take those jobs will live, on the assumption that they minimise their journeys to work. Local service activities are then located where they can serve the markets provided by workers in basic industries. Next workers in local service industries are located, as close as possible to where they work. The model has to be run through several times as more population, and then more local service jobs, are added at each step. The number of residents and the number of jobs of different kinds in each zone are constrained by the capacity of the zone. Although the distribution of service jobs and population between zones is mainly based on the length of journeys to work and shopping trips, environmental features and services available in each zone can also be taken into account.

The research of the Urban Research Unit in both Sydney and Melbourne (Vandermark, 1970; Neilson, 1972) confirmed that it is useful to distinguish two categories of suburban (that is non-CBD) private businesses, each with different locational needs. The first is commercial firms which deal directly with the public—mainly retailing and some services. They are found mainly in shopping centres and are very strongly market-oriented. Not only do they need to be accessible to their customers, they also prefer to be close to other similar activities which attract shoppers. Since an urban area can support only a limited number of large shopping centres, land within established centres becomes very valuable. Although the shopping centre needs to be reasonably convenient to its customers its precise location does not greatly affect its viability. Traditionally shopping centres were located on the main roads, and especially at main intersections. More recently these locations have become less attractive with the growth in traffic, and entrepreneurs have been able to establish large scale 'regional' shopping centres in almost any place where they can tap a large enough market and get a large enough site to provide parking and a large floor area on no more than two or three levels.

The second kind of business corresponds to Lowry's basic activity. It does not deal with the public and therefore can seek sites that are cheaper than those in commercial centres. Most wholesaling and manufacturing comes into this category. Its location is sometimes determined by linkages with other businesses and government authorities, either through transport of goods or through personal contacts. These factors tend to attract businesses towards the city centre or towards transport terminals. Frequently the availability of a suitable site, with appropriate zoning, is a major consideration. Another important factor for some is accessibility to a suitable labour supply. When industrial or wholesaling establishments move they often try to keep the same workers and suppliers by seeking another site in the same general area. Availability of labour is one reason why many large employers of clerical workers are located in the city centre.

The city centre also attracts a third type of employer who mainly wants contacts—flows of information rather than goods—with other businesses and with government authorities. Government authorities also want to be close to one another and to parliament. The city centre is almost the only place where retailers who want highly accessible shopping sites compete with other businesses that want contact with other activities. Part of the reason for this competition is that shops in the city centre cater for those who work there as well as those who travel from the suburbs. In addition the city centre is attractive to highly specialised retailers since it is accessible to most parts of the city. Only a few suburban centres have attracted a significant amount of employment in firms that put a high value on business contact (Alexander, 1976).

Many manufacturers are willing to locate wherever in a city they can get a suitable site and attract a suitable workforce. Industrial development frequently follows residential development, after a lag, into suburbs where there are blue collar workers. This kind of industrial development is no more a leader in setting the pattern of development than the shops that are found in each suburb. Some large manufacturers, such as the car assembly plants established in outer suburbs of Melbourne and Adelaide, have had an influence as they are large enough to be somewhat independent of local suppliers. They need to attract related industrial development and may even attract residential development to the vicinity. Investors and developers take the opportunity to provide for these demands.

Location decisions of employers have been partly responsible for the dispersal of jobs and activities from the city centre to the suburbs which was described in Chapter 4. This is encouraging residential development to spread even further and reduces the use of public transport in the journey to work since it cannot readily serve dispersed work places. It has also led to some geographic segmentation of labour markets in large cities.

The role of employers' location decisions in determining the pattern of urban development is therefore limited for at least two reasons. Firstly, such decisions are partly determined by the availability of suitable zoned sites and access to labour, and to that extent they follow rather than lead urban development. Secondly, access to job opportunities is not by any means the only determinant of where people live. For the most part investors in rental industrial premises and all but the largest industrial firms locate in zoned industrial areas, and prefer established areas.

Government employers can also be roughly subdivided according to the relative importance of three factors influencing their location. The first, accessibility to the local population, is very important for most local government services, education and some health, welfare and employment services. The second, access to labour supplies, is most important for such information processing activities as the Taxation Office (Lanigan, 1976). The third is access to minister's offices (usually in or near parliament), and other government and private activities. This is very important for the policy departments of state and federal governments. Although the location of government offices, like private employers, has been partly responsible for the concentration of jobs in the city centre, a few large government employers locate on the fringe. They include defence and research establishments, prisons and psychiatric hospitals, which are not likely to attract other development.

Developer Initiatives

Most of the initiatives for development and redevelopment in Australian cities are taken by private developers. They purchase land, arrange finance, seek permission to develop from the planning and servicing authorities, arrange to have the necessary services installed (or install them themselves) and find buyers for the completed development. In this very direct sense decisions of developers are the key decisions in urban development. It is their decisions which require service authorities to extend and amplify their service networks. Especially now that developers themselves are responsible for reticulation of services within a subdivision, they have even become somewhat less dependent on service authorities. In some Australian cities, for example Brisbane, where land use controls are used mainly for short-term regulation, an application from a developer can also initiate a land use planning decision. Developer decisions are at the centre of models of urban development produced at the University of North Carolina (Weiss *et al.*, 1966; Kaiser, 1968). In earlier chapters it was pointed out that householders and businesses can act as developers when they build their own houses, shops and factories. However, the developer who subdivides land or builds for sale initiates most development and is the subject of this section.

The hypothesis that private developers are the key decision-makers is an alternative to the hypothesis that consumer preferences are the guiding force. Like the latter this producer-oriented interpretation of the determinants of the pattern of development has its parallel in economics. Some economists argue that producers decide what is profitable to produce and manipulate tastes through promotion and advertising to persuade consumers that they want the goods being produced. Similarly, it can be argued, developers buy land where they can get it in large lumps at an acceptable price and promote the development to ensure that it is commercially successful. Part of the promotion might include providing a higher quality of residential environment than is available elsewhere. Perhaps the best example is the ex-urban subdivision with minimum services promoted by their developers as both a good investment and a rural retreat (Wagner, 1974).

An alternative interpretation of the role of developers is that, in order to make profits, they try to anticipate the preferences of their potential clients, and to seek development opportunities where those preferences can be satisfied. A good deal of research seems to suggest that most developers are guided, in seeking profitable development opportunities, by the experience of other developers and by their own previous experience. This would suggest that they will tend to follow the established pattern of development rather than initiate changes in the pattern (Vandermark and Harrison, 1972; Neilson, 1976).

Those who suggest that developers' decisions are important determinants of the way cities grow are usually referring to the pattern of development within cities. Developers have little influence on either residents' or employers' choice of location between cities, but they can and do promote retirement resorts and holiday home developments. Larger developers have more opportunity to influence the pattern of development than small ones since they can spread the costs of promotion and the provision of amenities to attract buyers over a larger volume of production. The increases in requirements for developers to service land have tended to squeeze the small developer out of the industry (Paterson, 1974), and as a result developers may increasingly be able to exercise an influence.

Even large developers are concerned to reduce their risks, and they do this partly by staging their developments so that investments in, and even decisions about, the later stages of development are not taken until the first stages are completed and the level of demand can be assessed. The situation where developers have influenced the pattern of development to the greatest extent is in the building of private enterprise new towns in the United States. The closest approach to them in Australia is large suburban developments such as Hooker's Centenary Estates in Brisbane. Most developers see themselves as catering for an existing demand rather than shaping demand, however.

Developers of industrial and commercial property probably innovate even less frequently than developers of residential estates. Private developers who build speculative industrial and commercial buildings or provide factory sites cater mainly for small manufacturers, retailers and investors. They are less likely to choose a location that departs from established areas than the large manufacturer or retailer. Large regional shopping centres are an exception, but in Australia, they almost always aim to serve established markets and therefore do not lead development. Speculative non-residential development is very largely confined to established, or at least zoned, industrial and commercial areas.

While few developers have much influence on the pattern of new development the options in the case of redevelopment are a good deal wider. For example, large areas of single family housing are convenient enough to public transport and other amenities to be suitable for flat redevelopment. The choice is somewhat limited by local government zoning restrictions, but in many municipalities there have been few controls. Speculative commercial and industrial redevelopment has also been of some importance though the larger redevelopments have frequently been initiated by prospective occupants. Central city office redevelopment has frequently been initiated by investors and developers. Since the market for office space is so highly localised these redevelopments have consolidated the pattern of development rather than changing it. Suburban office developments have been relatively insignificant (Alexander, 1976).

In their role in urban development the state housing authorities are much like private developers, but they are not so constrained by the demands of their clients. Because they can offer cheap housing, their clients provide, to some degree, a captive market. As a result the authorities have been able to undertake large new areas of development and to carry out high density redevelopment that has had a marked impact on the inner areas of Melbourne and, to a lesser extent, Sydney. Their fringe developments have been less innovative, though in South Australia the development of Elizabeth was a distinct departure from the previous pattern, and in the Sydney region the Housing Commission is pioneering the corridor development to the south-west.

Government Services

In the earlier part of this chapter the influence of the suburban railways on the shape of the major Australian cities was emphasised. It was also noted that very few suburban railways have been built in Australia since the 1920s, and most were built much earlier. The relatively minor proposed extensions and improvements are unlikely to have much influence on the pattern of development. Electrification of lines to more remote suburban areas and improved services can have some effect, but follow demand more often than leading it. Much of the investment in urban transport facilities in recent years has been in roads. They differ from railways in that road improvements increase access to much broader areas. Most investment in roads is in arterials and minor roads which, unlike suburban railway routes, provide a relatively low travel capacity, dispersed over the whole urban area. In addition the capacity of the road system can be increased in stages in response to increased demand.

Of all government services transport is most likely to influence the pattern of urban development. Indeed the interdependence of transport and land use is well recognised in urban research and policy making. Other services can also have an influence on the shape of development. For example, without mains sewerage only low density development will be possible, or development may be prohibited. The availability of good schools is often cited as one of the reasons people are attracted to live in particular suburbs, though this is probably less important in Australia, where schools are provided by the states, than in some other countries. Some people need to live close to the central city's hospitals, colleges or universities, although this affects only a limited number, and access to central facilities does not impose an absolute restraint on the extent to which the city spreads outwards. Most services, including electricity, water, telephones, schools, parks and local health facilities, are eventually provided more or less wherever they are demanded within the metropolitan area. The authorities responsible for them are required by their Acts to meet any reasonable demand for their services, and regard themselves as responding to development initiatives taken by others rather than stimulating or initiating development (Pickett, 1973).

There may be significant delays between development and the time when all services are provided. Delays have been most common in provision of sewerage but families have also had to wait for telephone connections. Roads have remained un-sealed, parks undeveloped and schools have become crowded before new ones were completed, but it appears that residents accept these delays as part of the pioneering life in a new suburb. Often they are matched by lags in private services. If the provision of sewerage lags more in some parts of a city than others it may discourage development. It may also have an indirect effect since planning authorities may be unwilling to ap-prove developments in areas which cannot be readily sewered.

Freeways, like railways, are by their nature built with a large capacity. Again like a railway, a freeway provides a high level of access to places close to the access points along its route. During the 1960s it appeared that the influence of freeways on the pattern of development might be like that of suburban railways earlier in the century. Extensive freeway networks have been planned for a number of Australian cities. They would have catered for travel along radial routes to the city centre, and also for the increasing demand for travel between suburbs arising from the spread of jobs, shopping and services to suburban areas. The freeway interchanges could have become, as they have in the United States, favoured locations for the development of employment and commercial centres.

Although parts of the networks were constructed in several cities, mounting op-position from residents whose housing and environment were threatened has led to a drastic slow-down in construction and the abandonment of many proposed routes within built-up areas (Commonwealth Bureau of Roads, 1974). On the other hand freeways are still being built on the urban fringes where it is not necessary to demolish housing and they do not threaten residential amenity. In those areas they can be a quite powerful influence encouraging development along particular corridors.

Elsewhere investment in road facilities is made to remove bottle-necks. In fact road authorities decide when a section of road needs to be improved by observing travel times on each section, and accident frequencies at intersections. These indicate the benefits from improvement, which are then compared with the costs. Costs are mainly a function of density of development, and vary markedly with distance from the city centre. Resources may occasionally be concentrated on a particular arterial route for a period, but travel times on different routes are not allowed to get too far out of balance.

On a different scale investment in roads has had a major effect on the pattern of development. In the first place road investment has allowed the gaps to be filled between the corridors of development along the suburban railways and arterial roads; additionally, road improvement has encouraged the spread of both population and jobs into the suburbs. The suburbanisation of jobs has had a profound influence. When goods transport by road became relatively cheap and efficient it became possible for manufacturers, wholesalers and large scale retailers to locate almost anywhere within an urban area without incurring very high transport costs. Previously costs rose rapid-ly with distance from railway stations and sidings.

The city centres still contain the highest concentration of jobs and a particularly high concentration of white collar jobs. Many of its workers live in middle or outer suburbs and rely on public transport to get to and from work. If public transport were allowed to deteriorate the city centre would become much less attractive to many employers. Improvements in rail services, such as the underground loop in Melbourne and the Eastern Suburbs Railway in Sydney, are designed mainly to cater for commuters and to maintain the viability of the city centre. Decisions about public transport services still have a very important influence on urban development.

Land Use Planning

The final hypothesis follows the theory of land use planning: it is decisions about permissible land use which determine the way a city grows and develops. Through their land use control powers, planning authorities can limit the spread of a city and can control the kinds of land uses permitted in particular areas. If the controls are sufficiently tight, it is possible for the planning authority to determine fairly precisely the use which will be permitted on every site by excluding other uses. Of course, while this procedure might work in controlling growth and change within an urban area, it is less powerful in influencing the growth of cities as a whole. The only way land use planning can influence this distribution is by limiting the land available for growth in an urban area as a whole. There are, of course, other ways in which regional planning can influence this distribution.

In practice land use planning in Australian cities has not seriously attempted to influence the inter-urban distribution of growth, and it has made only limited attempts to control the distribution of growth within cities (Harrison, 1974). There have been many attempts to restrict development in particular directions. The 'green belt' policy introduced by the Cumberland County Council (1948) for the Sydney region was probably the most ambitious and comprehensive. More recently land use controls have been used to restrict development in particular directions and in particular areas such as the hills face zone in Adelaide and the Dandenong Ranges in Melbourne. This has usually been a part of a corridor plan to encourage the growth of the cities in other directions. Land use controls have also been used to protect from development areas designated as open space, pending their acquisition, and to reserve routes for freeways from further development or redevelopment. They have been used to prevent industrial and commercial development in residential areas, and to prevent the sprawl of urban development along main routes and away from the built-up urban fringe. As mentioned above they have sometimes been used to restrict or prevent development in areas that cannot be sewered, though this policy has often been introduced after a good deal of development has already occurred in such areas and become a contingent liability for the sewerage authority.

Apart from pursuing these general objectives, land use planning has been mostly responsive rather than positive and directive. The objective has been to zone enough land for each kind of development, broadly in the areas where it is likely to be demanded. There are good reasons for such a planning procedure. Any more active policy would produce strong counter-pressures in the land market. Any attempt to control land use very precisely puts the owner of the land which is zoned for development in a monopoly position. Thus the Sydney green belt was blamed for escalating prices of land inside the belt. More recently the same charges have been levied against land use controls in general. Especially in the case of high density redevelopment, precise definition of permissible sites would be directly reflected in their price, so land use plans seldom specify at all precisely where redevelopment is to take place.

There has been some success in planning the areas in which industrial development will be permitted, and in consolidating existing industrial areas. Even in established areas there is increasing consolidation of the industrial zones as the remaining houses in such areas are replaced by factories, and factories which remain as 'nonconforming uses' in residential areas are phased out because they are not permitted to rebuild or extend. It can be argued that these policies have been too successful and have produced too much separation of home from work so that work journeys are unnecessarily long and working wives, for example, have difficulty finding jobs near home. Conversely, it can be argued just as forcefully that zoning has restrained the expansion of inner city industrial areas and has encouraged manufacturing to disperse to the suburbs where there is plenty of zoned industrial land closer to where industrial workers live.

Control over commercial development has been less effective. In new suburbs permission is usually given to the developer who makes the first application for a shopping centre in a suitable location. Many of the early post-war metropolitan plans nominated a number of existing suburban centres for development as major centres. Very few of them have developed to the extent planned, despite the very substantial growth of retailing and private services in the suburbs as a whole. Rather, a good deal of this type of development has occurred in new major regional shopping centres which have been located away from existing suburban centres and away from major public transport routes. In part this is due to a change in the technology of retailing which has favoured the large centre with good road access and plenty of parking, and which provides traffic-free pedestrian movement between shops—but land use planning has only been able to react to private proposals rather than determine the location of these centres.

City centre plans cannot be shown to have had very much effect. Indeed there have been few serious attempts to plan the development of central business districts. Once the limit to building heights imposed by the height of fire brigade ladders was removed, it became difficult to find criteria for control over the height and density of redevelopment. It is not surprising therefore, that density controls over office building have proved difficult to enforce. The best that has been achieved is some improvement in pedestrian circulation. When parking in the city centre became a serious problem, builders were required to provide parking in each new building, but when it was realised that this simply attracted more vehicles into the city centres, the policy was reversed in some cities and limits set on the amount of parking permitted in new buildings.

Land use planning has not been a very powerful influence over the pattern of urban development, mainly because land use controls themselves are negative planning tools and do not allow a planning authority to take much initiative. If the authorities tried to exercise more influence they would have encountered strong counter-pressures in the land market. Urban planning could be more influential if it incorporated the plans for the development of transport and other services as well as controls over the private use of land. Although each of the service authorities, and often the planning authority itself, feels bound to observe established trends in urban development, together they comprise a significant part of the total and could lead it rather than simply exercising controls.

There is increasing recognition of the interdependence of land use planning and provision of services, and there have been attempts to integrate them by including representatives of service authorities on planning authorities. Service authorities increasingly use planning powers to restrict developments in areas that are difficult to service. However, there have been few serious attempts in Australia to use the resources of the public sector in an integrated way to lead the pattern of development. In Canberra, Adelaide, and more recently in Sydney, the public sector lead has been more powerful, partly because of its ownership of land.

A different kind of urban planning can be exercised if the planning authority is able to purchase a significant proportion of the land needed for development. Although many Australian cities and towns were sited on crown land, most of it was subsequently sold to private owners. In Canberra, which was founded as the national capital in 1911, the site was purchased by the Federal Government before development commenced. As a result the roles of planning authority, servicing authority (at least for roads and hydraulic services) and developer have been combined so that urban planning is positive rather than negative. In most other cities the only government authorities which have been able to exercise this positive role by buying land for development have been the public housing authorities. Service authorities have also purchased land for their own needs but, as has been argued above, are mainly responsive to demands created by private developments. In Adelaide, however, the housing authority undertook a programme to provide cheap land for housing and industrial development as part of a plan to attract industry by providing cheap land and labour (Stretton, 1975, Ch.5 and Ch.6). Almost by accident this provided an opportunity to engage in positive planning of the city's development. One result was the satellite city of Elizabeth. Sydney is now attempting to use similar methods on a larger scale in the Campbelltown Corridor.

Interaction Between Decision-Makers

There is no clear leader in determining the pattern of urban development. In most Australian cities, urban development does not follow careful and detailed plans adopted by government. Nor is it purely a free market process; it cannot be, because government authorities play an important role as providers of services in urban areas. In addition the public accepts that governments should exercise some control over private development. In a mixed private-government system, decisions made by each of the different authorities, firms and individuals influence the development decisions of the others. The actual development that occurs is the result of these interactions. There appear to be three main kinds of interaction—market, administrative and political. Figure 9.1 summarises the paths through which the activities of each type of decision-maker influence the others.

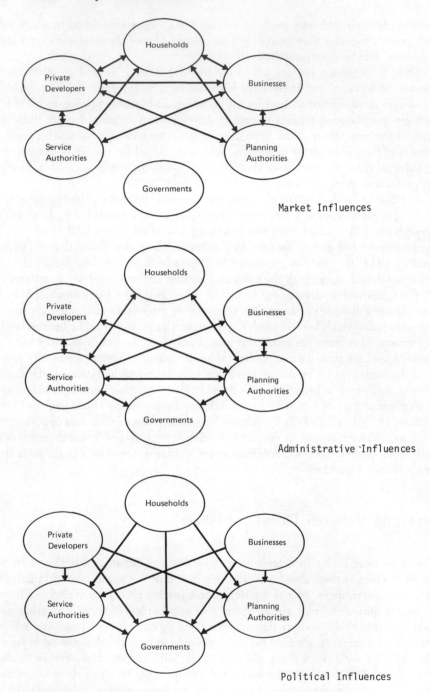

Figure 9.1 Relations between groups involved in urban development.

Markets

Even though urban development is by no means purely a market process, the market still plays the major role in encouraging private investors to provide houses, shops, factories and offices more or less as and where they are needed. The market demand originates with households, and businesses and private developers respond to profit-making opportunities. For example, an increase in the demand for flats in a particular part of a city will, in the first instance, lead to an increase in rents and prices. These increases will create profitable development and investment opportunities to which developers will respond by building flats on any available land. If there is no vacant land the price will have to rise to a level where it pays to buy established houses and demolish them to provide sites for new flats.

It was pointed out above that availability of a suitable site at a reasonable price is an important factor determining where businessmen locate. If the demand for factory space in an area increases, factory developments will increasingly compete with other activities for land. Left to its own devices the market will generally allocate vacant land to the use for which it is most valuable, as reflected in the price a user is prepared to pay. Once it is developed, of course, it is usually expensive to convert it from one use to another because buildings and services are specialised and have a long life.

Although the price private users are prepared to pay for land reflects the value they place on it, the situation is much more complex in the case of government service authorities—yet they use something like 40 per cent of all of the land in an urban area (Chapter 5) and they have to buy most of it in the market. Much of the publicly owned land is used for roads, parks or schools, which do not produce anything for sale, so it is difficult to even estimate its value to users. In addition some of the authorities need to buy particular pieces of land (for new road routes, for example) and could be held up to ransom by a seller unless they can use compulsory purchase powers. Nevertheless, the cost of land in different locations does have a significant influence on their location decisions, so schools and parks are not always located in the best places.

Markets influence the allocation of land to development at different times as well as to different uses. If a land owner or developer expects the value of a particular site to increase rapidly, because it will become attractive for commercial or high density development, it will be profitable for him to hold it vacant while awaiting that opportunity. Although speculative holding of land is often condemned, it can be useful in such a situation. The market similarly allocates different social groups to different localities. Once a suburb gets a reputation as a high-class residential area, land and house prices rise so that poorer families cannot afford to live there. Furthermore, it will not pay to build costly houses and flats in a poor area because most of the potential buyers in such an area will be poor families who will not be willing to pay the full cost of an expensive home. Therefore an expensive house in a poorer area can be a bad investment, as can a low cost house in an area where most buyers want a big one. In this way the market can reinforce a preference for rich and poor to live in different parts of a city.

Competing users express their preferences for locating at particular places through the property market, which acts as the main arbitrator between them. The market is, of course, conditioned by land use controls. Although the market for property is the most important, the markets for labour and for goods and services also influence location. They have less influence than the property market because people travel to work, to shop and to get services, and goods are transported from one part of the city to another, while land and buildings are immobile. Nevertheless transport and travel within an urban area is costly in both money and time, especially at peak periods when a lot of other people are also trying to use the limited capacity of the transport system. Even though wages may not vary within an urban area, it may be easier to recruit and retain workers in locations close to where they live. A shopping centre will have a larger turnover if it is accessible to its potential customers. Sometimes, of course, prices of goods are different—the corner shop can charge higher prices because it is more convenient.

While most goods and services supplied in the private market can be transported or can be collected by the user, some of the services produced by government authorities are provided to a particular location and cannot be transported. This is true of 'pipe and wire' services, transport routes and public transport. The value of property reflects the availability of these services along with access to other public services such as schools, and private services such as shops (Adams *et al.*, 1968).

Finally, as has been mentioned above, planning authorities cannot ignore the property market. Property prices reflect both established development rights and rights which owners expect to get in the future. Land use planning decisions that take away some of those rights involve a degree of expropriation, therefore land use plans generally recognise existing uses and only attempt to encourage the removal of the most clearly incompatible uses by designating them 'non-conforming', which usually prevents substantial additions or rebuilding. In a more general sense the property market limits the effectiveness of land use planning by responding to the scarcities created by land use controls.

The market performs a co-ordinative role between different developers and different users. It encourages activities which find advantages in locating close together to do so, but its role in relation to the public sector is ambiguous. Service authorities are constrained by the prices they have to pay, but they are not motivated by profits to locate in the 'best' place. Their ability to buy a site is limited by the size of their budget rather than by its value for providing the service. The property market and land use planning controls are essentially competitive ways of determining land use. When they exist together one usually becomes dominant (Neutze, 1975).

Administration

Since particular decisions about the location of services and about land use controls cannot be made in response to market demands, they are necessarily made in an administrative way in accord with some decision rules. These rules may range from a kind of market simulation such as benefit cost analysis to much simpler rules about the size of schools and the maximum distance children of different ages should have to travel. Benefit cost analysis has been used most in transport where the quality of the service is very variable and scarce resources have to be allocated between improvements to different parts of the system. For other services an administrative (or technical) decision is made about the standard at which the service is provided, and the authority tries to meet all demands at that standard.

Many of the administrative relationships between the public and the private sector in urban development are based on the application for permission to develop land for a particular use. There may also be formal provision for rezoning land from one permissible use to another, for registration of title, and for permission to build and to occupy a new building. The various stages of approval that must be obtained are used by public authorities as a source of information about likely future developments, to prevent unacceptable developments, to require any change in the proposed development, and to ensure that the developer installs services to the required standards and meets any charges for which he might be liable.

Because it takes time to increase the capacity and the area served, an authority needs some advance warning of increased demand. The lead time varies, from electricity where it is very short, to transport facilities where it can be very long. Many of the authorities carry out expensive demand projections in order to plan their investment programmes. The most notable examples are the transportation studies which have been carried out for all major Australian cities since about 1960. Service authorities are also informed when a planning authority approves an application to develop. This allows them to predict, at least a short time ahead, the demand for schools, pipe and wire services and other local facilities. Most government service authorities do not sell their products and therefore cannot simply respond to the market demand. For the same reason they cannot charge different prices in locations where their costs vary, and rely on the market to influence the location of the private developments they service. Development applications are referred to them not only for information but also for approval. If the location or the type of development proposed would be difficult or expensive to service, they will either oppose it or suggest that conditions are attached to make it easier or cheaper to service. Although developers are now responsible for the reticulation of a number of services within subdivisions, the authorities responsible for those services still need to ensure that the standards are acceptable since they will be responsible for operation and maintenance. They also have to make sure that the new subdivision can be linked into the existing network.

A variety of devices is used in attempts to achieve co-ordination between different government authorities involved in urban development. Co-ordination is difficult, partly because, as the previous chapter showed, authorities and departments of different levels of government are involved—it is not easy even among authorities responsible to the state governments which have the main responsibility for urban planning and servicing in Australia. Despite the fact that they need each others' services, and often serve the same customers, co-ordination is difficult if it requires an organisation to commit itself to an investment programme for a period into the future. Because of uncertainties about available funds and about political constraints, authorities value their freedom to manoeuvre. Interdepartmental committees are the standard way of trying to achieve co-ordination at the bureaucratic level. Conflicts between different authorities are ultimately resolved in cabinet if they involve a single level of government, or by intergovernmental negotiations.

Political Relationships

Most of the decisions of authorities are taken in pursuance of Acts, administrative rules or general policies laid down by the government concerned. Periodically, however, these rules are questioned and sometimes decisions have to be made which are not covered by the rules. Authorities also have to work within their budgets and have to be free to choose between alternative uses of funds. Many of the rules allow a good deal of discretion to the authority. Sometimes governments themselves make decisions on particular cases—this occurs most frequently at the local government level where the distinction between the executive and administrative functions of government is least clear. It occurs occasionally at higher levels of government when individuals or organisations make representations to ministers or members of parliament. Private developers, businessmen, business associations, individuals and groups in the community make representations to governments with respect to both individual policy decisions and more general policies.

Although representations to the government itself are the theoretically correct way to exert political pressure, it is common for interested parties to make representations to the authority directly responsible. One reason for this is the discretion the authorities have; another is that enlisting the support of the responsible authority is very useful in getting a favourable response at a political level. Examples are easy to find: developers press at all levels for their responsibilities in servicing to be reduced; parents press for a new school; retailers press for more parking facilities near their shopping centre and for roads which give better access.

Service and planning authorities get involved not only in the political relationships between the private and the public sector but also in political relationships between parts of the public sector. Some of these relate to different levels of government, as when a new airport is being sited, involving the Federal Government as responsible for air transport, the state government as responsible for linking surface transport, and both state and local governments as responsible for land use planning. On other occasions different authorities of the same government have different views on a policy issue because of their different responsibilities and objectives; for example a housing authority wants cheap land for housing while a planning authority wants to restrict urban sprawl by releasing land for development only a short time before it is needed. Different authorities can seek support not only within the bureaucracy but also among elected members and occasionally in the community at large.

Conclusion

Cities are complex systems, and urban development can only be understood as some of those complexities are understood. 'Development' is required so that the city can grow to meet the growing demands of its residents and can adapt to changes in the kinds of living environments people want and changes in the technology of production, consumption and transport of goods, information, energy and wastes. Cities are shaped by a number of markets, especially the property market, which allocates scarce space at different locations between competing users. The strictly market view of the city only provides a partial understanding of the process of development. Because many of the services that are produced in a city are provided by the public sector and paid for from taxes of various kinds, the city also reflects the results of a political and administrative process which allows the interests of the community as a whole, and group interests within it, to be taken into account in determining its development. Markets are good at reflecting individual but not collective interests.

Collective interests are involved not only in services such as education, police and fire protection, which have to be provided collectively, but also in the interests of other members of the community in the private development of individually owned pieces of land. Land use planning is the device used to try to avoid offence between neighbours. Because we live and work close together in cities we have rules to allow us to get the maximum advantages of living close together while avoiding the worst of its potential disadvantages. A forthcoming volume will look in more detail at collective aspects of urban development and at some of the broad policy issues which arise.

Bibliography

Items marked * are recommended for further reading.

Abbreviations

ABS   Australian Bureau of Statistics
AIUS   Australian Institute of Urban Studies
AGPS   Australian Government Publishing Service
ANU   Australian National University
BTE   Bureau of Transport Economics
CBCS   Commonwealth Bureau of Census and Statistics
CBR   Commonwealth Bureau of Roads
DURD   Department of Urban and Regional Development
MATS   Metropolitan Adelaide Transportation Study
MRPA   Metropolitan Region Planning Authority
SATS   Sydney Area Transportation Study

Adams, F.Gerard; Milgram, Grace; Green, Edward W., and Mansfield, Christine (1968): 'Undeveloped land prices during urbanisation: a micro-empirical study over time', *Review of Economics and Statistics*, Vol. 50, pp. 248–58.

Aird, W.V. (1961): *The Water Supply, Sewerage and Drainage of Sydney*, The Metropolitan Water, Sewerage and Drainage Board, Sydney.

Alexander, Ian (1976): 'The suburbanization of private sector office employment: fact or fiction?', in Linge, G.J.R. (ed.): *Restructuring Employment Opportunities in Australia*, Publication HG/11, Department of Human Geography, ANU, Canberra.

Allbut, Guy (1958): *A Brief History of some of the Features of Public Electricity Supply in Australia and the Formation and Development of the Electricity Supply Association of Australia 1918–1957*, Electricity Supply Association, Melbourne.

Allen, G.R. (1954): 'The "courbe des populations"; a further analysis', *Bulletin of the Oxford University Institute of Statistics*, Vol. 16, pp. 179–89.

Alonso, W. (1964): *Location and Land Use: Toward a General Theory of Land Rent*, Harvard University Press, Cambridge, Mass.

Andrews, R.B. (1953–6): 'Mechanics of the urban economic base', a series of articles in *Land Economics*, Vols. 30–2.

* Archer, R.W. (1976): *Planning and Managing Metropolitan Development and Land Supply*, Committee for Economic Development of Australia, Melbourne.

Atlas of Australian Resources (1973): Second Series, 'Land Use', Department of Minerals and Energy, Canberra.

ABS (1976): *Journey to Work and Journey to School, August 1974*, Ref. 17.5, Canberra.

Australian Housing Corporation (1976): *Defence Service Homes Scheme: Its Nature, History and Operations*, AGPS, Canberra.

AIUS (1975a): *Industrial Land in Sydney*, Canberra.

* AIUS (1975b): *Housing for Australia: Philosophies and Policies*, Canberra.

Barrett, B. (1971): *The Inner Suburbs*, Melbourne University Press, Melbourne.

Beesley, M.E., and Dalvi, M.Q. (1974): 'Spatial equilibrium and journey to work', *Journal of Transport Economics and Policy*, Vol. 8, pp. 197–222.

Bentley, Philip; Collins, D.J., and Drane, N.T. (1973): *The Incidence of the Australian Tax Structure*, Research Paper No. 34, School of Economic and Financial Studies, Macquarie University, Sydney.

Berry, Brian, and Garrison, William (1958): 'Alternative explanations of urban rank-size relationships', *Annals of the Association of American Geographers*, Vol. 47, pp. 83–91.

Birch, A., and Macmillan, D.S. (1962): *The Sydney Scene 1788–1960*, Melbourne University Press, Melbourne.

Bird, J. (1968): *Seaport Gateways of Australia*, Oxford University Press, London.

Black, John A. (1974): 'Techniques of land use/transportation planning in Australian cities', *Transportation*, Vol. 3, pp. 255–88.

* Bowman, M. (1976): *Local Government in the Australian States*, An Urban Paper, Department of Environment, Housing and Community Development, AGPS, Canberra.

Bromilow, F.J. (1975): 'The supply of land for urban purposes', Fifth Australian Building Research Congress, proceedings, reprinted in *The Developer*, August 1975, pp. 32–7.

Bromilow, F.J., and Meaton, M.L. (1974): *The Land Conversion Process*, AIUS, Canberra.

* Bunker, R.C. (1971): *Town and Country or City and Region*, Melbourne University Press, Melbourne.

BTE (1972): *Economic Evaluation of Capital Investment in Urban Public Transport*, Canberra.

BTE (1975): 'Urban passenger transport outlook', Transport Outlook Conference, Canberra, July 29–30.

Burgess, E.W. (1925): 'The growth of the city', in R.E. Park *et al* (eds), *The City*, University of Chicago Press, Chicago.

Burkitt, R. (Chairman) (1974): *Modern Housing Techniques*, A report to the Minister for Housing and Construction by the Australian Government Task Force to investigate modern housing techniques, AGPS, Canberra.

* Burnley, I.H. (ed.) (1974): *Urbanization in Australia: The Post-War Experience*, Cambridge University Press, Cambridge.

Butlin, N.G. (1959): 'Some structural features of Australian capital formation, 1861–1938/39', *Economic Record*, Vol. 35, pp. 389–415.

Butlin, N.G. (1962) *Australian Domestic Product, Investment and Foreign Borrowing, 1861–1938/39*, Cambridge University Press, Cambridge.
Butlin, N.G. (1964): *Investment in Australian Economic Development 1861–1900*, Cambridge University Press, Cambridge.

Cannon, M. (1966): *The Land Boomers*, Melbourne University Press, Melbourne.
Champion, A.G. (1975): *An Estimate of the Changing Extent and Distribution of Urban Land in England and Wales, 1950–70*, Research Paper RP 10, Centre for Environmental Studies, London.
Choi, C.Y., and Burnley, I.H. (1974): 'Population components in the growth of cities', in Burnley, I.H. (ed.) *Urbanization in Australia: The Post-War Experience*, Cambridge University Press, Cambridge.
Cities Commission (1975): *Studies in Australian Internal Migration 1966–71*, Occasional Paper No. 2, Canberra.
Cities Commission and Davis, J.R. (1975): *Melbourne at the Census, 1971: A Social Atlas*, Cities Commission, Canberra.
Clark, Nicholas (ed.) (1970): *Analysis of Urban Development*, Transport Section, Department of Civil Engineering, University of Melbourne.
Clawson, Marion (1971): *Suburban Land Conversion in the United States*, Johns Hopkins Press, Baltimore.
Cloher, D. Urlich (1975): 'A perspective on Australian urbanisation', in Powell, J.M., and Williams, M. (eds): *Australian Space, Australian Time*, Oxford University Press, Melbourne.
Coghlan, T.A. (1896): *A Statistical Account of the Seven Colonies of Australasia, 1895–96*, Government Printer, Sydney.
CBCS (1972): *Journey to Work and Journey to School, May 1970*, Ref. No. 17.5, Canberra.
CBR (1973): *Reports on Roads in Australia: 1973*, Melbourne.
CBR (1974): *Assessment of Freeway Plans: State Capital Cities*, Melbourne.
CBR (1975): *Report on Roads in Australia: 1975*, Melbourne.
Commonwealth Housing Commission (1944): *Final Report of the Commonwealth Housing Commission*, Department of Post-War Reconstruction, Canberra.
Cumberland County Council (1948): *The Planning Scheme for the County of Cumberland*, The Council, Sydney.

Davis, J.R., and Spearritt, Peter (1974): *Sydney at the Census, 1971: A Social Atlas*, Urban Research Unit, ANU, Canberra.
Davison, G. (1970): 'Public utilities and the expansion of Melbourne in the 1880s, *Australian Economic History Review*, Vol. 10, pp. 169–89.
Department of Housing (1968): *Flats: A Survey of Multi-unit Construction*, Canberra.
Department of Post-War Reconstruction (1949): *Regional Planning in Australia*, Canberra.
DURD (1974a): *Urban Land: Problems and Policies*, AGPS, Canberra.
DURD (1974b): *Urban Land Prices 1968–1974*, AGPS, Canberra.
DURD (1975): *Urban and Regional Development 1975–76*, 1975–76 Budget Paper No. 9, AGPS, Canberra.

Evans, A.W. (1973): *The Economics of Residential Location*, Macmillan, London.

Ewart, J.D. (1970): 'Semi-government loan finance in Victoria', *Economic Record*, Vol. 46, pp. 208–21.

Fagan, R.H. (1971): 'Government policy and the Australian metalliferous mining and processing industries', in Linge, G.J.R., and Rimmer, P.J. (eds): *Government Influence and the Location of Economic Activity*, Publication HG/5, Department of Human Geography, ANU, Canberra.

Grant, J., and Searle, G. (1957): *The Melbourne Scene 1803–1956*, Melbourne University Press, Melbourne.

Greenwood, G., and Laverty, J.R. (1959): *Brisbane 1859–1959*, The City Council, Brisbane,

Hall, Peter; Gracey, Harry; Drewett, Roy, and Thomas, Ray (1973): *The Containment of Urban England*, George Allen and Unwin, London.

Harris, Britton (1968): 'Quantitative models of urban development: their role in metropolitan policy-making', in Perloff, Harvey S., and Wingo, Lowdon (eds): *Issues in Urban Economics*, Resources for the Future, Washington DC.

Harrison, David, and Kain, John F. (1974): 'Cumulative urban growth and urban density functions', *Journal of Urban Economics*, Vol. 1, pp. 61–98.

Harrison, Peter (1974): 'Urban Planning', in Forward, Roy (ed.): *Public Policy in Australia*, Cheshire, Melbourne.

* Harrison, Peter (in press): 'Major urban areas', *Atlas of Australian Resources*, Department of Minerals and Energy, Canberra.

Hill, M.R. (1974): 'Housing finance institutions', in Hirst, R.R., and Wallace, R.H. (eds): *The Australian Capital Market*, Cheshire, Melbourne.

Hirsch, Werner Z. (1973): *Urban Economic Analysis*, McGraw-Hill, New York.

Housing Industry Association (1970): *The Structure and Operations of the Housing Industry in NSW*, Melbourne.

Housing Industry Association (1971): *A Study of Land Costs in Australia*, Melbourne.

Hutton, John (1970): *Building and Construction in Australia*, F.W. Cheshire, Melbourne.

Jeans, D.N. (1972): *An Historical Geography of New South Wales to 1901*, Reed Education, Sydney.

Johnson, Ken (1973a): 'The Melbourne and Metropolitan Board of Works', in Pickett, J.C.: *Public Authorities in Urban Development in Melbourne*, Urban Research Unit, ANU, Canberra.

Johnson, Ken (1973b): *People and Property in North Melbourne*, Urban Research Unit, ANU, Canberra.

Johnston, R.J. (1969): 'Some tests of a model of intra-urban population mobility: Melbourne, Australia', *Urban Studies*, Vol. 6, pp. 34–57.

* Johnston, R.J. (1971): *Urban Residential Patterns*, G. Bell and Sons, London.

Joint Study into Local Government Finances: Australia and New Zealand (1976), Report of the Joint Steering Committee appointed by the Local Government Ministers' Conference, Canberra.

Jones, F.L. (1969): *Dimensions of Urban Social Structure: The Social Areas of Melbourne, Australia*, ANU Press, Canberra.

* Jones, M.A. (1972): *Housing and Poverty in Australia*, Melbourne University Press, Melbourne.

Kaiser, E.J. (1968): *A Producer Model for Urban Growth*, Institute for Research in Social Science, University of North Carolina, Chapel Hill.

Kerr, Alex (1970): 'Urban industrial change in Australia, 1954 to 1966', *Economic Record*, Vol. 46, pp. 355–67.

King, R. (1973): *The Dimensions of Housing Need in Australia*, Occasional Paper No. 3, Ian Buchan Fell Bequest, University of Sydney.

Lampard, Eric E. (1968): 'The evolving system of cities in the United States: urbanisation and economic development', in Perloff, Harvey S., and Wingo, Lowdon (eds): *Issues in Urban Economics*, Resources for the Future, Washington DC.

Lanigan, P.J. (1976): 'The spatial reorganisation of a federal government department', in Linge, G.J.R. (ed.): *Restructuring Employment Opportunities in Australia*, Publication HG/11, Department of Human Geography, ANU, Canberra.

Lewis, G. (1973): *A History of the Ports of Queensland*, University of Queensland Press, Brisbane.

Linge, G.J.R. (1963): 'The location of manufacturing in Australia', in Hunter, Alex (ed.): *The Economics of Australian Industry*, Melbourne University Press, Melbourne.

Linge, G.J.R. (1965): *The Delimitation of Urban Boundaries*, Publication G/2, Department of Geography, Research School of Pacific Studies, ANU, Canberra.

Linge, G.J.R. (1975): 'The forging of an industrial nation: manufacturing in Australia 1788–1913', in Powell, J.M., and Williams, M. (eds): *Australian Space: Australian Time*, Oxford University Press, Melbourne.

Linge, G.J.R. (in press): *Industrial Awakening: A Geography of Manufacturing in Australia 1788 to 1900*, Thomas Nelson, Melbourne.

* Linge, G.J.R. (ed.) (1976): *Restructuring Employment Opportunities in Australia*, Publication HG/11, Department of Human Geography, ANU, Canberra.

Linge, G.J.R.; Rimmer, P.J., and Lance, G.N. (1976): 'Australia's evolving urban system: workforce structure, performance and implications', in Linge, G.J.R. (ed.): *Restructuring Employment Opportunities in Australia*, Publication HG/11, Department of Human Geography, ANU, Canberra.

* Logan, M.I.; Maher, C.A.; McKay, J., and Humphreys, J.S. (1975): *Urban and Regional Australia, Analysis and Policy Issues*, Sorrett, Malvern, Vic.

Lowry, Ira S. (1964): *A Model of Metropolis*, Memorandum RM–4035–RC, The Rand Corporation, Santa Monica, Calif.

* Mathews, Russel (1967): *Public Investment in Australia*, F.W. Cheshire, Melbourne.

Manvel, Allen D. (1968): 'Land use in 106 large cities', in *Three Land Research Studies*, Research Report No. 12, National Commission on Urban Problems, U.S. Government Printing Office, Washington DC.

McCarty, J.W. (1970): 'Australian capital cities in the nineteenth century', *Australian Economic History Review*, Vol. 10, pp. 107–37.

* McMaster, J.C., and Webb, G.R. (eds) (1976): *Australian Urban Economics*, Australia and New Zealand Book Co., Sydney.

MATS (1966): *Basic Data for Transportation Planning*, Adelaide.

MRPA (1969): *Perth Region Data Book 1966*, Perth.

MRPA (1975): *Perth Region Data Book 1971*, Perth.

Mills, E.S. (1967): 'An aggregative model of resource allocation in a metropolitan area', *American Economic Review*, Vol. 57 (Proceedings) pp. 197–210.

Mills, E.S. (1972a): *Studies in the Structure of the Urban Economy*, Johns Hopkins Press, Baltimore.

Mills, E.S. (1972b): *Urban Economics*, Scott Foresman, Glenview, Illinois.

Murphy, D.G. (1973): *Economic Aspects of Residential Subdivision*, AIUS, Canberra.

Mushkin, Selma J. (1972): 'An agenda for research', in Mushkin (ed.): *Public Prices for Public Products*, The Urban Institute, Washington DC.

Muth, R.F. (1969): *Cities and Housing*, University of Chicago Press, Chicago.

* National Population Inquiry (1975): *Population in Australia, a Demographic Analysis and Projection*, First Report, AGPS, Canberra.

Neilson, L.R. (1972): *Business Activities in Three Melbourne Suburbs*, Urban Research Unit, ANU, Canberra.

Neilson, L.R. (1976): 'Developers as conservative decision-makers', in McMaster, J.C., and Webb, G.R. (eds): *Australian Urban Economics*, Australia and New Zealand Book Co., Sydney.

* Neutze, Max (1965): *Economic Policy and the Size of Cities*, ANU Press, Canberra.

Neutze, Max (1971a): *People and Property in Randwick*, Urban Research Unit, ANU, Canberra.

Neutze, Max (1971b): *People and Property in Bankstown*, Urban Research Unit, ANU, Canberra.

Neutze, Max (1972a): *People and Property in Redfern*, Urban Research Unit, ANU, Canberra.

Neutze, Max (1972b): 'The cost of housing', *Economic Record*, Vol. 48, pp. 357–73.

Neutze, Max (1974): 'Local, regional and metropolitan government', in Mathews, R.L. (ed.): *Intergovernmental Relations in Australia*, Angus & Robertson, Sydney.

Neutze, Max (1975): 'Urban land policy in five western countries', *Journal of Social Policy*, Vol. 4, pp. 225–42.

New South Wales Planning and Environment Commission (1975): *Sydney Region Open Space Survey*, Research Study No. 1, Sydney.

Odgen, K.W., and Hicks, S.K. (eds) (1975): *Goods Movement and Goods Vehicles in Urban Areas*, CBR, Melbourne.

Pak-Poy, P.G., and Associates (1973): *Inner Suburban—Outer Suburban: A Comparison of Costs*, AIUS, Canberra.

* Parker, R.S., and Troy, P.N. (eds) (1972): *The Politics of Urban Growth*, ANU Press, Canberra.

Paterson, John (1970): 'Programming Urban Development' Ph.D. Thesis, ANU, Canberra.

Paterson, John, Urban Systems Pty Ltd (1972): *Melbourne's C.B.D. in the 1960s*, AIUS, Canberra.

Paterson, John, Urban Systems Pty Ltd (1974): *Melbourne Metropolitan Land Study*, Urban Development Institute of Australia, Victorian Branch, Melbourne.

Paterson, John (1975): 'A study of the comparative costs of providing public utilities and services in Melbourne and selected Victorian centres', in *Studies Commissioned by the Commonwealth/State Officers Committee on Decentralization*, AGPS, Canberra.

Pickett, J.C. (1973): *Public Authorities and Development in Melbourne*, Urban Research Unit, ANU, Canberra.

Prest, W. (1963): 'The electricity supply industry', in Hunter, Alex (ed.): *The Economics of Australian Industry*, Melbourne University Press, Melbourne.

Report of the Committee of Inquiry into Residential Land Development (1975): (Hayes Report) Government Printer, Melbourne.

Report on the Metropolitan Area of Adelaide, (1962): Prepared by the Town Planning Committee, Government Printer, Adelaide.

Report of the Metropolitan Town Planning Commission, (1929): The Commission, Melbourne.

Richardson, H.W. (1969): *Regional Economics*, Weidenfeld and Nicholson, London.

Rimmer, Peter J. (1975): *Urban Goods Movement*, CBR, Melbourne.

Robinson, K.W. (1962): 'Processes and patterns of urbanisation in Australia and New Zealand', *New Zealand Geographer*, Vol. 18, pp. 32–49.

Rose, A.J. (1966): 'Dissent from down-under: metropolitan primacy as the normal state', *Pacific Viewpoint*, Vol. 7, pp. 1–27.

* Sandercock, L.K. (1975): *Cities for Sale*, Melbourne University Press, Melbourne.

Siegan, Bernard H. (1970): 'Non-zoning in Houston', *Journal of Law and Economics*, Vol. 13, pp. 71–149.

Solomon, K.T. (1974): 'Roads and road use in Australia, statistical summary 1971', *Australian Road Research*, Vol. 5, No. 5, pp. 16–40.

Spearritt, P. (1976): 'An Urban History of Sydney, 1920–1950', Ph.D. Thesis, ANU, Canberra.

State Planning Authority of NSW (1965): *The Journey to Work*, Sydney.

State Planning Authority of NSW (1972): *The Journey to Work 1966*, Technical Bulletin No. 2, Sydney.

Stephenson, P.R. (1966): *A History and Description of Sydney Harbour*, Rigby, Adelaide.

Stephenson, Gordon, and Hepburn, J.A. (1955): *Plan for the Metropolitan Region, Perth and Fremantle*, Government Printing Office, Perth.

* Stilwell, F.J.B. (1974): *Australian Urban and Regional Development*, Australia and New Zealand Book Co., Sydney.

Stretton, Hugh (1974): *Housing and Government*, 1974 Boyer Lectures, Australian Broadcasting Commission, Sydney.

Stretton, Hugh (1975): *Ideas for Australian Cities*, (Second edition) Georgian House, Melbourne.

*SATS (1974): *Report* (Vols I to IV), Sydney.

Taits Electoral Directory of Australia and New Zealand (1929): Tait Publishing Co., Melbourne and Sydney.

Talbot, S., and Filmer, R. (1973): 'Demand for passenger motor vehicles', Industries Assistance Commission, Canberra.

Troy, P.N. (ed.) (1967): *Urban Redevelopment in Australia*, Urban Research Unit, ANU, Canberra.

Troy, P.N. (1971): *Environmental Quality in Four Sydney Suburban Areas*, Urban Research Unit, ANU, Canberra.

Troy, P.N. (1972): *Environmental Quality in Four Melbourne Suburbs*, Urban Research Unit, ANU, Canberra.

Troy, Patrick, and Neutze, Max (1969): 'Urban road planning in theory and practice', *Journal of Transport Economics and Policy*, Vol. 3, pp. 139–51.

Turner, I.A.H. (1967): 'The growth of Melbourne: an historical account', in Troy, P.N. (ed.): *Urban Redevelopment in Australia*, Urban Research Unit, ANU, Canberra.

Tyler, A.S. (1973): *Report on the Price of Land*, The Institute of Real Estate Development, Sydney.

*Urban Research Unit (1973): *Urban Development in Melbourne*, AIUS, Canberra.

Vandermark, Elzo (1970): *Business Actitivies in Four Sydney Suburbs*, Urban Research Unit, ANU, Canberra.

Vandermark, Elzo (1974): 'Urban renewal', in Burnley, I.H. (ed.): *Urbanisation in Australia: The Post-War Experience*, Cambridge University Press, Cambridge.

Vandermark, Elzo, and Harrison, Peter (1972): *Development Activities in Four Sydney Suburban Areas*, Urban Research Unit, ANU, Canberra.

Wagner, Claire (1974): *Rural Retreats*, An Urban Paper, Department of Urban and Regional Development, AGPS, Canberra.

Weiss, Shirley F.; Smith, John E.; Kaiser, Edward J., and Kenney, Kenneth B. (1966): *Residential Developer Decisions—A Focussed View of the Urban Growth Process*, Center for Urban and Regional Studies, Institute for Research in Social Science, University of North Carolina, Chapel Hill.

Wingo, Lowdon Jr. (1961): *Transportation and Urban Land*, Resources for the Future, Washington DC.

Winston, Denis (1957): *Sydney's Great Experiment*, Angus and Robertson, Sydney.

Zipf, George (1949): *Human Behaviour and the Principle of Least Effort*, Harvard University Press, Cambridge, Mass.

Index